Blackstone's
Police Q&A

General Police Duties 2023

Blackstone's
Police Q&A

General Police Duties 2023

Twenty-first edition

Anjali Howard and Andy Cox

OXFORD
UNIVERSITY PRESS

OXFORD
UNIVERSITY PRESS

Great Clarendon Street, Oxford, OX2 6DP,
United Kingdom

Oxford University Press is a department of the University of Oxford.
It furthers the University's objective of excellence in research, scholarship,
and education by publishing worldwide. Oxford is a registered trade mark of
Oxford University Press in the UK and in certain other countries

First published in 2022

Public sector information reproduced under Open Government Licence v3.0
(http://www.nationalarchives.gov.uk/doc/open-government-licence/open-government-licence.htm)

Published in the United States of America by Oxford University Press
198 Madison Avenue, New York, NY 10016, United States of America

British Library Cataloguing in Publication Data
Data available

ISBN 978-0-19-286998-2

DOI: 10.1093/law/9780192869982.001.0001

Printed and bound by
CPI Group (UK) Ltd, Croydon, CR0 4YY

Contents

Contents

Introduction

Before you get into the detail of this book, there are two myths about multiple-choice questions (MCQs) that we need to get out of the way right at the start:

1. that they are easy to answer;
2. that they are easy to write.

Take one look at a professionally designed and properly developed exam paper such as those used by the Police Promotion Examinations Board and the first myth collapses straight away. Contrary to what some people believe, MCQs are not an easy solution for examiners and not a 'multiple-guess' soft option for examinees.

That is not to say that *all* MCQs are taxing, or even testing—in the psychometric sense. If MCQs are to have any real value at all, they need to be carefully designed and follow some agreed basic rules.

And this leads us to myth number 2.

It is widely assumed by many people and educational organisations that anyone with the knowledge of a subject can write MCQs. You need only look at how few MCQ writing courses are offered by training providers in the UK to see just how far this myth is believed. Similarly, you need only to have a go at a few badly designed MCQs to realise that it is a myth nonetheless. Writing bad MCQs is easy; writing good ones is no easier than answering them!

There are several purposes for which MCQs are very useful. The first is in producing a reliable, valid and fair test of knowledge and understanding across a wide range of subject matter. Another is an aid to study, preparation and revision for such examinations and tests. The differences in objective mean that there are slight differences in the rules that the MCQ writers follow. Whereas the design of fully validated MCQs to be used in high-stakes examinations, which will effectively determine who passes and who fails, has very strict guidelines as to construction, content and style, less stringent rules apply to MCQs that are being used for teaching and revision. For that reason, there may be types of MCQ that are appropriate in the latter setting which would not be used in the former. However, in developing the MCQs for this book, the author has tried to follow the fundamental rules of MCQ design but would not claim to have replicated the level of psychometric rigour that is—and has to be—adopted by the type of examining bodies referred to previously.

These MCQs are designed to reinforce your knowledge and understanding, to highlight any gaps or weaknesses in that knowledge and understanding, and to help focus your revision of the relevant topics.

Good luck!

Blackstone's Police Q&As—Special Features

References to Blackstone's Police Manuals

Every answer is followed by a paragraph reference to Blackstone's Police Manuals. This means that once you have attempted a question and looked at an answer, the Manual can immediately be referred to for help and clarification.

Unique numbers for each question

Each question and answer has the same unique number. This should ensure that there is no confusion as to which question is linked to which answer. For example, Question 2.1 is linked to Answer 2.1.

Checklists

The checklists are designed to help you keep track of your progress when answering the multiple-choice questions. If you fill in the checklist after attempting a question, you will be able to check how many you got right on the first attempt and will know immediately which questions need to be revisited a second time. Please visit www. blackstonespoliceservice.com and click through to the Blackstone's Police Q&As 2023 page. You will then find electronic versions of the checklists to download and print out. Email any queries or comments on the book to: police@oup.com.

Acknowledgements

This book has been written as an accompaniment to Blackstone's Police Manuals, and will test the knowledge you have accrued through reading that series. It is of the essence that full study of the relevant chapters in each Police Manual is completed prior to attempting the Questions and Answers. As qualified police trainers, we recognise that students tend to answer questions incorrectly either because they don't read the question properly, or because one of the 'distracters' has done its work. The distracter is one of the three incorrect answers in a multiple-choice question (MCQ), and is designed to distract you from the correct answer and in this way discriminate between candidates: the better-prepared candidate not being 'distracted'.

So particular attention should be paid to the *Answers* sections, and students should ask themselves 'Why did I get that question wrong?' and, just as importantly, 'Why did I get that question right?' Combining the information gained in the *Answers* section together with rereading the chapter in the Police Manuals should lead to greater understanding of the subject matter.

The publisher and the author wish to thank Huw Smart and John Watson for their contributions to previous editions of this book.

1 | Stop and Search

QUESTIONS

Question 1.1

Constable DURAND was on patrol late at night and received a call concerning a person acting suspiciously near to a house. The control room informed the officer that neighbours had said that the premises had been empty and unoccupied for about six months, following the death of the elderly occupant, and that the property was for sale. The officer attended immediately and found DRAKE in the rear garden of the house, hiding in some bushes. The officer decided to search DRAKE for stolen or prohibited articles.

Did Constable DURAND have the power to search DRAKE under s. 1 of the Police and Criminal Evidence Act 1984 in these circumstances?

A No, searches in the garden of a dwelling are prohibited and the search was unlawful.

B Yes, DRAKE was in a garden of a house which was not being used as a dwelling and which was unoccupied; the search was lawful.

C No, searches must take place in a public place and the search was unlawful.

D Yes, there are no restrictions on searches which take place outside a dwelling; the search was lawful.

Question 1.2

Constable CORK attended a report of a theft in the High Street; a store detective had witnessed a female person removing two mobile phones from a display and walking out of the shop. The female was now being tracked by a CCTV operator, who reported that she was accompanied by two girls; one was about 5 years of age and the other was about 2 years of age and in a pushchair. As Constable CORK approached the suspect, she was told that she had placed one of the mobile phones in

1

the older child's pocket and had hidden the other in the pushchair. Constable CORK detained the female and the two children.

Which of the following statements is correct in relation to Constable CORK's power to search the two children, under s. 1 of the Police and Criminal Evidence Act 1984?

A Constable CORK could not search the children; because of their ages, they could not form the necessary criminal intent for this crime.

B Constable CORK could search the children provided she had reasonable grounds to suspect that she would find the stolen articles.

C Constable CORK could not search the children because they are in innocent possession of stolen articles.

D Constable CORK could search the pushchair because it is not a 'person'; however, she could not search the older child because that child could not form the necessary criminal intent for this crime.

Question 1.3

Constable LEE was on uniform mobile patrol and received a radio message from the control room. A member of the public had witnessed a theft from a vehicle and the suspect had got into a Renault car and driven off. A registration number was given and, a short while later, Constable LEE located the vehicle which was being driven in front of him. The officer stopped it and there was a single occupant, the vehicle driver, SAMPSON. The officer decided to search the Renault and SAMPSON.

In relation to the reasonable grounds for suspicion the officer would require before conducting a search under s. 1 of the Police and Criminal Evidence Act 1984, which of the following statements is correct?

A Constable LEE could search the vehicle regardless of whether she suspected there was any likelihood of finding stolen articles.

B Any grounds Constable LEE acted on should have been enough to give rise to reasonable suspicion in a 'reasonable person' and the information from the witness may provide such reasonable grounds for suspicion.

C The information from the witness may provide reasonable grounds for suspicion; however, any grounds Constable LEE acted on should have been enough to give rise to reasonable suspicion in any person with similar skills to the officer.

D Constable LEE could search the vehicle regardless of whether she believed there was any likelihood of finding stolen articles, provided it could be shown that the witness had reasonable grounds to suspect there was a likelihood of finding stolen articles.

Question 1.4

An authorisation is in place under s. 60 of the Criminal Justice and Public Order Act 1994. There were serious riots and looting on the Friday night when the authorisation was granted. On the Saturday night, intelligence suggests that further riots will take place over the whole weekend and into the following week, with gang members carrying knives and other weapons. Superintendent LEACH is the senior officer in charge of policing for the area and is considering whether or not the s. 60 authorisation should be extended.

In relation to such an extension, which of the following statements is correct?
A Superintendent LEACH may extend the authorisation on any number of occasions, for up to seven days each time.
B Superintendent LEACH may extend the authorisation period once, for a maximum period of 24 hours; further use of the powers would require a new authorisation.
C Superintendent LEACH may extend the authorisation period for 24 hours; further extensions may take place for 24-hour periods, up to a maximum of seven days.
D Superintendent LEACH may extend the authorisation period twice, for two 24-hour periods; further use of the powers would require a new authorisation.

Question 1.5

Constable WILLIS was on patrol in uniform in the early hours of the morning in an area where there had recently been outbreaks of serious public disorder between two gangs, who were known to carry weapons. An authorisation was in force, under s. 60 of the Criminal Justice and Public Order Act 1994, to stop and search persons in the locality. Constable WILLIS saw MOORE walking in the street wearing a ski mask which was concealing his face.

In what circumstances could Constable WILLIS ask MOORE to remove his mask?
A If he reasonably believed that MOORE was likely to be involved in violence.
B No further circumstances are required as an order is in force under s. 60.
C If he reasonably believed that MOORE was wearing the ski mask wholly or mainly to conceal his identity.
D If he reasonably believed that MOORE was carrying a dangerous instrument or an offensive weapon.

Question 1.6

A police control room received a report of a suspicious vehicle driving around at night. The informant stated that there were four male persons in the vehicle and that they were all wearing masks covering their faces. Constable BUNCE was on uniform mobile patrol and heard the observations for the vehicle. Shortly afterwards, the officer spotted the vehicle and began following it. Constable BUNCE was aware that there had recently been incidents of serious public disorder in the locality and that there was an order in force, under s. 60AA of the Criminal Justice and Public Order Act 1994, in the area.

Which of the following statements is correct?

A Constable BUNCE has the power to stop the vehicle under s. 60AA and if the occupants are wearing masks he could require the occupants to remove them.

B Constable BUNCE would have to use the general power under s. 163 of the Road Traffic Act 1988 to stop the vehicle; if the occupants were not wearing masks, the officer has a power to search a vehicle for items used to conceal a person's identity under s. 60AA.

C Constable BUNCE has the power to stop the vehicle under s. 60AA in order to require the occupants to remove their masks (if they are wearing them), or to search the vehicle for such items, if they are not wearing any.

D Constable BUNCE would have to use the general power under s. 163 of the Road Traffic Act 1988 to stop the vehicle; there is no power to search a vehicle for items used to conceal a person's identity under s. 60AA.

Question 1.7

DCs SHELBY and MINTO have attended at DARBY's home address to serve a Terrorism Prevention and Investigation Measures (TPIM) notice on him under s. 2 of the Terrorism Prevention and Investigation Measures Act 2011, to restrict his movements because of his suspected links to terrorism. The officers are considering searching DARBY when the notice has been served to ascertain whether there is anything on him that contravenes the measures specified in the notice.

Which of the following statements is correct in relation to any reasonable suspicion the officers must have before such a search can take place?

A The officers could not search DARBY in this situation as he is inside his home address.

B They do not require any reasonable grounds to suspect that DARBY has anything on him that contravenes the measures specified in the notice, regardless of whether or not they have a warrant.

C They require reasonable grounds to suspect that DARBY is in possession of articles connected with terrorism.

D They require reasonable grounds to suspect that DARBY is in possession of articles that could be used to threaten or harm any person.

Question 1.8

MIAH has previously been served with a Terrorism Prevention and Investigation
Measures (TPIM) notice under s. 2 of the Terrorism Prevention and Investigation
Measures Act 2011. The police are in possession of intelligence that MIAH has
obtained a mobile phone and has been communicating with people abroad, over
the internet. This is contrary to the measures specified in the TPIM notice. The intelligence suggests he is using the phone whilst away from his home and the police
have obtained a warrant to search MIAH for the phone.

Which of the following statements is correct in relation to the measures that
must be taken in order to conduct the search?

A The police may search MIAH on one occasion, within 28 days of the warrant
being issued.

B There is no time limit in which the police have to perform the search, but they
may only conduct it once.

C The police may search MIAH on more than one occasion if it is necessary to do so,
but must do so within 28 days of the warrant being issued.

D The police may search MIAH on one occasion, within three months of the warrant being issued.

Question 1.9

DUNN was stopped in the street by Constables MEEK and PHELAN, both male officers. The officers had reasonable suspicion that DUNN was in possession of stolen
jewellery as they had been conducting surveillance on him. They believed that the
jewellery was contained in a clear bag, hidden in his trousers or possibly his underwear. While they were speaking to him, a police van pulled up to see if they needed
assistance. The officers wish to search DUNN by requiring him to remove his trousers
or if necessary his underwear and thereby expose intimate body parts.

To what extent could the officers search DUNN in these circumstances?

A They could require DUNN to remove items of clothing that would involve the exposure of intimate body parts in the rear of the police van, provided it is out of
public view.

B They would have to take DUNN to a nearby police station if they want to remove his underwear and expose intimate body parts.

C They could take DUNN to a nearby police station or another nearby location which is out of public view, if they want to remove his underwear and expose intimate body parts.

D They could not remove DUNN's underwear anywhere; this would be a strip search which may not carried out under s. 1 of PACE.

Question 1.10

Constable DANIELLS, a male officer, and Constable NEVIN, a female officer, stopped BENTLEY in the car park of a shopping centre. The officers had reasonable suspicion that BENTLEY was in possession of stolen goods, having received information from a CCTV operator who had seen her shoplifting. The officers were in a police van at the time and had been told that BENTLEY was possibly hiding a stolen necklace in her coat pocket.

Which of the following statements is correct, according to the PACE Codes of Practice, in relation to searching BENTLEY?

A Only Constable NEVIN could search BENTLEY in these circumstances.

B Either officer could search BENTLEY, provided they were only searching her outer garments.

C Either officer could search BENTLEY, provided they were only searching her outer garments and the search took place out of public view.

D Only Constable NEVIN could search BENTLEY in these circumstances, although the search could take place in the presence of Constable DANIELLS.

Question 1.11

Constable BAIRD attended a suspicious incident reported by POOLE, a CCTV operator. POOLE saw two men acting suspiciously near a 4 x 4 vehicle, and saw one of the men hand the other what the CCTV operator believed to be an offensive weapon. He believed the offensive weapon was placed inside the cover of the spare wheel attached to the rear door of the vehicle. As a result of this information, Constable BAIRD attended the scene. When the officer arrived, the two men were not with the vehicle—it was unattended. Constable BAIRD searched the spare wheel (using his power of search under s. 1 of the Police and Criminal Evidence Act 1984), but found nothing inside.

Is Constable BAIRD required to supply a notice of this search under s. 2 of the Police and Criminal Evidence Act 1984?

A Yes, it should be placed on the vehicle and a copy sent to the registered owner.

B No, a notice is not required as the inside of the vehicle was not searched.

C No, as no damage was caused to the vehicle.

D Yes, a notice must be placed somewhere on the vehicle.

Question 1.12

Inspector SPINK receives high-quality intelligence from a trusted source that there is going to be a large fight between two gangs of men (armed with knives, baseball bats and other offensive weapons) outside the Saddlers Arms pub. The source states that one of the gangs (numbering approximately 20 men) will be arriving in a coach and provides the registration number of the coach. Inspector SPINK reasonably believes it is necessary to authorise the use of the power under s. 60 of the Criminal Justice Act 1994 to stop and search the coach and its occupants as it approaches the pub in order to prevent serious violence taking place.

Would Inspector SPINK be able to authorise the use of the power under s. 60 in these circumstances?

A Yes, although any authorisation given would be subject to an initial authorisation limit of 15 hours.

B No, the power can only be authorised by an officer of the rank of superintendent or above.

C Yes, although any authorisation given would be subject to an initial authorisation limit of 24 hours.

D No, the power can only be authorised by an officer of the rank of assistant chief constable (or commander in the Metropolitan Police or City of London Police).

Question 1.13

A trade dispute has broken out over the sacking of several members of staff working for Portan Holdings Ltd. The company owns two large factory premises located approximately 1 mile away from each other in separate police force areas. Protesters have gathered at both factory premises to demonstrate their opposition to the sackings and reliable information is received that some of the protesters are intent on causing trouble, planning to attack any member of the Portan Holdings Ltd management team they see and cause them serious injury. To achieve that aim, they have taken a number of offensive weapons to both factory premises and are waiting outside the premises. Consideration is being given to authorising the powers under s. 60 of the Criminal Justice and Public Order Act 1994 to cover the factories concerned and the areas surrounding them.

Could the power be authorised in this situation?

A No, as no incidents of serious violence have actually taken place.

B Yes, an officer from either of the police forces where the factories are located can authorise the power in both police force areas, as the grounds for such an authorisation are connected.

C No, as an authorisation under s. 60 of the Act must cover an entire force area rather than a smaller part of it.

D Yes, but as the power is to be used in response to a threat or incident that straddles police force areas, an officer from each of the forces concerned will need to give an authorisation.

Question 1.14

DC FISHLOCK (dressed in plain clothes) has attended the scene of a large public disorder incident. During the course of the disorder, an offence of wounding (contrary to s. 18 of the Offences Against the Person Act 1861) took place. The wounding offence occurred in the last 30 minutes and involved the victim being stabbed several times with a knife. In order to recover the weapon concerned, an authorisation under s. 60 of the Criminal Justice and Police Act 1994 has been granted. Whilst DC FISHLOCK is making inquiries in the street where the wounding took place, he sees OSBORN walking towards him; OSBORN is wearing a black mask which partially covers his face. DC FISHLOCK believes OSBORN is wearing the mask wholly for the purpose of concealing his identity.

Would DC FISHLOCK be able to require OSBORN to remove the mask and seize it?

A Yes, because DC FISHLOCK believes OSBORN is wearing the mask wholly for the purpose of concealing his identity.

B No, because DC FISHLOCK is dressed in plain clothes and this is a uniform power.

C Yes, because the powers under s. 60 of the Act have been authorised, this automatically means that the powers under s. 60AA of the Act are also available.

D No, because the only way the powers under s. 60AA of the Act would be available would be if they had been specifically authorised, i.e. subject to a 'standalone' authorisation.

Question 1.15

BARR is driving a Volkswagen Passat motor vehicle (owned by LOMBARDI). BARR parks the vehicle on the car park of the Hound pub, enters the pub and strikes up a conversation with STRANG (who, unknown to BARR, is a well-known handler of stolen goods). After having a drink, BARR leaves the pub, gets back into the Passat and drives off. Once he is out of sight of the pub, he is stopped by PC GUMBLE (who is on uniform mobile patrol) as the police have been keeping observations on STRANG inside the pub and suspect that he has sold stolen property to BARR. PC GUMBLE searches BARR and the Passat for stolen property (under s. 1 of the Police and Criminal Evidence Act 1984); no stolen property is found. PC GUMBLE fills out a single search record in respect of the search and provides a copy of it to BARR.

Has PC GUMBLE correctly followed the provisions of Code A of the Codes of Practice?

A No, as a separate search record is required for the search of BARR and the search of the vehicle.
B Yes, as the object and grounds for the search are the same, only one search record needs to be completed.
C No, as BARR is not the owner of the vehicle, a copy of the search record of the vehicle must also be sent to LOMBARDI (the owner of the vehicle) within three months from the date of the search.
D Yes, as the owner of the vehicle (LOMBARDI) would not be entitled to a copy of the record of search.

Question 1.16

PC PORTER is on uniform foot patrol when he is directed to an area where a burglary has just taken place. A description of the possible offender is circulated and while searching the area, PC PORTER sees MALIK, who matches the description circulated, walking towards him. PC PORTER decides to exercise his powers under s. 1 of the Police and Criminal Evidence Act 1984 and to search MALIK. When PC PORTER approaches and speaks to MALIK, it becomes obvious that MALIK is having difficulty understanding what the officer is saying to him.

With regard to the Police and Criminal Evidence Act 1984, which of the following statements is correct?

A As MALIK does not appear to understand what is being said to him, PC PORTER cannot search him.

B PC PORTER must give MALIK certain information which can be communicated before or during the course of the search.

C As MALIK does not appear to understand what is being said, PC PORTER must take reasonable steps to bring all relevant information to his attention before starting the search.

D As MALIK is having difficulty understanding what PC PORTER is saying, the officer need not attempt to explain anything to him and he may search MALIK without communicating the usual information required.

Question 1.17

PC ASHCROFT (a male officer) and PC HOLLAND (a female officer) are on uniform mobile patrol in a marked police van which has no windows in the rear so the inside of the van cannot be seen from the street. They are directed to attend an incident of burglary where the offender has stolen a large amount of property including a mobile phone, watch and wallet. A description of the suspect is circulated and as the officers get closer to the scene of the offence they see TYLER (a male), who closely matches the description of the suspect, running along a street. The officers manage to stop TYLER and are considering whether to search him using the power under s. 1 of the Police and Criminal Evidence Act 1984 as they reasonably suspect they will find stolen articles on TYLER's person.

Thinking about the issues in respect of s. 1 of the Police and Criminal Evidence Act 1984 and Code A of the Codes of Practice, which of the following comments is correct?

A If the search involves the removal of no more than TYLER's outer coat, jacket and gloves then either officer could carry out a search of TYLER in the street in those circumstances.

B As TYLER is a male, only PC ASHCROFT could carry out a s. 1 search in these circumstances.

C The officers could place TYLER in the rear of the police vehicle and require him to remove his T-shirt but only if both officers are present.

D If it were necessary, a search involving the exposure of TYLER's intimate parts could take place in the rear of the police vehicle (as long as PC HOLLAND is not present).

ANSWERS

Answer 1.1

Answer **B** — Under s. 1(2) of the Police and Criminal Evidence Act 1984, a constable:

(a) may search—
  (i) any person or vehicle;
  (ii) anything which is in or on a vehicle, for stolen or prohibited articles or any article to which subsection (8A) below applies or any firework to which subsection (8B) below applies; and
(b) may detain a person or vehicle for the purpose of such a search.

Searches in gardens of dwellings are not prohibited altogether; under s. 1(4), where a person is in a garden or yard occupied with and used for the purposes of a dwelling or on other land so occupied and used, a constable may not search him/her in the exercise of the power conferred by this section unless the constable has reasonable grounds for believing:

(a) that he/she does not reside in the dwelling; and
(b) that he/she is not in the place in question with the express or implied permission of a person who resides in the dwelling.

Answers A and C are therefore incorrect.

There *are* restrictions on searches which take place outside a dwelling by virtue of s. 1(4); therefore, answer D is incorrect.

General Police Duties, paras 3.1.4.1, 3.1.4.2

Answer 1.2

Answer **B** — Under s. 1(2) of the Police and Criminal Evidence Act 1984, a constable:

(a) may search—
  (i) any person or vehicle;
  (ii) anything which is in or on a vehicle, for stolen or prohibited articles or any article to which subsection (8A) below applies or any firework to which subsection (8B) below applies; and
(b) may detain a person or vehicle for the purpose of such a search.

Paragraph 2.2A of Code A states that:

The exercise of these stop and search powers depends on the likelihood that the person searched is in possession of an item for which they may be searched; it does not depend

11

on the person concerned being suspected of committing an offence in relation to the object of the search.

Paragraph 2.2A further states that a police officer who has reasonable grounds to suspect that a person is in innocent possession of a stolen or prohibited article, controlled drug or other item for which the officer is empowered to search, may stop and search the person even though there would be no power of arrest. Answers C and D are therefore incorrect.

This would even apply when a child under the age of criminal responsibility (10 years) is suspected of carrying any such item, even if they knew that person had it. Answers A and D are incorrect for this reason also.

General Police Duties, paras 3.1.4.1, 3.1.4.2

Answer 1.3

Answer **B** — Under PACE Code C, para. 2.1(a), a constable must have reasonable grounds to suspect that the relevant articles would be found, before the powers under s. 1 of the Police and Criminal Evidence Act 1984 can be exercised.

The courts have accepted that reasonable grounds for suspicion can arise from information given to an officer by a colleague, an informant or even anonymously (*O'Hara* v *Chief Constable of the Royal Ulster Constabulary* [1997] AC 286). There is no requirement to prove that the witness had a reasonable suspicion, or whether they had any particular skills and answers C and D are incorrect.

The courts have held that it must be shown that any such grounds on which an officer acted would have been enough to give rise to that suspicion in a 'reasonable person' (*Nakkuda Ali* v *Jayaratne* [1951] AC 66).

However, the mere existence of such circumstances or evidence is not enough. The officer must actually have a 'reasonable suspicion' that the relevant articles will be found. If, in fact, the officer knows that there is little or no likelihood of finding the articles, the power could not be used (*R* v *Harrison* [1938] 3 All ER 134). Answer A is therefore incorrect.

General Police Duties, paras 3.1.4.3, 3.1.4.4

Answer 1.4

Answer **B** — Under s. 60 of the Criminal Justice and Public Order Act 1994, if a police officer of or above the rank of inspector reasonably believes that incidents of serious violence may take place in his/her area, or that people are carrying dangerous instruments or offensive weapons in the area or that a single incident of serious violence has taken place involving the use of a dangerous instrument or offensive weapon, then he/she may give an authorisation to stop any pedestrian and/or vehicle and search him/her and/or the vehicle for offensive weapons or dangerous instruments.

A direction to *extend* the period authorised under the power may be given only once. This extension is for a maximum period of 24 hours and thereafter further use of the powers requires a new authorisation. In the context of this question, the extension may be granted on the Saturday night, but if intelligence suggests further incidents will take place on the Sunday and Monday night, a new authorisation may be put in place on the Sunday, which can be extended to the Monday if necessary.

Answers A, C and D are incorrect for these reasons.

General Police Duties, paras 3.1.4.5, 3.1.4.6

Answer 1.5

Answer **C** — Under s. 60AA(1) of the Criminal Justice and Public Order Act 1994, where an authorisation under s. 60 is in force, a constable in uniform may require any person to remove any item which the constable reasonably believes that person is wearing wholly or mainly for the purpose of concealing his/her identity. The power is not absolute, as the constable has to reasonably believe that the person is wearing the item wholly or mainly to conceal his/her identity (therefore answer B is incorrect). There is no need, however, for the constable reasonably to believe that the person is carrying a dangerous instrument or an offensive weapon, or that the person is likely to be involved in violence, in order to exercise the power under s. 60AA(1). Those matters would have been considered before the authorisation was granted under s. 60. Answers A and D are therefore incorrect.

General Police Duties, para. 3.1.4.9

Answer 1.6

Answer **D** — Under s. 60AA of the Criminal Justice and Public Order Act 1994, a constable in uniform may require any person to remove any item which the constable reasonably believes that person is wearing wholly or mainly for the purpose of concealing his/her identity. However, there is no specific power under this section to stop vehicles and therefore answers A and C are incorrect.

There is no power to search for face coverings etc. under s. 60AA. The Divisional Court has held that the predecessor to this power (the old s. 60(4A)) neither involved nor required a 'search' and that, therefore, the provisions of s. 2 of the Police and Criminal Evidence Act 1984 did not apply (*DPP* v *Avery* [2001] EWHC 748 (Admin)).

The court went on to hold that although the power amounted to a significant interference with a person's liberty, it was justified by the type of situation envisaged by the legislators, whereby the police may need to call upon the law. Clearly, if an item is found during a lawful search for other articles (say, under s. 60(4)) which does not require any 'reasonable belief' by the officer, face coverings and masks could then be seized under s. 60AA(2)(b). As there is no accompanying power of search under s. 60AA, answer B is incorrect.

Given that this is a power for police officers in uniform, the general power to stop vehicles under s. 163 of the Road Traffic Act 1988 could be used.

General Police Duties, paras 3.1.4.9, 3.1.4.13

Answer 1.7

Answer **B** — Paragraph 3 of sch. 5 to the Terrorism Prevention and Investigation Measures Act 2011 allows a constable to detain an individual to be searched under the following powers:

- para. 6(2)(a) when a TPIM notice is being, or has just been, served on the individual for the purpose of ascertaining whether there is anything on the individual that contravenes measures specified in the notice;
- para. 8(2)(a) in accordance with a warrant to search the individual if that search is necessary to determine whether an individual is complying with measures specified in the notice (see para. 2.20); and
- para. 10 to ascertain whether an individual in respect of whom a TPIM notice is in force is in possession of anything that could be used to threaten or harm any person.

The officers in the question are exercising their powers under para. 6(2)(a) which allows them to search DARBY. The power is exercisable anywhere (including DARBY's house) making answer A incorrect.

Paragraph 2.19 of the PACE Code of Practice in relation to sch. 5 states that when exercising his/her powers of search, there is no requirement for the constable to have reasonable grounds to suspect that the individual has been, or is, contravening any of the measures specified in the TPIM notice; or is not complying with measures specified in the TPIM notice; or is in possession of anything that could be used to threaten or harm any person.

In summary, the officers can simply search DARBY because they are attending to serve the TPIM notice on him, and answers A, C and D are incorrect.

General Police Duties, paras 3.1.4.1, 3.1.4.14

Answer 1.8

Answer **A** — Paragraph 8(2)(a) of sch. 5 to the Terrorism Prevention and Investigation Measures Act 2011 allows a constable to detain and search an individual in accordance with a warrant, if that search is necessary to determine whether an individual is complying with measures specified in the notice.

Paragraph 2.20 of the PACE Code of Practice in relation to sch. 5 states that a search of an individual on warrant under the power mentioned must be carried out within 28 days of the issue of the warrant and:

- the individual may be searched on one occasion only within that period;
- the search must take place at a reasonable hour unless it appears that this would frustrate the purposes of the search.

This means that answer A is correct, and answers B, C and D are incorrect.

General Police Duties, para. 3.1.4.14

Answer 1.9

Answer **C** — Code C, para. 3.5 of the PACE Codes of Practice states that there is no power to require a person to remove any clothing in public other than an outer coat, jacket or gloves (except under s. 60AA of the Criminal Justice and Public Order Act 1994 which empowers a constable to require a person to remove any item worn to conceal identity).

Paragraph 3.6 states that where, on reasonable grounds, it is considered necessary to conduct a more thorough search (e.g. by requiring a person to take off a T-shirt or trousers), this must be done out of public view, for example in a police van or police station if there is one nearby.

Paragraph 3.7 states that searches involving exposure of intimate parts of the body may be carried out only at a nearby police station or other nearby location which is out of public view (but not a police vehicle). Answers A and B are therefore incorrect.

This paragraph goes on to say that a search involving exposure of intimate parts of the body must be conducted in accordance with the requirements of Annex A to Code C (strip searches), but that an intimate search may not be authorised or carried out under any stop and search powers. However, what the officers propose to do may be conducted under s. 1 at either of the locations described previously. Answer D is therefore incorrect.

General Police Duties, para. 3.1.5

Answer 1.10

Answer **B** — Code C, para. 3.5 of the PACE Codes of Practice states that there is no power to require a person to remove any clothing in public other than an outer coat, jacket or gloves (except under s. 60AA of the Criminal Justice and Public Order Act 1994 which empowers a constable to require a person to remove any item worn to conceal identity).

A search in public of a person's clothing which has not been removed must be restricted to superficial examination of outer garments. This does not, however, prevent an officer from placing his/her hand inside the pockets of the outer clothing or feeling round the inside of collars, socks and shoes if this is reasonably necessary in the circumstances to look for the object of the search or to remove and examine any item reasonably suspected to be the object of the search. For the same reasons, subject to the restrictions on the removal of headgear, a person's hair may also be searched in public.

The only time the gender of the officer is mentioned in this Code is when it relates to conducting a more thorough search. Paragraph 3.6 states that where on reasonable grounds it is considered necessary to conduct a more thorough search (e.g. by requiring a person to take off a T-shirt), this must be done out of public view, for example in a police van or police station if there is one nearby.

This paragraph goes on to say that any search involving the removal of more than an outer coat, jacket, gloves, headgear or footwear or any other item concealing identity, may only be made by an officer of the same sex as the person searched and may not be made in the presence of anyone of the opposite sex unless the person being searched specifically requests it.

This means that Constable DANIELLS can search BENTLEY and so answers A and D are therefore incorrect.

There is no requirement to conduct a search of outer garments out of public view and answer C is incorrect.

General Police Duties, para. 3.1.5

Answer 1.11

Answer **D** — Section 2(6) of the Police and Criminal Evidence Act 1984 states that 'on completing the search of an unattended vehicle, or anything in or on such a vehicle, a constable shall leave a notice', making answers B and C incorrect.

There may be occasions when officers have to force entry into a vehicle in order to search it. On such an occasion, the officer must, if practicable, leave the vehicle secure (Code A, para. 4.10). However, in this scenario the officer has not needed to force entry, this means that the vehicle has not been damaged as a result of the search. Section 2(7) states that 'the constable shall leave the notice inside the vehicle unless it is not reasonably practicable to do so without damaging the vehicle'.

There is no obligation on the officer to send a notice to the registered owner's address, and therefore answer A is incorrect.

General Police Duties, paras 3.1.5.2, 3.1.6.2

Answer 1.12

Answer **C** — The power under s. 60 of the Criminal Justice and Public Order Act 1994 can be authorised by an officer of the rank of inspector or above, making answers B and D incorrect. The initial authorisation of the power can last up to 24 hours (correct answer C), making answer A incorrect.

General Police Duties, paras 3.1.4.4, 3.1.4.5

Answer 1.13

Answer **D** — An authorisation under s. 60 can be given if a police officer of or above the rank of inspector reasonably believes that:

- incidents involving serious violence may take place in any locality in his/her police area, and that it is expedient to give an authorisation under this section to prevent their occurrence; or
- an incident involving serious violence has taken place in England and Wales in his/her police area and that a dangerous instrument or offensive weapon used in the incident is being carried in any locality in his/her police area by a person and it is expedient to give an authorisation under this section to find the instrument or weapon; or
- where persons are carrying dangerous instruments or offensive weapons in any locality in his/her police area without good reason, he/she may give an authorisation that the powers conferred by this section are to be exercisable at any place within that locality for a specified period not exceeding 24 hours.

The authorisation is not limited to situations where incidents of serious violence have taken place, making answer A incorrect.

It is for the authorising officer to determine the geographical area in which the use of the powers is to be authorised (this may encompass an entire police force area, but not necessarily so), making answer C incorrect. If the area specified is smaller than the whole force area, the officer giving the authorisation should specify either the streets which form the boundary of the area or a divisional boundary within the force area.

Answer B is incorrect as if the power is to be used in response to a threat or incident that straddles police force areas, an officer from *each* of the forces concerned will need to give an authorisation (correct answer D).

General Police Duties, para. 3.1.4.6

Answer 1.14

Answer **B** — The powers under s. 60AA can be authorised as a 'stand-alone' power, but they are also available when the powers under s. 60 of the Criminal Justice and Public Order Act 1994 are authorised. This means that when a s. 60 authorisation is made, the powers under s. 60AA of the Act are also automatically available, meaning that answer D is incorrect. This would seem to make answer C correct—that is not the case. It is correct that the powers under s. 60AA would be available in the area where the s. 60 authorisation has been granted, but the important element here is that the powers under s. 60 (and s. 60AA) are only granted to an officer in uniform. So the fact that the powers under s. 60AA are available and the fact that DC FISHLOCK believes OSBORN is wearing the mask wholly for the purpose of concealing his identity are irrelevant (answers A and C are incorrect). If DC FISHLOCK were in uniform, then the officer could use the power—*he is not*, so the power is not available to the officer.

General Police Duties, paras 3.1.4.8 to 3.1.4.11

Answer 1.15

Answer **B** — A record is required for each person and each vehicle searched. However, answer A is incorrect as if a person is in a vehicle and both are searched, and the object and the grounds for the search are the same, only one record need be completed (correct answer B (Code A, para. 4.5)). So in these circumstances PC GUMBLE would comply with Code A of the Codes of Practice. The owner of the vehicle is entitled to a copy of the search record (if one is made) but the Act does not require that they are sent the copy of the search record only that they can have a copy if they ask for one (s. 3(8)), making answers C and D incorrect.

General Police Duties, paras 3.1.6.1 to 3.1.6.2

Answer 1.16

Answer **C** — Code A of the Codes of Practice (para. 3.11) states that if a person does not appear to understand what is being said, or there is any doubt about their ability to understand English, the officer must take all reasonable steps to bring the relevant information (constable's name etc.) to the person's attention, making answer D incorrect. The relevant information must be given *before* starting the search (making answer B incorrect). The fact that MALIK does not understand the officer does not preclude the use of the powers under s. 1 of the Police and Criminal Evidence Act 1984, making answer A incorrect.

General Police Duties, para. 3.1.5.1

Answer 1.17

Answer **A** — There would be nothing wrong with an everyday s. 1 search taking place in the street in such circumstances. The officers reasonably suspect that they will find stolen articles on TYLER and have legitimate justification for the use of the power. When the power is being used to carry out a search that involves the removal of no more than the outer coat, jacket and gloves etc., then a male may search a female and vice versa (answer A). There is no requirement for such a search to be made by a person of the same sex, making answer B incorrect. Answer C is incorrect as if the officers did require TYLER to remove his T-shirt this would have to be done out of the public domain and only by an officer of the same sex. Officers or persons of the opposite sex may not be present unless the person searched specifically requests it. Answer D is incorrect as a search involving intimate body parts cannot take place in a police vehicle.

General Police Duties, para. 3.1.5

2 | Entry, Search and Seizure

Question 2.1

Police officers entered premises under the authority of a warrant issued under the Misuse of Drugs Act 1971. The premises were empty when the warrant was executed. While they were conducting the search for evidence relating to the unlawful supply of controlled substances, they came across other property which appeared to be stolen. A discussion took place as to how the officers should deal with the property as it was not covered in the warrant and the original reason for the search.

Which of the following statements is correct in relation to the correct application of the officers' powers and how they should deal with the suspected stolen property?

A The purpose of the entry was to find evidence relating to the unlawful supply of controlled drugs; officers may not seize suspected stolen goods in these circumstances.

B The purpose of the entry was to find evidence relating to the unlawful supply of controlled drugs; officers would require an additional authorisation under the Police and Criminal Evidence Act 1984 to seize suspected stolen goods in these circumstances.

C Provided the original entry by the officers was lawful, they may seize suspected stolen goods while on the premises, even if that was not the original purpose for entry.

D Provided the original entry by the officers was lawful, they may only seize other goods while on the premises which are connected with, or similar to, the offence suspected, even if that was not the original purpose for entry.

Question 2.2

DCs COHEN and VARDY work on a specialist team investigating organised crime groups in their region. PEARSON was arrested for a series of armed robberies and was in police detention; a search of his office premises was authorised under s. 18 of the Police and Criminal Evidence Act 1984 (PACE). The officers attended the office premises owned by PEARSON to search for evidence connecting him to the robberies. At the premises, they produced a copy of the search authorisation to MANNINGS, who worked for PEARSON. MANNINGS pointed out to the officers that their names did not appear on the authorisation and demanded they disclose who they were and the station they worked at before they conducted the search.

Which of the following statements is correct in relation to the searches of premises under Code B of the PACE Codes of Practice?

A MANNINGS is entitled to know the officers' identities before the search; they should either be disclosed on the PACE authorisation or the officers should identify themselves.

B The officers' identities should be disclosed unless they reasonably believe that recording or disclosing their names might put them in danger.

C The officers are not investigating a case linked to terrorism, where it is reasonably believed that recording or disclosing their names might put them in danger; therefore their identities must be disclosed.

D The officers' identities should be disclosed unless an inspector has authorised in writing that he/she reasonably believes that recording or disclosing their names might put them in danger.

Question 2.3

DC HALL is investigating an allegation that FRISK, who owns a building company, paid bribes to officers in a local authority planning department over a number of years, to push through planning applications. DC HALL has recovered evidence from a search of FRISK's offices and anticipates seizing numerous documents and computers at the local authority offices. DC HALL is seeking a multiple entry search warrant but is uncertain how many visits will be required to complete the evidence-gathering process.

Which of the following statements is correct in relation to the type of warrant DC HALL is seeking?

A DC HALL must state the maximum number of entries desired in the application for the warrant.

B DC HALL may apply for a warrant authorising unlimited entries in these circumstances, because the maximum number is unknown.

C DC HALL is not required to specify the number of entries desired; the warrant will automatically authorise unlimited entries.

D DC HALL is not required to specify the number of entries desired; an inspector may authorise further entries if necessary.

Question 2.4

DC GRANT is investigating a case involving a series of frauds. It is suspected that PEDERSON has been involved in the production of counterfeit coins and notes. PEDERSON has a large base of operations as a contractor for a major national building firm. He has a main office for legitimate business and a home address for which DC GRANT has obtained an all premises warrant which authorised the search of these. During the search of PEDERSON's home address, DC GRANT has recovered documents that suggest PEDERSON owns two other premises where evidence may be found.

Which of the following comments is correct in relation to the all premises warrant DC GRANT possesses and a search of the other two premises?

A The other two premises may be searched provided entry to those premises is authorised by an inspector in writing.

B The other two premises may be searched provided entry to those premises is authorised by a superintendent in writing.

C The other two premises could not be searched under the all premises warrant; DC GRANT will have to apply to a magistrate for another all premises warrant to search those premises.

D The other two premises can be searched provided entry to those premises is authorised by an inspector in writing or, if one is not readily available, the senior officer on duty.

Question 2.5

DC GOMEZ was the officer in charge of a search which was conducted at MALONEY's home address. Officers entered the premises by force under the authority of a warrant to search for property stolen from a recent burglary at a jeweller's shop. The search team found several items of jewellery matching the description of the stolen goods and these were seized as evidence. MALONEY was not present when the search took place and DC GOMEZ established that there was no other person available who appeared to be in charge of the premises; however, the officer forgot to leave a copy of the warrant in a prominent place in the premises.

Given that DC GOMEZ has failed to follow the requirements of s. 16(7) of PACE by not leaving a copy of the warrant in a prominent place, which of the following statements is correct?

A The search was unlawful; this may result in the exclusion of any evidence obtained under the warrant and officers could be made to return the jewellery to MALONEY.

B This is a minor deviation from the terms of the warrant which would not render the search unlawful or result in the exclusion of any evidence obtained.

C The search was unlawful; this may result in the exclusion of any evidence obtained under the warrant, but officers could not be made to return the jewellery to MALONEY.

D The search was unlawful, but a failure to follow the requirements of s. 16 will not result in the exclusion of any evidence obtained under the warrant.

Question 2.6

A number of large parties have been taking place on weekends and officers suspect that COOKSLEY is the organiser. The location of the events changes every week and intelligence suggests that COOKSLEY is dealing Class A drugs from a tent that is erected at each venue, which also contains the sound equipment for the parties. Officers have information that COOKSLEY transports the equipment and drugs to the venues in the back of a van. They are considering applying for a warrant under the Misuse of Drugs Act 1971 to search the vehicle and tent for drugs. However, COOKSLEY's address is unknown and officers will have to wait until the following weekend for intelligence on the next venue.

Which of the following statements is correct in relation to the officers' intentions?

A Only the tent is a 'premises' in respect of a search warrant; there is no power to apply for a warrant to search a vehicle in this way.

B Both the tent and the vehicle are 'premises' and officers could apply for a search warrant in respect of both.

C Neither the tent (which is a moveable structure) nor the vehicle are 'premises' in respect of a search warrant; officers will have to use other powers to search them.

D Officers will have to use other powers to search both the tent and the vehicle; a search warrant requires a location to be specified in it before one can be issued.

Question 2.7

DC PRICE is investigating a fraud case and has uncovered evidence that a number of solicitors from a local firm may be involved. The officer has applied to a justice of the peace for a warrant under s. 8 of the Police and Criminal Evidence Act 1984 to enter and search the solicitors' offices for evidence relating to the offence. DC PRICE has reasonable cause to believe that there may be communications between solicitors and clients referring to the fraud. The officer is aware that there may be a substantial amount of paper and computer records on the premises and is anticipating having to use powers under s. 50 of the Criminal Justice and Police Act 2001 to seize and sift evidence.

Which of the following statements is correct in relation to items subject to legal privilege which may be on the premises?

A Any communication between solicitors and clients is subject to legal privilege and cannot be searched for or seized under the terms of a warrant.

B Any items found that relate to criminal offences are not subject to legal privilege and may be searched for or seized.

C A warrant cannot authorise a search for legally privileged material and, if such material is inadvertently seized, it would render the search unlawful.

D The possession of a warrant under s. 8 authorises any material found on the premises to be seized and sifted.

Question 2.8

Late at night, Constable CLYNE was in uniform following a motor vehicle on a road, which was not displaying any lights. The officer activated the sirens and blue lights to the police vehicle, attempting to get the other vehicle to stop. However, the other vehicle accelerated away from Constable CLYNE and was lost after a period of time. About an hour later, the officer attended the address of the registered owner of the vehicle. The vehicle concerned was found outside the address and Constable CLYNE knocked on the door to speak to the occupant(s)—there was no reply. There were lights on at the premises and Constable CLYNE believed that the driver was inside the premises.

Given that Constable CLYNE may have had reasonable grounds for believing that the driver was on the premises, was there a power of entry in these circumstances?

A No, the driver had not been involved in an accident which involved injury to any person.

B Yes, the driver of the vehicle failed to stop when required to do so by a constable in uniform.

C No, Constable CLYNE was not in immediate pursuit of the driver of the vehicle.

D Yes, but only if Constable CLYNE had reason to believe that the driver was unfit to drive through drink or drugs.

Question 2.9

Constable BROWN has attended the scene of a road traffic collision where a van had collided with a parked and unattended car at the side of the road. The parked car had sustained substantial damage and the driver of the van had made off from the collision, leaving the van at the scene of the accident. People at the scene stated that they had followed the van for some time and they believed the driver was drunk from the manner of driving they had witnessed. Also, they had seen the driver drinking from cans of lager while driving on the road and throwing empty cans out of the window. Constable BROWN was considering searching the van for evidence that the driver had been drinking, using the power under s. 32 of the Police and Criminal Evidence Act 1984.

Which of the following statements is correct in relation to any power Constable BROWN may have to search the vehicle in these circumstances?

A Constable BROWN may not search the vehicle under this section; it is restricted to searching for articles which may assist a person to escape from lawful custody.

B Constable BROWN may search the vehicle under this section for anything which might be evidence relating to an offence.

C Constable BROWN may not conduct a search under this section; it is restricted to searching people or premises and not vehicles.

D Constable BROWN may not conduct a search under this section; the driver has not been arrested for an indictable offence.

Question 2.10

Constable ELLIS attended a dwelling burglary in progress at 2 am. On arrival, the officer was told that the householders had disturbed the suspect, who had escaped through the back door into the rear garden. They had seen the suspect carrying a bag, believed to have contained items stolen from their house. The victims' rear garden was enclosed and was adjacent to several other houses; it was believed that the suspect had climbed over fences and escaped through the other gardens on to the main street nearby. Whilst making a search of the area, Constable ELLIS received a message that GRAFF had been arrested in a street nearby, by other officers, and that he matched the suspect's description. However, this person was not carrying a bag as described by the witnesses. Constable ELLIS intended returning to the crime scene to search the neighbours' gardens for the bag, to try to link it to GRAFF.

What authority, if any, would Constable ELLIS require in order to search neighbours' gardens in these circumstances?

A Constable ELLIS would require the occupiers' permission unless she was in immediate pursuit of a suspect.

B Constable ELLIS would not require the occupiers' permission as this may cause disproportionate inconvenience to the person concerned.

C Constable ELLIS would not require the occupiers' permission as this may cause disproportionate inconvenience to the investigation.

D Constable ELLIS would require the statutory authority of a warrant or through PACE (s. 17, 18 or 32). Otherwise she would require the occupiers' permission.

Question 2.11

Constable ALLEN has attended WALTER's home address to serve him with a Terrorism Prevention and Investigation Measures (TPIM) notice, under s. 2 of the Terrorism Prevention and Investigation Measures Act 2011, to restrict his movements because of his suspected links to terrorism. The TPIM requires WALTER to reside at the address on the notice and prohibits him from travelling overseas. The notice also contains a list of people that WALTER is not to contact. On serving the notice, Constable ALLEN decided that WALTER's address should be searched to discover anything that might breach any measures specified in the TPIM notice.

Which of the following statements is correct in relation to whether Constable ALLEN may search WALTER's address?

A A search of premises in connection with a TPIM notice may only be made under warrant.

B A search of premises may only be made in connection with a TPIM notice without a warrant where the person has absconded.

C A search of premises may only be made in connection with a TPIM notice without a warrant if it is conducted for the purposes of finding the individual on whom the notice is to be served.

D A search of premises may be made without a warrant at the time of serving a TPIM notice, to ascertain whether there is anything in the premises that contravenes measures specified in the notice.

ANSWERS

Answer 2.1

Answer **C** — Where police officers enter premises lawfully (including where they are there by invitation), they are on the premises for all lawful purposes (*Foster* v *Attard* [1986] Crim LR 627). This means that they can carry out any lawful functions while on the premises even if that was not the original purpose for entry. For instance, if officers entered under a lawful power provided by the Misuse of Drugs Act 1971, they may carry out other lawful functions which would include a general power under s. 19(3) of the Police and Criminal Evidence Act 1984 to seize anything which is on the premises if the officers have reasonable grounds for believing that it is evidence in relation to an offence which they are investigating or any other offence and that it is necessary to seize it in order to prevent the evidence being concealed, lost, altered or destroyed.

Answers A, B and D are therefore incorrect.

General Police Duties, para. 3.2.1

Answer 2.2

Answer **B** — Code B, para. 2.9 of the PACE Codes of Practice relating to searches of premises by police officers states:

Nothing in this Code requires the identity of officers, or anyone accompanying them during a search of premises, to be recorded or disclosed:

(a) in the case of enquiries linked to the investigation of terrorism; or
(b) if officers reasonably believe recording or disclosing their names might put them in danger.

In these cases, officers should use warrant or other identification numbers and the name of their police station.

Paragraph 2.9 places the decision-making powers in respect of disclosing their identity (when they are investigating specific offences covered in para. 2.9(b)) firmly with the officers—or the people accompanying them—who are conducting the search.

The purpose of para. 2.9(b) is to protect those involved in serious organised crime investigations or arrests of particularly violent suspects when there is reliable information that those arrested or their associates may threaten or cause harm to the officers or anyone accompanying them during a search of premises—in cases of doubt, an officer of inspector rank or above should be consulted.

Whilst the search under s. 18 must be authorised by an inspector, there is no specific requirement for him/her to authorise the non-disclosure of the officer's identification in writing prior to the search and answers A and D are incorrect.

Whilst this paragraph does apply to cases linked to the investigation of terrorism, it is not exclusive in respect of non-disclosure of the identification of the officers conducting the search and answer C is therefore incorrect.

General Police Duties, paras 3.2.3, 3.2.3.1

Answer 2.3

Answer **B** — Section 15(2)(iii) of the Police and Criminal Evidence Act 1984 states:

> if the application is for a warrant authorising entry and search on more than one occasion, the ground on which he applies for such a warrant, and whether he seeks a warrant authorising an unlimited number of entries, or (if not) the maximum number of entries desired.

Therefore, an officer will normally be required to specify the number of entries desired and the warrant will *not* automatically authorise unlimited entries. Answer C is therefore incorrect.

On the other hand, s. 15(2)(iii) does provide some flexibility in case the number of entries is unknown (answer A is therefore incorrect).

Section 16(3B) of the Act deals with the authority required from an inspector in relation to multiple entry warrants. Under this section, premises may not be entered or searched for a second or any subsequent time under a warrant which authorises multiple entries unless a police officer of at least the rank of inspector has authorised that in writing. The section does not give an inspector the power to authorise multiple entries; on the contrary, it places a restriction on such warrants so that each entry must be authorised by an inspector, even when multiple entries have been authorised by a magistrate. Answer D is therefore incorrect.

General Police Duties, paras 3.2.3.2, 3.2.3.3

Answer 2.4

Answer **A** — Section 16 of the Police and Criminal Evidence Act 1984 states:

> (3A) If the warrant is an all premises warrant, no premises which are not specified in it may be entered or searched unless a police officer of at least the rank of inspector has in writing authorised them to be entered.

There is no provision under this section for a senior officer on duty to authorise entry to new premises if an inspector is not readily available and there is no requirement for a superintendent to sign the authorisation. Answers B and D are therefore incorrect.

Also, there will be no requirement for the officer to apply to a magistrate for another all premises warrant to search those premises. Answer C is therefore incorrect.

General Police Duties, para. 3.2.3.3

Answer 2.5

Answer **A** — Section 16(7) of PACE states that if there is no person present who appears to the constable to be in charge of the premises, he/she shall leave a copy of the warrant in a prominent place on the premises. There was a clear breach of the terms of the warrant by DC GOMEZ in this case, which means that any entry and search made under a warrant will be unlawful. Further, a failure to follow the requirements of ss. 15 and 16 of PACE may result in the exclusion of any evidence obtained under the warrant. Answer D is therefore incorrect.

Where officers failed to provide the occupier of the searched premises with a copy of the warrant, they were obliged to return the property seized during the search (*R v Chief Constable of Lancashire, ex parte Parker* [1993] QB 577). As this is a possibility, answer C is incorrect.

Very minor departures from the letter of the warrant will not render any search unlawful (*Attorney-General of Jamaica v Williams* [1998] AC 351); however, *Parker* suggests that failing to provide a copy of the warrant would not be considered a *minor* departure from the requirement to do so under s. 16, therefore answer B is incorrect.

General Police Duties, paras 3.2.3.3, 3.2.3.6

Answer 2.6

Answer **B** — Section 23 of PACE states that 'premises' include any place, and in particular:

(a) any vehicle, vessel, aircraft or hovercraft;
(b) any offshore installation;
(c) any renewable energy installation;
(d) any tent or moveable structure.

Answers A and C are therefore incorrect.

Since 'premises' includes any place, officers are not restricted by the fact that they are not yet aware of the location of the party, and therefore answer D is incorrect.

General Police Duties, para. 3.2.3.4

Answer 2.7

Answer **B** — Section 10(1) of the Police and Criminal Evidence Act 1984 states that subject to subs. (2), 'items subject to legal privilege' means:

(a) communications between a professional legal adviser and his client or any person representing his client made in connection with the giving of legal advice to the client;
(b) communications between a professional legal adviser and his client or any person representing his client or between such an adviser or his client or any such representative and any other person made in connection with or in contemplation of legal proceedings and for the purposes of such proceedings; and
(c) items enclosed with or referred to in such communications and made—
    (i) in connection with the giving of legal advice; or
    (ii) in connection with or in contemplation of legal proceedings and for the purposes of such proceedings, when they are in the possession of a person who is entitled to possession of them.

Generally, material which falls within the definition in s. 10(1) is subject to legal privilege, which means that it cannot be searched for or seized. However, items held with the intention of furthering a criminal purpose are no longer subject to this privilege (s. 10(2)). Occasions where this will happen are very rare, but could include instances where a solicitor's firm is the subject of a criminal investigation (*R v Leeds Crown Court, ex parte Switalski* [1991] Crim LR 559). Answer A is therefore incorrect.

Although a warrant cannot authorise a search for legally privileged material, the fact that such material is inadvertently seized in the course of a search authorised by a proper warrant does not render the search unlawful (*R v HM Customs & Excise, ex parte Popely* [2000] Crim LR 388). Answer C is therefore incorrect.

Possession of a warrant under s. 8 does not authorise police officers to seize *all* material found on the relevant premises to be taken away and 'sifted' somewhere else (*R v Chesterfield Justices, ex parte Bramley* [2000] QB 576). Officers using seize and sift powers will have to be able to show that it was essential (rather than simply convenient or preferable) to do so. Answer D is incorrect.

General Police Duties, paras 3.2.3.7, 3.2.3.8, 3.2.8.7

Answer 2.8

Answer **B** — There are a number of powers to enter premises under s. 17 of the Police and Criminal Evidence Act 1984, including circumstances associated with the offence under s. 4 of the Road Traffic Act 1988 (unfit through drink or drugs). However, under s. 17(1)(c)(iiia), provided the constable has reasonable grounds for

2. Entry, Search and Seizure

believing that the person whom he/she is seeking is on the premises, the constable may enter for the purposes of arresting a person for an offence under s. 163 of the Road Traffic Act 1988 (failure to stop when required to do so by constable in uniform). Answers A and D are therefore incorrect.

There are further powers under s. 17(d) to recapture a person who is unlawfully at large and whom the officer is pursuing; however, the power to enter premises under s. 17(iiia) does not require the constable to be in 'immediate pursuit' and answer C is incorrect.

General Police Duties, para. 3.2.5.1

Answer 2.9

Answer **D** — Under s. 32(2)(a) of the Police and Criminal Evidence Act 1984, a constable may search an arrested person for anything:

(i)   which he might use to assist him to escape from lawful custody; or
(ii) which might be evidence relating to an offence.

Under s. 32(2)(b), if the offence for which he/she has been arrested is an indictable offence, there is a further power to enter and search any premises in which the person was when arrested or immediately before he/she was arrested for evidence relating to the offence.

The section is not restricted to conducting a search for articles which may assist a person to escape from lawful custody; it may also be used to search for evidence of an offence, so answer A is incorrect.

Section 23 of PACE states that for the purpose of the Act, premises includes any vehicle, vessel, aircraft or hovercraft. Answer C is therefore incorrect.

The use of this power is restricted to searching a person or premises *after* he/she has been arrested for an indictable offence, which means that answer B is incorrect. It is worth noting that because the offence suspected is a summary offence, the officer would not have been able to utilise this search power even if the driver had remained at the scene.

General Police Duties, para. 3.2.5.2

Answer 2.10

Answer **B** — Generally, Code B of the PACE Codes of Practice deals with the search of premises through the statutory authority of a warrant or through PACE (s. 17, 18 or 32). However, para. 5 of this Code deals with searches with the consent of the occupier or the person 'entitled to grant consent'.

Paragraphs 5.1 to 5.3 deal with how such consent should be obtained; however, para. 5.4 states that it is unnecessary to seek consent if this would cause disproportionate inconvenience *to the person concerned*. Answer C is incorrect, as it is the inconvenience to the occupier that matters.

Paragraph 5.4 is intended to apply when it is reasonable to assume innocent occupiers would agree to, and expect, police to take the proposed action, e.g. if:

- a suspect has fled the scene of a crime or to evade arrest and it is necessary quickly to check surrounding gardens and readily accessible places to see if the suspect is hiding;
- police have arrested someone in the night after a pursuit and it is necessary to make a brief check of gardens along the pursuit route to see if stolen or incriminating articles have been discarded.

Therefore, it would be reasonable for Constable ELLIS to search the gardens without the occupiers' permission, even though she was not in immediate pursuit of a suspect, because to have woken the entire street in the middle of the night to search for a bag may have seemed disproportionate in these circumstances. This search could have been conducted *without* the statutory authority of a warrant or other powers derived from PACE. Answers A and D are therefore incorrect.

General Police Duties, paras 3.2.5.1, 3.2.6, 3.2.6.1

Answer 2.11

Answer **D** — Terrorism Prevention and Investigation Measures (TPIMs) are a civil preventative measure, issued under s. 2 of the Terrorism Prevention and Investigation Measures Act 2011, which are intended to protect the public from the risk posed by suspected terrorists who can be neither prosecuted nor, in the case of foreign nationals, deported, by imposing restrictions intended to prevent or disrupt their engagement in terrorism-related activity.

Section 24 gives effect to sch. 5. The schedule provides for powers of entry, search, seizure and retention in a number of scenarios relating to TPIM notices. These include:

Without a warrant:

- the power to search *without a search warrant in para.* 5 (for the purposes of serving TPIM notice), finding the individual on whom the notice is to be served;
- the power to search *without a search warrant in para.* 6 (at time of serving TPIM notice), ascertaining whether there is anything in the premises that contravenes measures specified in the notice;

- the power to search *without a search warrant under para.* 7 (suspected absconding), ascertaining whether a person has absconded or if there is anything on the premises which will assist in the pursuit or arrest of an individual in respect of whom a TPIM notice is in force who is reasonably suspected of having absconded.

With a warrant:

- in relation to the power to search *under a search warrant issued under para.* 8 (for compliance purposes), determining whether an individual in respect of whom a TPIM notice is in force is complying with measures specified in the notice.

Therefore, searches *may* take place without a warrant for several reasons and answers A, B and C are incorrect.

General Police Duties, para. 3.2.11

3 | Powers of Arrest

QUESTIONS

Question 3.1

MOSS is taking a case to the European Court of Human Rights, alleging a breach of Art. 5 of the Convention (the right to liberty and security). The circumstances are that SMITH had been arrested for attempting to enter the United Kingdom illegally and had been detained in a temporary centre, pending an application to enter the country as an asylum seeker. MOSS's argument is that his arrest and detention were unnecessary because he had family with strong roots in the United Kingdom and that he was not a flight risk.

What does Art. 5 of the European Convention on Human Rights state about the 'necessity' of such an arrest, in these circumstances?

A The State is not required to demonstrate that an arrest is 'necessary' in these circumstances.

B The State is required to demonstrate that all arrests are 'necessary', even in these circumstances.

C The State is required to demonstrate that all arrests are 'necessary', for the purposes of bringing the person before the competent legal authority.

D The State is required to demonstrate that all arrests are 'necessary', for the purposes of bringing the person before the competent legal authority on reasonable suspicion of having committed an offence.

Question 3.2

O'SHEA commits an offence of theft from a warehouse. He is seen committing the offence on CCTV by CURTIS who runs out of an office (where he is monitoring the CCTV cameras) and into the warehouse. He sees O'SHEA walking towards an exit in the warehouse and suspecting that O'SHEA will make off before a constable can assume responsibility for O'SHEA and that it would not be reasonably practical for a constable to arrest O'SHEA, CURTIS arrests O'SHEA for theft. The police later attend the scene and CURTIS speaks to PC LATIMER telling the officer that the reason he arrested O'SHEA was because a theft had been committed and he knew that O'SHEA was guilty of the offence.

Considering the power of arrest under s. 24A of the Police and Criminal Evidence Act 1984, was CURTIS correct to arrest O'SHEA in these circumstances?

A No, as CURTIS only suspected that O'SHEA would make off before a constable could assume responsibility for him.

B Yes, as CURTIS knows an indictable offence has been committed and that O'SHEA is guilty of the offence.

C No, as the power of arrest under s. 24A is only available when the offence the person is arrested for is triable on indictment only.

D Yes, because CURTIS suspects that it would not be reasonably practicable for a constable to arrest O'SHEA.

Question 3.3

Constable POTTER was called to a domestic disturbance at the home of HENDERSON and LeBOW. On the officer's arrival, HENDERSON was shouting loudly at LeBOW and making threats. Constable POTTER arrested HENDERSON for a breach of the peace and HENDERSON began struggling violently. Constable POTTER later recorded the facts in a pocket notebook, noting that HENDERSON had not been cautioned at the time of the arrest because of the violent struggle.

Which of the following statements is correct in relation to the requirement to caution a person, according to the PACE Codes of Practice?

A There was a requirement for Constable POTTER to caution HENDERSON because she was not cautioned immediately before the arrest.

B There was no requirement for Constable POTTER to caution HENDERSON at the time of arrest because she was not being arrested for an offence.

C Constable POTTER was required to caution HENDERSON at the time of arrest because she was not in the process of escaping from the officer.

D There was no requirement for Constable POTTER to caution HENDERSON at the time of arrest; because of her behaviour, however, the officer was required to caution her as soon as practicable afterwards.

Question 3.4

Constable O'NEIL is being investigated for a misconduct offence of excessive use of force during the lawful arrest of COLLINS for an offence of robbery. COLLINS sustained a fractured wrist when handcuffs were being applied and has made a complaint of assault against the officer. The Professional Standards Department has submitted a file to the Crown Prosecution Service and is awaiting a charging decision.

What would the situation be in relation to COLLINS's arrest if Constable O'NEIL is found guilty of assault in these circumstances?

A If Constable O'NEIL is found guilty in court of assault, it would automatically render the arrest unlawful.

B If Constable O'NEIL is not charged with assault but proven at a misconduct hearing to have used excessive force, it would automatically render the arrest unlawful.

C Even if the force used by Constable O'NEIL amounted to an assault and/or misconduct, it would not render an otherwise lawful arrest unlawful.

D Constable O'NEIL would have to be found guilty in court of assault *and* found to have used excessive force in a misconduct hearing for the arrest to be declared unlawful.

Question 3.5

Constable HAYWOOD stopped JENNINGS for a motoring offence on a road. The officer conducted a PNC check on the vehicle and discovered it was not registered to JENNINGS. Constable HAYWOOD then tried to obtain personal details but, although JENNINGS responds with a name and address, she does so in a reluctant and hesitant manner causing Constable HAYWOOD to have reasonable grounds to doubt the authenticity of the details and cause the officer to consider that an arrest may be necessary under s. 24(5) of the Police and Criminal Evidence Act 1984.

What does Code G of the PACE Codes of Practice state about the steps Constable HAYWOOD should now take?

A Code G expressly requires Constable HAYWOOD to warn JENNINGS that she will be arrested if she fails to give her correct name and address.

B If practicable, Constable HAYWOOD should issue a warning which points out JENNINGS's offending behaviour and explain why, if she does not stop, the consequences may make her arrest necessary.

C Code G expressly requires Constable HAYWOOD to warn JENNINGS that unless she provides documentary evidence regarding her name and address she will be arrested.

D Constable HAYWOOD does not need to issue any type of warning and should arrest JENNINGS in these circumstances.

Question 3.6

DOWNEY works as a security guard in a shopping centre. Whilst at work on a busy afternoon at the weekend, he saw FENTON walking towards the public car park outside. It was clear to DOWNEY that, from the way she was staggering, FENTON was drunk. DOWNEY saw FENTON approach a car with the keys in her hand and begin to open the driver's door. DOWNEY decided to detain her before she could drive the vehicle. DOWNEY made a 'citizen's arrest' on FENTON (for an offence of being in charge of a mechanically propelled vehicle whilst unfit (contrary to s. 4 of the Road Traffic Act 1988)) as she stood alongside the car and then contacted the police on his mobile phone.

Did DOWNEY have the power to arrest FENTON in these circumstances (under s. 24A of the Police and Criminal Evidence Act 1984)?

A Yes, provided it was not reasonably practicable for a constable to make the arrest instead.

B No, a member of the public only has the power to arrest a person to prevent them from committing an indictable offence.

C Yes, regardless of whether there was a constable available to make the arrest instead.

D No, a member of the public only has the power to arrest a person when an indictable offence is being committed or has been committed.

Question 3.7

THORPE was arrested for an assault and following a period of detention was charged, fingerprinted, photographed and had provided a sample of DNA. Following THORPE's conviction in court two months later, it was discovered that an administrative error had occurred and the DNA sample had been lost. This information was forwarded to Inspector MARDEN in the Custody Services Department, with a request that a further DNA sample be obtained from THORPE for the database.

Section 63A of the Police and Criminal Evidence Act 1984 provides a power of arrest without warrant to obtain samples from people in certain circumstances; would the use of this power be suitable in these circumstances?

A Yes, a DNA sample has been taken but it is no longer available.

B No, provided the sample THORPE gave was sufficient for analysis.

C Yes, because THORPE has now been convicted of a recordable offence.

D No, there is no power to take a second sample from someone when they have previously provided one during the investigation.

Question 3.8

Constable FRENCH, an officer from Police Scotland working from Dumfries Police Station, was pursuing a vehicle which was stolen from the Dumfries and Galloway Divisional area. The vehicle crossed the Scottish border into Cumbria Constabulary's area, in England, where it eventually stopped. Before officers from Cumbria Constabulary arrived at the scene, Constable FRENCH arrested the driver, KELLY (this would be a lawful arrest in Scotland).

What action should now be taken in respect of KELLY?

A KELLY must be taken to the nearest designated station in Scotland, where the original offence took place.

B KELLY must be taken to the nearest designated station in England, where the arrest took place.

C KELLY must be taken to the nearest designated station in Scotland or to the nearest designated police station in England.

D KELLY should be further arrested by an officer from Cumbria Constabulary and be taken to the nearest designated station in England.

Question 3.9

BENTLEY was in police detention waiting to appear in court. He had been arrested for a warrant which had been issued by the court for failing to appear to answer a charge of burglary. BENTLEY asked to see the duty inspector to make a complaint against Constable MOORE who had arrested him the previous evening. The foundation for BENTLEY's complaint was that Constable MOORE was not in possession of the warrant when she arrested him, and that she did not tell him he was under arrest.

If BENTLEY's case was genuine, has Constable MOORE acted unlawfully in these circumstances?

A Yes, Constable MOORE should have been in possession of the warrant at the time of the arrest and she should have informed BENTLEY that he was under arrest.

B No, there was no requirement for Constable MOORE to have been in possession of the warrant at the time of the arrest or to have informed BENTLEY that he was under arrest.

C Yes, although there was no requirement for Constable MOORE to have been in possession of the warrant at the time of the arrest, she should have informed BENTLEY that he was under arrest.

D Yes, Constable MOORE should have been in possession of the warrant at the time of the arrest, although it was not necessary for her to inform BENTLEY that he was under arrest.

Question 3.10

DC SHARPE was interviewing HUNTER for a burglary. The officer suspected that HUNTER had committed more than one burglary but only had reasonable grounds to arrest him for the one offence. In the interview, HUNTER provided DC SHARPE with reasonable grounds to suspect he should be arrested for two other offences. At that time, the officer made a decision that HUNTER would be further arrested for those offences but not until after the interview. HUNTER was actually arrested for the further offences two hours after the interview concluded.

Considering s. 31 of the Police and Criminal Evidence Act 1984, which of the following statements is correct in relation to the timing of HUNTER's arrest?

A HUNTER should have been arrested when DC SHARPE had reasonable grounds to suspect him of further offences; the officer has acted unlawfully.

B HUNTER should have been arrested when DC SHARPE made the decision to arrest him for the further offences; the officer has acted unlawfully.

C HUNTER should have been arrested before the end of the interview; the officer has acted unlawfully.

D DC SHARPE has acted lawfully; there was no requirement to arrest HUNTER before the officer did so.

Question 3.11

MILLS had been detained by Constable GROVES for an offence of burglary which occurred an hour ago. MILLS matched the description of a person seen running away from the scene; the officer informed him he was under arrest and, after caution, MILLS replied, 'It couldn't have been me, I was in my mate's house. Take me round there now and he'll tell you I was there.'

Section 30(1A) of the Police and Criminal Evidence Act 1984 requires a person to be taken by a constable to a police station as soon as practicable after the arrest. Would the information provided by MILLS allow Constable GROVES to deviate to his friend's address before taking him to the station?

A Yes, this may be a valid reason for not taking a person to a police station as soon as practicable after the arrest, provided the matter required immediate investigation.

B No, the only reason not to take a person to a police station as soon as practicable after the arrest is to recover evidence relating to an indictable offence for which he/she has been arrested.

C No, a person must be taken to a police station as soon as practicable after the arrest on every occasion.

D No, there are circumstances in which a person may not be taken to a police station as soon as practicable after the arrest; however, checking an alibi would not amount to such an exception.

Question 3.12

VIZARD has been working for a charity organisation as a health care worker based in Monrovia (Liberia) for the past five years. On a Christmas break, VIZARD returns to her home in London but several days after arriving home she begins to feel extremely unwell and visits a hospital. At the hospital, she is examined and diagnosed with Ebola virus disease (an extremely infectious and dangerous condition). Due to the nature of the disease, there is extreme concern about the spread of the disease as well as concern for the health of VIZARD.

Can VIZARD be detained under Art. 5 of the European Convention on Human Rights?

A No, as Art. 5 does not provide any power to arrest or detain; it simply sets out certain circumstances where the general right to liberty may be interfered with by some existing lawful means.

B Yes, as Art. 5 provides a power of detention when it is necessary and proportionate to deprive a person of their liberty in order to prevent the spread of infectious diseases.

C No, as Art. 5 would not be applicable to this situation as whilst it provides numerous powers to arrest (if the arrest is for a lawful and legitimate reason), it does not address issues connected to the continued detention of an individual.

D Yes, if it could be shown that releasing VIZARD from the hospital would be likely to be detrimental to public health.

Question 3.13

PC BABBINGTON is a probationary constable and is on patrol with PS RABY (an experienced police officer with 20 years' service). They see JACKSON running away from a male who is on the ground bleeding from a head injury. A passing paramedic immediately attends to the male and PC BABBINGTON and PS RABY exit their police vehicle and chase JACKSON who has run into a nearby alley. PC BABBINGTON is faster than PS RABY and catches up to JACKSON. Seeing blood on JACKSON's knuckles, he stops him and says 'Mate, you're nicked for assault'.

Considering s. 28 of the Police and Criminal Evidence Act 1984, which of the following statements is correct?

A When a person is arrested using the powers under the Police and Criminal Evidence Act 1984, that person must be told that he/she is under arrest and given the grounds for the arrest unless it is not practicable to do so. These requirements do not have to be satisfied when arresting a person using other powers.

B When a person is arrested by a constable and it is obvious to that person that he/she has been arrested, the constable does not actually have to tell that person that he/she has been arrested.

C A failure by a police officer to comply with the requirements of s. 28 of the Police and Criminal Evidence Act 1984 will not make the arrest unlawful.

D The requirement to indicate to a person the fact that he/she has been arrested might be met by using a colloquialism, such as 'You're nicked' or 'You're locked up', providing the person understands its meaning.

ANSWERS

Answer 3.1

Answer **A** — Article 5(1) of the European Convention on Human Rights states:

> Everyone has the right to liberty and security of person. No one shall be deprived of his liberty save in the following cases and in accordance with a procedure prescribed by law.

Under Art. 5(1)(c), it must be demonstrated that the arrest or detention of a person was effected for the purpose of bringing him/her before the competent legal authority on reasonable suspicion of having committed an offence or when it is reasonably considered necessary to prevent him/her committing an offence or fleeing after having done so.

However, other subsections in Art. 5 do not require the arrest to be made for the purpose of bringing the person before the competent legal authority. Under Art. 5(1)(f), the lawful arrest or detention of a person may be made:

> to prevent his effecting an unauthorised entry into the country or of a person against whom action is being taken with a view to deportation or extradition.

Answers C and D are therefore incorrect.

In the case of *R (On the Application of Saadi) v Secretary of State for the Home Department* [2002] UKHL 41, the House of Lords ruled that, unlike part of Art. 5(1)(c), Art. 5(1)(f) does *not* require that detention has to be necessary in order to be justified. As a result, the temporary detention of asylum seekers, pending their application to remain in the United Kingdom, is not of itself unlawful. Answer B is therefore incorrect.

General Police Duties, para. 3.3.2

Answer 3.2

Answer **A** — Section 24A of the Police and Criminal Evidence Act 1984 states:

(1) A person other than a constable may arrest without a warrant—
   (a) anyone who is in the act of committing an indictable offence;
   (b) anyone whom he has reasonable grounds for suspecting to be committing an indictable offence.
(2) Where an indictable offence has been committed, a person other than a constable may arrest without a warrant—
   (a) anyone who is guilty of the offence;
   (b) anyone whom he has reasonable grounds for suspecting to be guilty of it.

(3) But the power of summary arrest conferred by subsection (1) or (2) is exercisable only if—

   (a) the person making the arrest has reasonable grounds for believing that for any of the reasons mentioned in subsection (4) it is necessary to arrest the person in question; and

   (b) it appears to the person making the arrest that it is not reasonably practicable for a constable to make it instead.

(4) The reasons are to prevent the person in question—

   (a) causing physical injury to himself or any other person;

   (b) suffering physical injury;

   (c) causing loss of or damage to property; or

   (d) making off before a constable can assume responsibility for him.

Answer C is incorrect as the power of arrest is available in relation to an 'indictable' offence—one that can be tried either way or on indictment (theft being such an offence)—it is not restricted to an offence that is triable on indictment only. It is correct that an indictable offence has been committed and CURTIS knows O'SHEA is guilty of it (answer B) and it is also correct that CURTIS suspects that it would not be reasonably practicable for a constable to arrest O'SHEA (answer D) but both answers are wrong because the power under s. 24A can only be exercised if the person making the arrest has reasonable grounds for *believing* that for any of the reasons mentioned in subs. (4) it is necessary to arrest the person in question—CURTIS suspected. Answer A is correct.

General Police Duties, para. 3.3.8

Answer 3.3

Answer **B** — Code C, para. 10.4 of the PACE Codes of Practice requires that a person must be cautioned on arrest or further arrest. There are exceptions to the requirement to administer the caution and these are:

- where it is impracticable to do so by reason of the person's condition or behaviour at the time; or
- where he/she has already been cautioned immediately before the arrest in accordance with Code C, para. 10.1 (requirement to caution where there are grounds to suspect commission of an offence).

However, consideration also needs to be given to Code G which states that the Code will not apply where a person is being arrested for a warrant or other matters, such as a breach of bail. It also states that the Code does not apply when a person is being arrested under a common law power to stop or prevent a breach of the peace. The caution should be given if it is intended to question a person about an 'offence' and, since this is not a requirement for an arrest which is meant to simply place a person before the court, a caution is not required regardless of any other exceptions in Code C. Answers A and C are therefore incorrect.

Section 28(5) of PACE allows that a person need not be informed of the reason or grounds for his/her arrest if it was not reasonably practicable by reason of his/her having escaped from arrest before the information could be given. However, this exception is not listed in Code C, para. 10.4, which relates to cautions. Answer C is incorrect for this reason also.

There is nothing in Code C requiring a person to be cautioned as soon as practicable after their arrest, if they were not cautioned at the time, and therefore answer D is incorrect.

General Police Duties, paras 3.3.3.1, 3.3.3.2

Answer 3.4

Answer **C** — Section 117 of the Police and Criminal Evidence Act 1984 allows the use of reasonable force when making an arrest. Section 3 of the Criminal Law Act 1967 also allows the use of such force as is reasonably necessary in the arrest of people and the prevention of crime.

For an arrest to be lawful, it must be 'necessary' under s. 24 of the Police and Criminal Evidence Act 1984 and this is the test that a court would apply. The court will consider all of the circumstances, which include the circumstances as the arresting officer believed them to be at the time; the force may even be lethal. The use of excessive force, while amounting to possible misconduct and assault, does not render an otherwise lawful arrest unlawful (*Simpson* v *Chief Constable of South Yorkshire* (1991) 135 SJ 383).

Answers A, B and D are therefore incorrect.

General Police Duties, para. 3.3.3.3

Answer 3.5

Answer **B** — Code G, para. 2.9 of the PACE Codes of Practice states:

When it is practicable to tell a person why their arrest is necessary (as required by paragraphs 2.2 and 3.3), the constable should outline the facts, information and other circumstances which provide the grounds for believing that their arrest is necessary and which the officer considers satisfy one or more of the statutory criteria in subparagraphs (a) to (f).

A warning is not expressly required by para. 2.9, but officers should, if practicable, consider whether to issue a warning which points out the person's offending behaviour and explains why, if the person does not stop, the resulting consequences may make his/her arrest necessary. Such a warning might:

- if heeded, avoid the need to arrest; or
- if ignored, support the need to arrest and also help to prove the mental element of certain offences, for example the person's intent or awareness, or help to rebut a defence that he/she was acting reasonably.

Answers A, C and D are incorrect for this reason.

General Police Duties, paras 3.3.5.4, 3.3.5.6

Answer 3.6

Answer **D** — Under s. 24A of the Police and Criminal Evidence Act 1984, certain powers of arrest are provided for any person. Section 24A states:

(1) A person other than a constable may arrest without a warrant—
   (a) anyone who is in the act of committing an indictable offence;
   (b) anyone whom he has reasonable grounds for suspecting to be committing an indictable offence.
(2) Where an indictable offence has been committed, a person other than a constable may arrest without a warrant—
   (a) anyone who is guilty of the offence;
   (b) anyone whom he has reasonable grounds for suspecting to be guilty of it.
(3) But the power of summary arrest conferred by subsection (1) or (2) is exercisable only if—
   (a) the person making the arrest has reasonable grounds for believing that for any of the reasons mentioned in subsection (4) it is necessary to arrest the person in question; and
   (b) it appears to the person making the arrest that it is not reasonably practicable for a constable to make it instead.
(4) The reasons are to prevent the person in question—
   (a) causing physical injury to himself or any other person;
   (b) suffering physical injury;
   (c) causing loss of or damage to property; or
   (d) making off before a constable can assume responsibility for him.

Section 24A(4)(d) of PACE does allow a member of the public to make a 'citizen's arrest', where it is not reasonably practicable for a constable to make it instead; however, unlike the powers of arrest available to police officers (which apply to all offences), the 'citizen's' power of arrest only applies where the relevant offence is *indictable*. An offence under s. 4 of the Road Traffic Act 1988 is a summary only offence. Answers A and C are therefore incorrect.

Under s. 24A, a person other than a constable may make such an arrest when an indictable offence *is* being committed, or *has* been committed; the power to make a preventative arrest (i.e. where an indictable offence is *about* to be committed) only applies to police officers. Answer B is therefore incorrect.

General Police Duties, para. 3.3.8

Answer 3.7

Answer **B** — Section 63A of the Police and Criminal Evidence Act 1984 provides a power of arrest without warrant in respect of people who:

- have been charged with/reported for a recordable offence and who have not had a sample taken or the sample was unsuitable/insufficient for analysis;
- have been convicted of a recordable offence and have not had a sample taken since conviction;
- have been so convicted and have had a sample taken before or since conviction but the sample was unsuitable/insufficient for analysis.

Whether the person has been charged or convicted, the only reason to arrest them to take samples is when the sample has not previously been taken or, if it has been taken, it was insufficient for analysis. However, a sample may not be taken simply because it has been lost by the police. Answers A and C are incorrect.

Answer D is incorrect because there *is* a power to take a second sample from someone, when they have previously provided one during the investigation, but it cannot be done in the circumstances described.

General Police Duties, para. 3.3.9.4

Answer 3.8

Answer **C** — The Criminal Justice and Public Order Act 1994 (ss. 136 to 140) makes provision for officers from one part of the United Kingdom to go into another part of the United Kingdom to arrest someone there in connection with an offence committed within their jurisdiction, and gives them powers to search on arrest.

A Scottish police officer may arrest someone suspected of committing an offence in Scotland who is found in England, Wales or Northern Ireland if it would have been lawful to arrest that person had he/she been found in Scotland. Since this power is granted to Constable FRENCH, there is no requirement for an officer from an English police force to further arrest KELLY and therefore answer D is incorrect.

Where an officer from a Scottish police force has arrested someone suspected of committing an offence in Scotland, who is found in England, the officer must take the person to the nearest convenient designated police station in Scotland *or* to the nearest convenient designated police station in England or Wales (see s. 137(7)).

Section 137(7) goes on to say that the person must be taken to the police station as soon as reasonably practicable. This would suggest that the arrested person should be taken to the nearest police station if the distance to one or another is too great. Since the arresting officer has a choice of police stations, answers A and B are incorrect.

General Police Duties, para. 3.3.9.5

Answer 3.9

Answer **C** — Warrants issued in connection with 'an offence' do not need to be in the possession of the officer executing them at the time. Answers A and D are therefore incorrect.

However, the requirement under s. 28 of the Police and Criminal Evidence Act 1984 to tell a person why he/she is being arrested, *does* apply to arrests under warrant. Answers B and D are incorrect for this reason also.

General Police Duties, paras 3.3.3.1, 3.3.10

Answer 3.10

Answer **D** — Section 31 of the Police and Criminal Evidence Act 1984 states that where:

(a) a person—
   (i) has been arrested for an offence; and
   (ii) is at a police station in consequence of that arrest; and
(b) it appears to a constable that, if he were released from that arrest, he would be liable to arrest for some other offence,
   he shall be arrested for that other offence.

In *R v Samuel* [1988] QB 615, the Court of Appeal said that the purpose of the s. 31 requirement was to prevent the release and immediate re-arrest of an offender—therefore, the court noted, s. 31 did not prevent any further arrest from being delayed until the release of the prisoner for the initial arrest was imminent.

Therefore, there was no requirement to arrest HUNTER at any time before he was actually arrested. The only obligation under s. 31 is that the person should not be released from police detention and then re-arrested when there were sufficient grounds to arrest that person before he/she was released. Answers A, B and C are therefore incorrect.

General Police Duties, para. 3.3.11

Answer 3.11

Answer **A** — Section 30 of the Police and Criminal Evidence Act 1984 states:

(1) Subsection (1A) applies where a person is, at any place other than a police station—
    (a) arrested by a constable for an offence, or
    (b) taken into custody by a constable after being arrested for an offence by a person other than a constable.
(1A) The person must be taken by a constable to a police station as soon as practicable after the arrest.

Section 30(1A) allows the officer to delay taking the arrested person to a police station where his/her presence elsewhere is necessary in order to carry out such investigations as it is reasonable to carry out immediately. Where there is such a delay, the reasons for it must be recorded when the person first arrives at the police station (s. 30(11)). Section 30(10) was confirmed in *R* v *Kerawalla* [1991] Crim LR 451, where the court held that if the matter can wait, the exception will not apply and the person must be taken straight to a police station. Answer C is therefore incorrect.

In *Dallison* v *Caffery* [1965] 1 QB 348, it was held that taking an arrested person to check out an alibi before going to a police station *may* be justified in some circumstances. Answer D is therefore incorrect.

Section 18(5)(a) of the Act allows a premises to be searched before the person is taken to a police station for evidence related to an indictable offence for which the person has been arrested or some other indictable offence which is connected with or similar to that offence. However, this is an *additional* power to the one under s. 30(10) and answer B is incorrect.

General Police Duties, paras 3.3.5.1, 3.3.5.3, 3.3.12

Answer 3.12

Answer **A** — A person may be deprived of their liberty for a number of legitimate and lawful reasons.

Article 5 of the Convention states:

1. Everyone has the right to liberty and security of person. No one shall be deprived of his liberty save in the following cases and in accordance with a procedure prescribed by law:
    (a) the lawful detention of a person after conviction by a competent court;

(b) the lawful arrest or detention of a person for non-compliance with the lawful order of a court or in order to secure the fulfilment of any obligation prescribed by law;

(c) the lawful arrest or detention of a person effected for the purpose of bringing him before the competent legal authority on reasonable suspicion of having committed an offence or when it is reasonably considered necessary to prevent his committing an offence or fleeing after having done so;

(d) the detention of a minor by lawful order for the purpose of educational supervision or his lawful detention for the purpose of bringing him before the competent legal authority;

(e) the lawful detention of persons for the prevention of the spreading of infectious diseases, of persons of unsound mind, alcoholics or drug addicts or vagrants;

(f) the lawful arrest or detention of a person to prevent his effecting an unauthorised entry into the country or of a person against whom action is being taken with a view to deportation or extradition.

A person can only be deprived of his/her general right to liberty under one of the conditions set out in the permitted grounds in Art. 5(1)(a)–(f), and even then that deprivation must be carried out in accordance with a *procedure prescribed by law*. Article 5 does not provide a power of arrest or detention, making answers B, C and D incorrect. Article 5 relates to a multitude of situations where an individual has been arrested or detained but does not provide any power to arrest or detain; it simply sets out certain circumstances where the general right to liberty may be interfered with by some existing lawful means. Whatever its extent, Art. 5(1)(e) is likely to be narrowly applied by the courts and the mere fact that an individual has, for example, an infectious disease, will not of itself justify his/her 'detention'.

General Police Duties, para. 3.3.2

Answer 3.13

Answer **D** — In the case of *R* v *Fiak* [2005] EWCA Crim 2381, it was held that an arrest was not rendered unlawful by the police officer's failure to use the word 'arrest'. The requirement may be met with the use of a colloquialism, provided that the person is familiar with it and understands its meaning (e.g. 'you're locked up' or 'you're nicked' (*Christie* v *Leachinsky* [1947] AC 573)).

Answer A is incorrect as whether an arrest is made under the Police and Criminal Evidence Act 1984 *or not*, s. 28 of the Act makes it clear that the person must be told that they are being arrested and the grounds for the arrest. The requirement for a person to be informed that he/she is under arrest applies regardless of whether the fact of the arrest is obvious, making answer B incorrect. A failure to comply with s. 28 will make an arrest unlawful (see e.g. *Dawes* v *DPP* [1994] Crim LR 604), making answer C incorrect.

General Police Duties, para. 3.3.3.1

4 | Protection of People Suffering from Mental Disorders

QUESTIONS

Question 4.1

Constable MURPHY was called to an incident in the High Street. On arrival, the officer came across ALLINGTON, who was sitting in a public fountain. The officer made inquiries with people in a crowd that had gathered and consequently was considering dealing with ALLINGTON under s. 136 of the Mental Health Act 1983.

Considering powers under s. 136 of the Act, which of the following statements is correct?

A Constable MURPHY may arrest ALLINGTON under s. 136 for her own safety.

B Constable MURPHY may remove ALLINGTON under s. 136 for her own interests or for the protection of other persons.

C Constable MURPHY may remove ALLINGTON under s. 136 if she represents a danger to herself.

D Constable MURPHY may remove ALLINGTON under s. 136 if she represents a danger to herself or other members of the public.

Question 4.2

HENDERSON was taken from a busy shopping centre to a hospital by Constable ANDREWS. The officer had removed HENDERSON to the hospital using powers under s. 136 of the Mental Health Act 1983 because of concerns over his mental well-being. The officer had taken HENDERSON there to have him assessed under the Act.

Considering s. 136 of the Mental Health Act 1983, what is 'the permitted period of detention' in relation to HENDERSON?

A A period of 24 hours beginning at the time HENDERSON arrives at the hospital (the place of safety).

B A period of 36 hours beginning at the time HENDERSON arrives at the hospital (the place of safety).

C A period of 48 hours beginning at the time HENDERSON arrives at the hospital (the place of safety).

D A period of 72 hours beginning at the time HENDERSON arrives at the hospital (the place of safety).

Question 4.3

Magistrates have issued a warrant under s. 135(1) of the Mental Health Act 1983 in relation to SHORT, whose family have been concerned that his mental health has deteriorated significantly recently. The warrant authorises SHORT to be removed to a place of safety.

Which of the following statements is correct in relation to the execution of the warrant issued by the court?

A The warrant must be executed by a constable, who must be accompanied either by a mental health professional or a registered medical practitioner.

B The warrant must be executed either by a mental health professional or a registered medical practitioner, who may ask for a constable to be present if there is reason to believe SHORT may become violent.

C The warrant may be executed either by a constable or a mental health professional, who must be accompanied by a registered medical practitioner.

D The warrant must be executed by a constable, who must be accompanied by an approved mental health professional and by a registered medical practitioner.

ANSWERS

Answer 4.1

Answer **B** — Section 136 of the Mental Health Act 1983 creates a power for police officers to remove such a person under certain conditions. Under s. 136(1), if a person appears to a constable to be suffering from mental disorder and to be in immediate need of care or control, the constable may, if he/she thinks it necessary to do so *in the interests of that person or for the protection of other persons*, remove that person to a place of safety.

Section 136 does not mention danger—this power is more to do with caring for individuals and removing them to a place where they can receive appropriate treatment. Answers C and D are therefore incorrect.

Further, there is no power of arrest under s. 136—the person is not being dealt with for an offence, rather, they are being removed to the most appropriate location to deal with their illness. Answer A is therefore incorrect.

General Police Duties, para. 3.4.2

Answer 4.2

Answer **A** — Where a person has been removed to a place of safety by a constable, under s. 136 of the Mental Health Act 1983, he/she may be detained there for a permitted period of detention. The 'permitted period of detention' means the period of *24 hours* beginning at the time when the person arrives at the hospital (the place of safety (s. 136(2A)(a)(i))).

Answers B, C and D are therefore incorrect.

General Police Duties, para. 3.4.2

Answer 4.3

Answer **D** — Under s. 135(1) of the Mental Health Act 1983, where there is reasonable cause to suspect that a person believed to be suffering from a mental disorder:

(a) has been, or is being ill-treated or neglected, or
(b) is unable to care for himself/herself and is living alone,

a warrant may be issued by a magistrate authorising a *constable* to enter any premises specified and to remove the person to a place of safety.

Answers B and C are therefore incorrect.

In doing so, the officer *must* be accompanied by an approved mental health professional and by a registered medical practitioner. Answer A is therefore incorrect.

General Police Duties, para. 3.4.3

5 | Offences Relating to Land and Premises

QUESTIONS

Question 5.1

A new football stadium is being built on the outskirts of a town. Vehicles belonging to the building company have been parked in an enclosed warehouse situated adjacent to the building site, which is due to be demolished after the stadium is completed. Environmental protesters have been attempting to stop the building work. The builders arrived for work one morning and as they opened the doors to the warehouse, 20 protesters stormed into the warehouse. Ten of the protesters chained themselves to vehicles, intending to disrupt the building work. The other ten protesters caused criminal damage to some of the machinery in the warehouse. Building work was disrupted for several hours as the police were called to remove them.

Have the protesters committed an offence under s. 68 of the Criminal Justice and Public Order Act 1994 (aggravated trespass) in these circumstances?

- **A** No, as the protesters were not on land in the open air.
- **B** Yes, all of the protesters have committed the offence in these circumstances.
- **C** No, as the protesters were not on land where the building work was due to take place.
- **D** Yes, but only the protesters who caused criminal damage have committed the offence.

Question 5.2

OSMAND and WREN entered a building site as trespassers; they were protesting against the construction of a new shopping centre. They had with them a large concrete tube which they placed on the ground in the middle of the site. OSMAND

and WREN then connected their arms through the tube with a padlocked chain. Inspector CARTER was the senior officer to arrive and concluded that they had committed an offence contrary to s. 68 of the Criminal Justice and Public Order Act 1994 (aggravated trespass) and directed them to leave. OSMAND and WREN stated that they were unable to leave because they had no key to the padlock. Eventually a locksmith was called to the scene and, when they were released, OSMAND and WREN were arrested for failing to leave when directed under s. 69 of the Act. They were charged with the offence under s. 69(3) and, later in court, they claimed that they had a reasonable excuse for failing to leave as soon as practicable—that they were unable to do so until they were released.

In relation to OSMAND and WREN's defence, which of the following statements is correct?

A They did not leave the site when directed to leave so the defence will fail.

B They had a reasonable excuse for failing to leave the land as soon as practicable and would have a defence to the offence in this situation.

C Their activities frustrated the police utilising their powers under this Act so the defence will fail.

D It is a defence for the accused to show that he/she was not a trespasser but there is no defence of 'reasonable excuse' to the offence under s. 69 of the Act.

Question 5.3

John and Lesley NESBITT (husband and wife) wish to protest against the building of several new houses on private land near to their home. They make several signs illustrating their opposition to the construction and enter a field next to the construction site. The field is common land. They shout at workers on the building site intending to disrupt their building work. PC VOLT (an officer in uniform) is sent to the incident. The NESBITTs are extremely polite to the officer but tell him in no uncertain terms that they are doing nothing wrong and that there is nothing he can do to stop them exercising their lawful rights.

Would PC VOLT be able to remove John and Lesley NESBITT from the common land using the power under s. 69 of the Criminal Justice and Public Order Act 1994 (power to remove persons)?

A No, the power to remove John and Lesley NESBITT would not be available to PC VOLT as it must be authorised by an officer of at least the rank of inspector.

B Yes, if PC VOLT reasonably believes that John and Lesley NESBITT intend to trespass on the building site (private land) and disrupt the lawful activity that is taking place there.

C No, the power is not available to PC VOLT as John and Lesley NESBITT are not committing the offence of aggravated trespass (under s. 68 of the Act) nor are they simply trespassing on land.

D Yes, if PC VOLT reasonably suspects that John and Lesley NESBITT intend to trespass on the building site (private land) and disrupt the lawful activity that is taking place there.

Question 5.4

Sergeant KENNEDY and PC MONTEIRO (both on uniform mobile patrol) are directed to a field owned by BECKFORD. BECKFORD is complaining that JUKES and GOODHEW are trespassing on her land having turned up in a van, pitching a tent on her land and telling her they are intent on living there despite the fact that she has told them to leave as they have no right to be on the land. She asks the officers to remove JUKES and GOODHEW from the land.

Could JUKES and GOODHEW be directed to leave the land under s. 62A of the Criminal Justice and Public Order Act 1994?

A Yes, PC MONTEIRO or Sergeant KENNEDY may give such a direction.

B No, as JUKES and GOODHEW do not have one or more caravans with them.

C Yes, but it is Sergeant KENNEDY (as the senior police officer at the scene) who gives such a direction.

D No, as JUKES and GOODHEW have not caused any damage to the land or intimidated the land owner and/or her agent.

Question 5.5

PERSHORE is homeless and living on the street. He is sleeping rough opposite a house owned and lived in by DRAYCOTT and his family. PERSHORE sees DRAYCOTT and his family packing their car and leaving to go on holiday. PERSHORE notices that the family have left a front window of the house open and, once they have left and knowing the house is empty, PERSHORE enters the house. It is his intention to live in the house while the DRAYCOTTs are on holiday. PERSHORE has been in the house for two days when he sees a friend of his, HEBBORN, who is also homeless, walking past the house. PERSHORE tells HEBBORN what has happened with the house and invites HEBBORN into the house, telling him he can stay as long as he likes. HEBBORN says that he will stay in the house. A neighbour of the DRAYCOTTs has seen the two men talking outside the DRAYCOTTs' house and calls the police. A short time later, PC SMITH (on uniform patrol) arrives at the scene.

Which of the following comments is correct in respect of the offence of squatting (contrary to s. 144 of the Legal Aid, Sentencing and Punishment of Offenders Act 2012)?

A PERSHORE has committed the offence but HEBBORN has not as HEBBORN does not enter the premises as a trespasser.

B The offence has not been committed by either man as there was no violence used (against property or a person) in order to secure entry to the premises.

C PC SMITH has a power to enter and search the DRAYCOTTs' house (under s. 17 of the Police and Criminal Evidence Act 1984) for the purpose of arresting PERSHORE and HEBBORN for the offence of squatting.

D The offence has not been committed as neither PERSHORE nor HEBBORN were 'holding over' after the end of a lease or licence in relation to the premises.

Question 5.6

Eight people are trespassing on land (a field) owned by BUSHELL. They drove onto the field in three 4 × 4 vehicles, each vehicle towing a caravan, and they have been camped on the field for two days. BUSHELL asked them to leave but they told him they were going to live on the land for at least a month. He calls the police control room for assistance. Sergeant COOPER attends and speaks to the trespassers. They confirm to him that they will be living on the land for around a month and expect further family members to join them shortly.

Could a direction to leave the land (under s. 61 of the Criminal Justice and Public Order Act 1994) be given to the eight trespassers?

A Yes, such a direction will be given by the senior police officer present at the scene.

B No, such a direction can only be given if damage has been caused to the land by one or more of the trespassers.

C Yes, such a direction will be given by an officer of the rank of inspector or above.

D No, such a direction can only be given if one or more of the trespassers has used or threatened violence towards the occupier, a member of his/her family or an employee or agent of the occupier.

Question 5.7

Five vans (four towing caravans) containing 20 people drive on to private land owned by TINNION. GUNBY is driving one of the vans and he pulls up outside a large agricultural building on the land (a barn) and breaks open the door causing damage to it in the process. All of the vehicles drive into the barn—the common purpose of the 20 people is to reside in vans and caravans in the barn for a week. TINNION arrives at the barn and asks all of the people to leave; they refuse, so TINNION calls the police.

Could the 20 people be directed to leave the barn (under s. 61 of the Criminal Justice and Public Order Act 1994)?

A Yes, but the direction would have to be given by an officer in uniform.

B No, only GUNBY can be directed to leave as he is the only person who has caused damage to the building.

C Yes, and such a direction could be given by an officer of any rank.

D No, because the people are in a barn and the direction to leave does not apply to buildings.

Question 5.8

SMITH is a tenant in a house owned by GLASER. The tenancy agreement is at an end and SMITH should have left the house but he has not (he is 'holding over') and is still living in the house without paying rent. SMITH leaves the house to get some shopping and is out for several hours before returning to the house. In that time, GLASER has called the police to the house and PC GOODWIN (on uniform patrol) has attended the scene. GLASER demands that PC GOODWIN enter the house and arrest SMITH for the offence of squatting in a residential building.

In relation to the offence of squatting in a residential building (contrary to s. 144 of the Legal Aid, Sentencing and Punishment of Offenders Act 2012), which of the following comments is correct?

A PC GOODWIN could not do as GLASER demands as no power of entry exists to enter and arrest a person for this offence.

B The offence has not been committed by SMITH in this situation.

C PC GOODWIN could enter the premises but would need to be authorised to do so by an officer of or above the rank of inspector.

D The offence has not been committed as no force was used by SMITH to enter the premises.

Question 5.9

LAKE is at work, he is the caretaker of a university. He spends the morning completing some maintenance to the entry gates of the university. The gates are usually open as the students will attend the site at various times of day, and night. As LAKE completes this, he drives up towards the sports hall and can see that a group of about 30 men are playing rugby on one of the university's playing fields without the permission of the university. LAKE contacts the police and PC RAYWORTH attends the scene.

Has the offence of causing or permitting nuisance on educational premises (contrary to s. 547(1) of the Education Act 1996) been committed in these circumstances?

A No, as it does not apply to university premises.

B Yes, and PC RAYWORTH has the power to require the men to leave the premises under the Act.

C No, as the activity is taking place on a playing field rather than in a building used for educational purposes.

D Yes, and PC RAYWORTH can assist LAKE to remove the men from the premises under the Act.

Question 5.10

IRWIN was treated in the casualty department of a hospital, after falling and spraining a wrist. Although the injuries were not serious, IRWIN was convinced his treatment was of poor quality and returned to the hospital about four hours after being discharged and insisted on complaining to a hospital administrator. IRWIN began causing a disturbance and because the hospital staff were worried about their safety, they called the police. POWELL, the on-duty security guard, became aware of the disturbance and decided to deal with IRWIN before the police arrived. POWELL was a duly authorised NHS staff member.

Would POWELL have the authority to remove IRWIN from the premises before the arrival of the police?

A No, only a constable could do so because IRWIN would be classed as a patient complaining about medical treatment.

B Yes, either POWELL, a constable or any NHS staff member could do so because IRWIN was not a patient waiting for medical advice.

C Yes, either POWELL or a constable could do so because IRWIN was not a patient waiting for medical advice.

D No, having received treatment less than eight hours ago, IRWIN may not be ejected from the premises.

ANSWERS

Answer 5.1

Answer **B** — Under s. 68(1) of the Criminal Justice and Public Order Act 1994, a person commits the offence of aggravated trespass if he/she trespasses on land and, in relation to any lawful activity which persons are engaging in or are about to engage in on that or adjoining land, does there anything which is intended by him/her to have the effect:

(a) of intimidating those persons or any of them so as to deter them or any of them from engaging in that activity,
(b) of obstructing that activity, or
(c) of disrupting that activity.

Therefore, their actions were sufficient to obstruct and disrupt the activity and all of the protesters commit the offence (correct answer B).

General Police Duties, para. 3.5.2

Answer 5.2

Answer **B** — Section 68(1) of the Criminal Justice and Public Order Act 1994 states that a person commits the offence of aggravated trespass if he trespasses on land and, in relation to any lawful activity which persons are engaging in or are about to engage in on that or adjoining land, does there anything which is intended by him/her to have the effect:

(a) of intimidating those persons or any of them so as to deter them or any of them from engaging in that activity,
(b) of obstructing that activity, or
(c) of disrupting that activity.

It is a defence for the accused to show that he/she was not trespassing on the land, or had a reasonable excuse for failing to leave the land as soon as practicable or for again entering the land as a trespasser (s. 69(4)), making answer D incorrect.

In circumstances similar to this question, the court quashed the appellants' convictions for failing to leave a shop premises as soon as practicable when so directed by the police, because they were physically unable to move until they had been unchained, and had left as soon as this was done. Answer A is therefore incorrect.

The court also held that the activities of the trespassers in *Nero* v *DPP* [2012] EWHC 1238 (Admin) and *Richardson* v *DPP* [2014] UKSC 8 were designed to disrupt the shop's trade, not to frustrate the operation of s. 69; the fact that they had voluntarily (and deliberately) placed themselves in a situation in which they could not leave when directed was held to be irrelevant so answer C is therefore incorrect.

General Police Duties, paras 3.5.2 to 3.5.2.2

Answer 5.3

Answer **C** — Section 69 of the Criminal Justice and Public Order Act 1994 states:

(1) If the senior police officer present at the scene reasonably believes—
  (a) that a person is committing, has committed or intends to commit the offence of aggravated trespass on land; or
  (b) that two or more persons are trespassing on land and are present there with the common purpose of intimidating persons so as to deter them from engaging in a lawful activity or of obstructing or disrupting a lawful activity,
  he may direct that person or (as the case may be) those persons (or any of them) to leave the land.

The power under s. 69 can be authorised by the senior officer present (making answer A incorrect). The power is only available in the above circumstances and as John and Lesley NESBITT are doing nothing wrong (they have not committed the offence of aggravated trespass nor are they trespassing on land), the power is not available no matter what PC VOLT suspects or believes, making answer C correct and answers B and D incorrect.

General Police Duties, paras 3.5.2, 3.5.2.1

Answer 5.4

Answer **C** — Section 62A of the Criminal Justice and Public Order Act 1994 creates a power for a *senior police officer* (that would be the sergeant and not the PC—making answer A incorrect) to direct people to leave land and remove any vehicle or other property with them on that land.

Section 62A states:

(1) If the senior police officer present at a scene [in this case Sergeant KENNEDY] reasonably believes that the conditions in subsection (2) are satisfied in relation to a person and land, he may direct the person—
  (a) to leave the land;
  (b) to remove any vehicle and other property he has with him on the land.
(2) The conditions are—
  (a) that the person and one or more others ('the trespassers') are trespassing on the land;
  (b) that the trespassers have between them at least one vehicle on the land;
  (c) that the trespassers are present on the land with the common purpose of residing there for any period;

5. Offences Relating to Land and Premises

(d) if it appears to the officer that the person has one or more caravans in his possession or under his control on the land, that there is a suitable pitch on a relevant caravan site for that caravan or each of those caravans;

(e) that the occupier of the land or a person acting on his behalf has asked the police to remove the trespassers from the land.

JUKES and GOODHEW do not have a caravan with them but that does not matter— the direction can still be given, making answer B incorrect. There is no need for damage or intimidation activities to take place, making answer D incorrect.

General Police Duties, para. 3.5.5

Answer 5.5

Answer **C** — This offence is committed when a person is in a residential building (the home of the DRAYCOTT family) as a trespasser having entered as a trespasser and the person knows or ought to know that he/she is a trespasser and that the person is living in the building or intends to live there for any period. So when PERSHORE enters the house and lives there for two days, he commits the offence. The fact that one person (HEBBORN) has the permission of another person (PERSHORE), who is a trespasser, to enter the premises does not prevent that person (HEBBORN) from being a trespasser (s. 144(4)), meaning answer A is incorrect. The offence does not require violence to secure entry in order to be committed, making answer B incorrect. Section 144(2) of the Act states that the offence of squatting is not committed by a person 'holding over' after the end of any lease or licence (even if the person leaves and re-enters the building). That may have relevance to those who have had a lease but it would not be relevant to PERSHORE and HEBBORN, making answer D incorrect. Section 17 of PACE 1984 provides police officers with the power to enter and search premises for the purpose of arresting a person for the offence of squatting in a residential building.

General Police Duties, para. 3.5.6

Answer 5.6

Answer **A** — The Criminal Justice and Public Order Act 1994, s. 61 states:

(1) If the senior police officer present at the scene reasonably believes that two or more persons are trespassing on land and are present there with the common purpose of residing there for any period, that reasonable steps have been taken by or on behalf of the occupier to ask them to leave and—

(a) that any of those persons (i) in the case of trespassing on land in England and Wales has caused damage, disruption or distress (see subsection (10)); (ii) in the case of trespassing on land in Scotland, and has caused damage to the land or to property on the land or used threatening, abusive or insulting words or behaviour towards the occupier, a member of his family or an employee or agent of his, or

(b) in either case that those persons have between them six or more vehicles on the land, he may direct those persons, or any of them, to leave the land and to remove any vehicles or other property they have with them on the land.

The direction can be given if the circumstances in s. 61(1)(a) or (b) apply, meaning that answers B and D are incorrect. The direction will be given by the 'senior officer present at the scene'—this could be of any rank, making answer C incorrect.

General Police Duties, para. 3.5.4

Answer 5.7

Answer **C** — The Criminal Justice and Public Order Act 1994, s. 61 states:

(1) If the senior police officer present at the scene reasonably believes that two or more persons (i) in the case of persons trespassing on land in England and Wales, has caused damage, disruption or distress (see subsection (10)); (ii) in the case of persons trespassing on land in Scotland, and are trespassing on land and are present there with the common purpose of residing there for any period, that reasonable steps have been taken by or on behalf of the occupier to ask them to leave and—

(a) that any of those persons has caused damage to the land or to property on the land or used threatening, abusive or insulting words or behaviour towards the occupier, a member of his family or an employee or agent of his, or

(b) in either case that those persons have between them six or more vehicles on the land, he may direct those persons, or any of them, to leave the land and to remove any vehicles or other property they have with them on the land.

'Land' does not include buildings other than agricultural buildings or scheduled monuments, so the barn would be 'land' for the purposes of s. 61, making answer D incorrect. If the conditions in s. 61(1)(a) or (b) are met, then 'those persons, or any of them' can be directed to leave, making answer B incorrect. The direction does not have to be given by an officer in uniform (answer A is incorrect); it is given by the 'senior police officer present' and that could be any rank (correct answer C).

General Police Duties, para. 3.5.4

Answer 5.8

Answer **B** — The Legal Aid, Sentencing and Punishment of Offenders Act 2012, s. 144 states:

(1) A person commits an offence if—

(a) the person is in a residential building as a trespasser having entered it as a trespasser,

(b) the person knows or ought to know that he or she is a trespasser, and

(c) the person is living in the building or intends to live there for any period.

(2) The offence is not committed by a person holding over after the end of a lease or licence (even if the person leaves and re-enters the building).

Section 144(2) tells you that SMITH cannot commit the offence (correct answer B).

General Police Duties, para. 3.5.6

Answer 5.9

Answer **A** — There is no power under s. 547(1) to remove anyone who commits the offence under s. 547(1) of the Education Act 1996 making answers B and D incorrect. A playing field would be 'premises' for the purposes of the offence, making answer C incorrect. The offence applies to premises that provide primary and secondary education—not university premises (making answer A correct).

General Police Duties, para. 3.5.7

Answer 5.10

Answer **C**— Section 119(1) of the Criminal Justice and Immigration Act 2008 creates an offence of causing a nuisance or disturbance to an NHS staff member who is working on NHS premises and then failing to leave when required to do so by a constable or an NHS staff member. This section will only apply to people who are not on the NHS premises for the purpose of obtaining medical advice, treatment or care for themselves.

Section 120 of the 2008 Act provides a power for a constable or authorised person to remove a person who has committed an offence under s. 119. Although a non-authorised NHS staff member may ask a person to leave, this does not extend to a power of removal of a person who refuses. Answer B is therefore incorrect.

An authorised officer cannot remove the person if it is reasonably believed that he/she is in need of medical advice etc. or that such removal would endanger that person's mental or physical health (s. 120(4)). However, a person ceases to be on NHS premises for the purpose of obtaining medical advice, treatment or care for him/herself in the following two circumstances:

- once the person has received the medical advice (s. 119(3)(a));
- if the person has received the medical advice etc. during the last eight hours (s. 119(3)(b)).

Having received treatment less than eight hours previously, IRWIN is not a patient and may be ejected from the premises. Answers A and D are therefore incorrect.

General Police Duties, para. 3.5.8

6 | Licensing and Offences Relating to Alcohol

QUESTIONS

Question 6.1

CALE is the chair of a residents' association on a housing estate. The Anchor public house on the estate has caused considerable concern recently due to the number of public order incidents that have occurred in the vicinity of the premises on weekends. CALE and other residents have raised the issue several times in meetings with local police groups as their perception is that the police and the local authority are reluctant to take action against the licensee. CALE is now demanding that the premises licence be reviewed.

In which circumstances could a review of the premises licence take place?

A A review of a licence may take place if the licensee is failing to take sufficient measures to prevent public nuisance, or where the police consider that measures put in place to prevent crime and disorder are not being effective.

B A review of a licence may only take place if the licensee is failing to take sufficient measures to prevent crime and disorder.

C A review of a licence may take place if the licensee has been convicted of offences under the Licensing Act 2003.

D A review of a licence may take place if there have been more than three public order incidents directly connected to the premises in question in the last six months.

Question 6.2

Constable READING is on patrol in uniform with Constable STEVENS when they hear information over the force radio that the local snooker club is holding a tournament event that evening. The operator asks any patrols in the area to pay passing attention to the club as at the last event there was some disorder resulting from recreational drugs taken on-site. The club has made assurances that it now has procedures in place to stop this, and to control disorderly behaviour. Later in the evening, they are passing the area and Constable READING slows the police vehicle to enable Constable STEVENS to look in through the club windows. Constable STEVENS suspects that licensing offences are taking place and they stop, park and enter the club.

Section 97 of the Licensing Act 2003 provides a power of entry for a constable to enter and search any premises which hold a club premises certificate. What restrictions are placed on this power of entry and search?

A Entry is allowed to detect licensing offences or to prevent a breach of the peace only.

B Entry is allowed to prevent a breach of the peace only.

C Entry is allowed to detect licensing offences, to search for offences relating to the supply of drugs or to prevent a breach of the peace.

D Entry is allowed to search for offences relating to the supply of drugs or to prevent a breach of the peace only.

Question 6.3

Constable KHAN was on duty as part of a plain-clothes team of police officers, working with LEWIS, a licensing officer from the local authority and a person authorised under the Licensing Act 2003. The team was tasked with visiting public houses in the locality to check the activities of licensed premises. They arrived at the Royal Oak public house at 10.50 pm and identified themselves (as a police officer and licensing officer) to GEORGE, the door supervisor, and asked to enter the premises. GEORGE refused, stating that the premises were about to close. The operating schedule stated that the premises should close at 11 pm.

Does either Constable KHAN or LEWIS have the power to enter the premises using reasonable force under the Licensing Act 2003?

A No, the power to enter by reasonable force is restricted to uniformed police officers only.

B Constable KHAN only; LEWIS does not have a power to enter by force in these circumstances.

C Yes, both have the power to enter using reasonable force in these circumstances.

D Yes, Constable KHAN and LEWIS have a power of entry but only if they have reason to believe that offences are being committed.

Question 6.4

The police have been called to a call centre where NUGENT works. When the officers arrived, they entered a private part of the building where entry was restricted to employees of the company. They were told by PRENTICE (NUGENT's manager) that NUGENT had returned to the office at lunchtime and was drunk. NUGENT had started an argument with her line manager and when they approached her they could see she was clearly drunk and acting in a disorderly manner.

Could the officers arrest NUGENT for an offence of being drunk and disorderly under s. 91(1) of the Criminal Justice Act 1967?

A No, the offence must be committed in a public place.

B Yes, the offence may be committed anywhere.

C No, the offence may not be committed inside a building.

D Yes, because NUGENT was not inside a dwelling at the time.

Question 6.5

Constable MURRAY was called to an incident in the Dog public house. The licensee led the officer to the toilet area where they saw LEWIS who was slumped in a corner in a drunken condition, covered in vomit. The officer tried to wake LEWIS but was unable to do so as he was so drunk. The officer was considering arresting LEWIS for being found drunk.

Does Constable MURRAY have the power to deal with LEWIS under s. 12 of the Licensing Act 1872 (being found drunk)?

A No, the offence must be committed in a public place.

B Yes, the offence may be committed anywhere.

C No, the offence may not be committed in a building.

D Yes, the offence may be committed on licensed premises.

Question 6.6

GREEN owns an off-licence which is being monitored by the local Neighbourhood Policing Team because of complaints that alcohol is being sold to young people on a regular basis. During an operation in March, the police caught GREEN selling alcohol to ZENDEN, aged 16. The following month (April), the police again detected GREEN selling alcohol to ZENDEN on one other occasion.

Would GREEN's behaviour amount to an offence under s. 147A of the Licensing Act 2003 (persistently selling alcohol to children under the age of 18)?

A Yes, GREEN has sold alcohol to a person under 18 on two or more occasions within a period of three consecutive months.

B No, GREEN has not sold alcohol to a person under 18 on three or more occasions in three consecutive months.

C Yes, and this is a 'strict liability' offence so GREEN would not have any defence available in answer to a charge under s. 147A of the Act.

D No, GREEN has not sold alcohol to a person under 18 on four or more occasions in three consecutive months.

Question 6.7

Whilst on patrol in a park in the evening, Constable MANNING saw a group of four young people, all drinking from bottles of beer. The officer discovered that three of the group were 17 years of age and the youngest, GRANT, was under 15. Constable MANNING confiscated the alcohol from the group and disposed of it.

What does s. 1 of the Confiscation of Alcohol (Young Persons) Act 1997 state about the actions Constable MANNING should now take?

A Constable MANNING may take names and addresses from all of the group and may remove GRANT to his place of residence or a place of safety.

B Constable MANNING must take names and addresses from all of the group and must remove GRANT to his place of residence or a place of safety.

C Constable MANNING shall require all the persons in the group to state their names and addresses and may remove GRANT to his place of residence or a place of safety.

D Constable MANNING must take names and addresses from all of the group and may remove everyone in the group to their place of residence or a place of safety.

Question 6.8

Constable SINGH was walking through a park when he came across two young people who were intoxicated. He discovered they were 15 years old and that they had been given drink by HAWKINS. Constable SINGH intercepted HAWKINS (who is 20 years old) who was walking in the park, and saw that he was in possession of several cans of lager. Constable SINGH reasonably suspects that HAWKINS intends the lager to be consumed by persons under the age of 18 in the park.

Does Constable SINGH have any powers to deal with HAWKINS in these circumstances under s. 1 of the Confiscation of Alcohol (Young Persons) Act 1997?

A Yes, he has the power to confiscate the alcohol from HAWKINS and shall also require HAWKINS to state his name and address.

B Yes, he has the power to demand HAWKINS's name and address.

C No, he has no powers as HAWKINS is not under 18.

D No, he has no powers as HAWKINS is not in the company of a person under 18 to whom he intends to supply the alcohol.

Question 6.9

The police have conducted a series of test-purchase operations over a period of a month at the Cherry Tree public house, due to suspected under-age drinking. The officers conducting the exercise have reported that GREEN, the premises licence holder, served alcohol to five under-age drinkers during this period. The duty inspector considers that an offence has been committed under s. 147A of the Licensing Act 2003, and a closure notice should be served on GREEN to prevent further sales to young people.

Which of the following statements is correct, in relation to such a notice, under s. 169A of the Act?

A The inspector may authorise a closure notice provided GREEN accepts responsibility for the offence under s. 147A.

B The inspector may authorise a closure notice in these circumstances alone.

C A superintendent may authorise a closure provided GREEN accepts responsibility for the offence under s. 147A.

D A superintendent may authorise a closure provided there is a realistic prospect of prosecuting GREEN for an offence under s. 147A.

Question 6.10

Staff from a Neighbourhood Policing Team have been meeting with partners from the local authority to discuss problems relating to ongoing serious anti-social behaviour on a housing estate. Consideration is being given to making a Public Spaces Protection Order to assist the partners in dealing with the problem.

Which of the following statements is correct in relation to making such an order under s. 59 of the Anti-social Behaviour, Crime and Policing Act 2014?

A The order may be made either by a superintendent or an equivalent person in the local authority, provided it can be demonstrated that they have consulted with each other.

B The order must be made and publicised by the local authority in consultation with the chief officer of police, the Police and Crime Commissioner and any representatives of the local community they consider appropriate.

C The order may be made either by a superintendent or an equivalent person in the local authority provided it can be demonstrated that they have consulted with each other and publicised the details of the order locally.

D The order may be made either by an inspector or an equivalent person in the local authority in consultation with any representatives of the local community they consider appropriate.

Question 6.11

Local licensing officers working in partnership have met urgently on a Saturday morning to discuss the Carpenters Arms public house, which has been the location of serious disorder over the last three weekends. A closure notice had been issued to the licence holder the previous evening following a fight between two rival gangs at the premises. The officers are preparing a file to take to court to apply for a closure order to prevent the premises opening again that night because intelligence had shown that further violence is likely to occur.

Which of the following statements is correct in relation to an application for a closure order under s. 160 of the Licensing Act 2003?

A The application may be made by an inspector or an equivalent person from the local authority.

B The application may be made by a superintendent or an equivalent person from the local authority.

C The application may only be made by a superintendent.

D The application may only be made by a member of the licensing authority for the area.

Question 6.12

A closure order has been made in respect of the Heathcock public house which has been the location of serious disorder over the weekend. The request was made for the order to allow the local licensing authority to meet urgently to discuss the problems at the premises and any potential solutions.

If the order was granted, how long would it last, according to s. 160 of the Licensing Act 2003?

A The premises could be closed for a period not exceeding 24 hours.

B The premises could be closed for a period not exceeding 48 hours.

C The premises could be closed for a period not exceeding 7 days.

D The premises could be closed for a period not exceeding 14 days.

Question 6.13

Constable WARREN works as a licensing officer based in a co-located office with the local authority Licensing Department. Constable WARREN has attended premises in High Street with CANTEBURY, a local authority licensing officer. They have received intelligence that NEWMAN is using the premises for the unlicensed sale of alcohol. Their intention is to gather evidence and, if necessary, close the premises down.

Section 19 of the Criminal Justice and Police Act 2001 allows for a closure notice to be served in respect of unlicensed premises. In respect of this power, which of the following statements is correct?

A A closure notice may be served by Constable WARREN only, provided this is done in consultation with the local authority (which would include consulting with CANTEBURY).

B Either Constable WARREN or CANTEBURY could serve a closure notice in these circumstances.

C A closure notice may only be served by an inspector; neither Constable WARREN nor CANTEBURY has the authority to do so in these circumstances.

D A closure notice may only be authorised by a magistrate; either Constable WARREN or CANTEBURY would have to apply to the court for such a notice.

ANSWERS

Answer 6.1

Answer **A** — A premises licence may be reviewed by a licensing authority where it is considered that a licensee is failing to take sufficient measures to prevent public nuisance, or where the police consider that measures put in place to prevent crime and disorder are not being effective.

Answers B, C and D are therefore incorrect.

General Police Duties, para. 3.6.4.1

Answer 6.2

Answer **D** — Under s. 97(1) of the Licensing Act 2003, where a club premises certificate has effect in respect of any premises, a constable may enter and search the premises if he/she has reasonable cause to believe:

(a) that an offence under section 4(3)(a), (b) or (c) of the Misuse of Drugs Act 1971 (supplying or offering to supply, or being concerned in supplying or making an offer to supply, a controlled drug) has been, is being, or is about to be, committed there, or

(aa) that an offence under section 5(1) or (2) of the Psychoactive Substances Act 2016 (supplying or offering to supply, a psychoactive substance) has been, is being, or is about to be, committed there, or

(b) that there is likely to be a breach of the peace there.

This section does not allow a constable to enter the premises to detect licensing offences; therefore, answers A and C are incorrect. Entry is allowed (using reasonable force if necessary) in order to detect offences under the Misuse of Drugs Act 1971, or if a breach of the peace is likely to occur in the premises. Answers A and B are incorrect for this reason.

General Police Duties, para. 3.6.4.3

Answer 6.3

Answer **C** — Under s. 179 of the Licensing Act 2003, where a constable or an authorised person has reason to believe that any premises are being, or are about to be, used for a licensable activity, he/she may enter the premises with a view to seeing whether the activity is being, or is to be, carried on under and in accordance with an authorisation (s. 179(1)). A person exercising the power conferred by this section may, if necessary, use reasonable force (s. 179(3)). Since the power under this section is not restricted to police officers, answer B is incorrect. Also, there is no requirement for a police officer to be in uniform; therefore, answer A is incorrect.

There is a separate power, under s. 180 of the Act, for a constable to enter premises in order to investigate offences. A constable may enter by reasonable force under this section. However, s. 179 shows that a constable or authorised person may enter premises using reasonable force simply to make sure that licensing activities are being carried out within the law. Answer D is therefore incorrect.

(Note that an authorised person exercising the powers conferred on him/her must, if so requested, produce evidence of his/her authority to exercise the power.)

General Police Duties, para. 3.6.5

Answer 6.4

Answer **A** — Under s. 91(1) of the Criminal Justice Act 1967, a person commits an offence if, in a public place, he/she is guilty, while drunk, of disorderly conduct. Since the offence may only be committed in a public place, answers B, C and D are incorrect.

General Police Duties, para. 3.6.8

Answer 6.5

Answer **D** — Under s. 12 of the Licensing Act 1902, every person found drunk in any highway or other public place, whether a building or not, or on any licensed premises, shall be liable.

The offence may not be committed 'anywhere', but may be committed inside a building or in a licensed premises. Answers B and C are therefore incorrect.

Similarly, the offence is not restricted to public places only; for example, a licensed premises which is closed may not be a public place; however, a person may be found drunk on the premises after everyone else has left and the offence may be committed in those circumstances. Answer A is therefore incorrect.

General Police Duties, para. 3.6.9

Answer 6.6

Answer **A** — Under s. 147A(1) of the Licensing Act 2003, a person is guilty of an offence if:

(a) on 2 or more different occasions within a period of 3 consecutive months alcohol is unlawfully sold on the same premises to an individual aged under 18.

It is 'unlawfully sold' if the person making the sale believed the individual to be under 18 or did not have reasonable grounds for believing him/her to be 18 or over (a defence to the offence, making answer C incorrect).

The offence is committed if alcohol is sold on 'two or more different occasions'. Answers B and D are therefore incorrect.

General Police Duties, para. 3.6.10

Answer 6.7

Answer **C** — Under s. 1 of the Confiscation of Alcohol (Young Persons) Act 1997, apart from the power to confiscate any alcohol from young people under the age of 18 under subss. (1) and (2) in certain conditions (which applied in this case), a constable has further duties and powers, as follows:

(1AA) A constable who imposes a requirement on a person under subsection (1) shall also require the person to state the person's name and address.
(1AB) A constable who imposes a requirement on a person under subsection (1) may, if the constable reasonably suspects that the person is under the age of 16, remove the person to the person's place of residence or a place of safety.

The duty to ask for the person's name and address under s. 1(1AA) is not just a power, it is a requirement and answer A is incorrect.

On the other hand, the constable is not *required* to remove a person under 16 to their place of residence or a place of safety and this power is not available to the rest of the people in the group, who were over 16. Answers B and D are therefore incorrect.

General Police Duties, para. 3.6.11.3

Answer 6.8

Answer **A** — Under s. 1(1) of the Confiscation of Alcohol (Young Persons) Act 1997, a constable who reasonably suspects that a person who is in a relevant place is in possession of alcohol, may confiscate the alcohol if:

(a) the person is under 18; or
(b) the person intends that any of the alcohol shall be consumed by a person under 18 in a relevant place; or
(c) the person is with or has recently been with a person under 18 and that person has recently consumed alcohol in the relevant place.

Under s. 1(6), a 'relevant place' is:

- any public place, other than licensed premises; or
- any place, other than a public place, to which that person has unlawfully gained access;

and for this purpose a place is a public place if, at the material time, the public or any section of the public has access to it—on payment or otherwise—as of right or by virtue of express or implied permission.

Alcohol may be confiscated from a person who is over 18 if he/she has committed an act mentioned under paras (b) and (c)—the power is designed to prevent alcohol either being consumed by, or supplied to, people under 18 (therefore answer D is incorrect). Answer C is therefore incorrect.

Note that subs. (1AA) of the Act states that a constable exercising the power under s. 1 *shall* require the person to state their name and address.

General Police Duties, para. 3.6.11.3

Answer 6.9

Answer **D** — Section 169A of the Licensing Act 2003 provides that a senior police officer (of the rank of superintendent or higher), or an inspector of weights and measures, may give a closure notice where there is evidence that a person has committed the offence of persistently selling alcohol to children at the premises in question. Answers A and B are therefore incorrect.

A further condition exists under s. 169A—the superintendent must consider that the evidence is such that there would be a realistic prospect of conviction if the offender was prosecuted for it. Answer C is therefore incorrect.

General Police Duties, para. 3.6.11.4

Answer 6.10

Answer **B** — Under s. 59 of the Anti-social Behaviour, Crime and Policing Act 2014, a local authority may make a Public Spaces Protection Order if satisfied on reasonable grounds that activities carried on in a public place within the authority's area have had, or are likely to have, a detrimental effect on the quality of life of those in the locality.

The power to make the order lies with the local authority. Answers A, C and D are therefore incorrect.

General Police Duties, para. 3.6.12.1

Answer 6.11

Answer **C** — Under s. 160(1) of the Licensing Act 2003, where there is or is expected to be disorder in any local justice area, a magistrates' court acting in the area may make an order requiring all premises which are situated at or near the place of the disorder or expected disorder, and in respect of which a premises licence or a temporary event notice has effect, to be closed for a period, not exceeding 24 hours, specified in the order.

A magistrates' court may make an order under this section only on the application of a police officer who is of the rank of superintendent or above (s. 160(2)).

Answers A, B and D are therefore incorrect.

General Police Duties, para. 3.6.14

Answer 6.12

Answer **A** — Under s. 160(1) of the Licensing Act 2003, where there is or is expected to be disorder in any local justice area, a magistrates' court acting in the area may make an order requiring all premises which are situated at or near the place of the disorder or expected disorder, and in respect of which a premises licence or a temporary event notice has effect, to be closed for a period, not exceeding 24 hours, specified in the order.

Answers B, C and D are therefore incorrect.

General Police Duties, para. 3.6.14

Answer 6.13

Answer **B** — Under s. 19 of the Criminal Justice and Police Act 2001, where a constable is satisfied that any premises (including land or any place whether covered or not):

- are being used or
- have been used within the last 24 hours
- for the unlicensed sale/exposure for sale
- of alcohol
- for consumption on or in the vicinity of the premises

he/she may serve a closure notice.

This power is available to any police officer of any rank; therefore, Constable WARREN does not need to call an inspector or go to court. Answers C and D are therefore incorrect.

In addition, under s. 19, the power to serve a notice is available to any police officer of any rank and *may also be exercised by the relevant local authority*. Answer A is therefore incorrect.

General Police Duties, para. 3.6.15

QUESTIONS

Question 7.1

BLANCO, aged 19, is the subject of an injunction under s. 34 of the Policing and Crime Act 2009, having been involved in gang-related drug-dealing activity. One of the conditions of the injunction is that he is to stay away from a park where members of the gang often gather. PC McCAIG is on uniform patrol and sees BLANCO, on his own, in the park. Reasonably suspecting that BLANCO is in breach of the provisions of the injunction, PC McCAIG arrests BLANCO.

Considering the issues surrounding injunctions under s. 34 of the Act, which of the following comments is correct?

A PC McCAIG should not have arrested BLANCO unless he reasonably believes BLANCO is in breach of the provisions of the injunction.

B BLANCO must be brought before a judge or the court that granted the injunction with 24 hours of his arrest.

C PC McCAIG should not have arrested BLANCO unless he was in the company of at least three other gang members.

D BLANCO must be brought before a judge or the court that granted the injunction as soon as is practicable.

Question 7.2

CURRY, aged 14, and STROUD, aged 16, have both been involved in gang-related activity. CURRY has engaged in gang-related violence and STROUD has encouraged

CURRY to engage in the gang-related violence. Consideration is being given to applying to a court for an injunction against CURRY and STROUD under s. 34 of the Policing and Crime Act 2009 to prevent them from engaging in further gang-related activities.

Who, if anyone, could an injunction be made against?

A CURRY only.

B STROUD only.

C CURRY and STROUD.

D Neither CURRY nor STROUD.

Question 7.3

The police and local authority are holding a strategy meeting to discuss McCANN, who is 10 years of age. Numerous referrals have been made to the anti-social behaviour coordinator over several months, showing evidence that McCANN has been acting in an anti-social manner towards PATEL, an elderly next-door neighbour who lives alone.

Given that McCANN has acted in an anti-social manner against PATEL, could a civil injunction under Pt 1 of the Anti-social Behaviour, Crime and Policing Act 2014 be applied for in these circumstances?

A Yes, provided McCANN's conduct amounts to anti-social behaviour, an injunction may be granted.

B No, even if the conduct amounts to anti-social behaviour, an injunction cannot be granted because of McCANN's age.

C Yes, if the conduct amounts to anti-social behaviour an injunction may be granted; McCANN's age is not relevant in an application for a civil injunction.

D No, because only one person in another household has been affected by McCANN's behaviour.

Question 7.4

The court has granted a civil injunction against KANE, aged 19, for conduct which amounted to anti-social behaviour. The court has decided that because drug misuse had been a major cause of the behaviour that led to the injunction being made, it would be appropriate for KANE to comply with a drug rehabilitation programme.

What is the maximum period of time the court can specify for KANE to comply with the injunction?

A A maximum period of six months.

B A minimum period of 12 months.

C A maximum period of two years.

D There is no maximum period.

Question 7.5

BAKER is 13 years of age and is being considered for an application for a civil injunction for dealing with anti-social behaviour. BAKER has been drinking alcohol in public places and becoming abusive to passers-by. BAKER is also joined by JAE who is aged 19. JAE will drink alcohol with BAKER and behave in an anti-social manner. Constable MEEKIN is preparing a written application for both BAKER and JAE.

When considering the requirements under s. 18(2) of the Anti-social Behaviour, Crime and Policing Act 2014, which of the following statements is correct?

A Constable MEEKIN should direct the court to hear both applications together as they are connected.

B A youth court must not accept an adult application, both applications will be made to the High Court or County Court.

C Constable MEEKIN should submit BAKER's application to the youth court and JAE's to the High Court or County Court.

D The youth court may give permission for the application in relation to JAE to be made there.

Question 7.6

MURRAY, aged 21, was convicted by the magistrates' court for an offence contrary to s. 5 of the Public Order Act 1986, following abusive behaviour towards an elderly neighbour, and was convicted for the offence. Prior to sentence, the court heard that MURRAY was alcohol-dependent and was regularly involved in abusing people in the street when drunk. Several intervention initiatives had been attempted but had failed because of MURRAY's continuous drinking.

In relation to Criminal Behaviour Orders (under s. 330 of the Sentencing Code (Sentencing Act 2020)), which of the following comments is correct?

A As MURRAY has been convicted for the offence, a Criminal Behaviour Order cannot be made as matters are finalised.

B A court will automatically be able to make a Criminal Behaviour Order because MURRAY has been convicted of a relevant offence.

C A Criminal Behaviour Order can only be made if the prosecutor applies for it on the advice of the police or the local authority.

D A prosecutor can make a request for a Criminal Behaviour Order in this situation regardless of the wishes of the police or local authority.

Question 7.7

The court has granted a Criminal Behaviour Order against SHAW, aged 16, for con-duct which amounted to anti-social behaviour. The court has decided that because drunkenness had been a significant contributing factor to the behaviour that led to the Criminal Behaviour Order being made, it would be appropriate for the order to require SHAW not to consume alcohol in a public place.

Which of the following statements is correct in relation to the time period the court can specify for SHAW to comply with the order?

A The order should be set for a minimum period of six months.

B The order should be set for a minimum period of one year.

C The order should be set for a minimum period of two years.

D There is no minimum period for the order to be set.

Question 7.8

Constable DONAHUE is the community beat officer on a housing estate which has been suffering an ongoing youth annoyance problem outside a small shopping centre. One bank holiday weekend, the police were called to the location to deal with intimida-tion and annoyance towards shopkeepers and customers, on average ten times a day. Constable DONAHUE was on duty on the bank holiday Monday and visited the shop-ping centre during the afternoon. There were two youths present who the officer knew were the main instigators. After speaking to the shopkeepers, Constable DONAHUE is satisfied on reasonable grounds that there will be further harassment that afternoon and evening. Constable DONAHUE was considering whether an authorisation should be given to use the dispersal power under s. 35 of the Anti-social Behaviour, Crime and Policing Act 2014, to disperse the two youths before the problem escalated again.

Would such an authorisation be appropriate in these circumstances?

A No, because there are only two people present.

B Yes, because there are two or more people present.

C No, this power may only be authorised when anti-social behaviour is actually taking place.

D Yes, an authorisation can be given but that must be by an officer of at least the rank of inspector.

Question 7.9

Constable DEAN was on patrol at 7.30 pm in a housing estate where, following incidents of significant and persistent anti-social behaviour, a dispersal notice had been issued. Constable DEAN saw PURSE, aged 15, and CHALMERS, aged 16, staggering around shouting loudly and clearly drunk. Constable DEAN was concerned that they would continue to act in an anti-social manner if left at the location.

Would Constable DEAN have the power to take PURSE and CHALMERS home in these circumstances, utilising powers under s. 3 of the Anti-social Behaviour, Crime and Policing Act 2014 (power to remove people to their place of residence)?

A No, this power would only be available in relation to PURSE.

B No, these powers only apply between the hours of 9 pm and 6 am.

C Yes, as they are likely to commit anti-social behaviour.

D Yes, provided they have been instructed to leave the area and have refused.

Question 7.10

PCSO McLEAN works on a Neighbourhood Policing Team and has been consulting with the local authority about a shop on a housing estate which has been the subject of numerous complaints in recent neighbourhood meetings. The shop is open late every night and young people congregate outside depositing litter in the street. PCSO McLEAN has spoken to the shop owner several times, who has stated that the local authority is tasked with clearing up litter not business owners. Consideration is being given to issuing the owner with a Community Protection Notice under Pt 5 of the Anti-social, Crime and Policing Act 2014.

Which of the following statements is correct in relation to the issuing of such a notice?

A The notice may only be issued by the local council as this is an environmental issue.

B The notice may be issued by the local council or any police constable.

C The notice may be issued by the local council or any police constable, provided it has been authorised by an inspector.

D The notice may be issued by the local council or the police, including designated PCSOs.

Question 7.11

Constable ELSOM is part of a Neighbourhood Policing Team and has been liaising with the local authority about premises that have been subject to a number of complaints at public meetings because of persistent anti-social behaviour problems. A closure notice has been issued in respect of the premises and an application is being prepared for a closure order to be issued by the court.

When must the application for a closure order be heard by a magistrates' court?
A Within 24 hours of the closure notice being issued.
B Within 48 hours of the closure notice being issued.
C Within 72 hours of the closure notice being issued.
D Within 96 hours of the closure notice being issued.

Question 7.12

Reliable intelligence is received that a large gathering of youths is planned to take place on a housing estate. The intelligence states that a number of high-powered vehicles will be used to race around the housing estate and that this racing will be watched and encouraged by over 100 youths. This intelligence is passed to Inspector EMERY who is considering using the powers under Pt 3 of the Anti-social Behaviour, Crime and Policing Act 2014 to authorise a dispersal order (under s. 34 of the Act) to counter and reduce the likelihood of anti-social behaviour occurring.

Could Inspector EMERY authorise the dispersal power in this situation?
A Yes, although any authorisation would be limited to a maximum period of 48 hours.
B No, as the power can only be authorised by an officer of the rank of superintendent or above.
C Yes, although the power to direct people to leave the specified area can only be used when the person concerned has committed an act of anti-social behaviour.
D No, as the power under s. 34 can only be authorised when anti-social behaviour has actually taken place.

Question 7.13

An authorisation under s. 34 of the Anti-social Behaviour, Crime and Policing Act 2014 has been granted in respect of a shopping precinct. The intelligence that gave rise to the authorisation being granted included information that youths would be causing criminal damage to buildings using cans of spray paint. During the time period that authorisation under s. 34 is valid, PC NIELD (on uniform foot patrol in the shopping precinct) lawfully stops and searches AYLING (who is 15 years old) using the power of stop and search under s. 1 of the Police and Criminal Evidence Act 1984. During the course of the search, the officer finds a can of spray paint in a bag that AYLING is carrying. PC NIELD directs AYLING to leave the shopping precinct and not to return for 24 hours.

Would PC NIELD be able to seize the can of spray paint from AYLING using powers under the Anti-social, Crime and Policing Act 2014?

A No, as an authorisation under s. 34 provides a power to disperse individuals or groups from an area—it does not provide a power to seize items.

B Yes, the can of spray paint can be seized and retained indefinitely.

C No, the power of seizure associated with the authorisation relates to the seizure of alcohol alone.

D Yes, but it must not be returned to AYLING before the exclusion period (in this case 24 hours) is over.

Question 7.14

A parenting order has been imposed on the parents of a child who has been involved in anti-social behaviour. Part of this order is a programme of counselling.

For how long can this counselling last?

A One month.

B Three months.

C Six months.

D Twelve months.

Question 7.15

AUDREY is a particularly unruly 15-year-old, in relation to whom the courts are considering a parenting order. Owing to her misbehaviour at home, AUDREY's uncle and aunt are currently looking after her but they have no legal guardianship.

Can a parenting order be imposed on AUDREY's uncle and aunt?

A Yes, for the time being, they are caring for AUDREY.

B Yes, provided the court's opinion is that they are caring for AUDREY.

C No, the order can be imposed on the biological parents only.

D No, as they do not have legal guardianship.

Question 7.16

LEWIS, aged 9, committed an act of criminal damage. The local authority applied to a family court for a Child Safety Order (under s. 11 of the Crime and Disorder Act 1998) in respect of LEWIS.

If the family court granted the application, what is the maximum time period such a 'Child Safety Order' placing LEWIS under the supervision of a responsible officer would run for?

A Six months.

B Twelve months.

C Eighteen months.

D Twenty-four months.

Question 7.17

MOORE is 17 years of age and has been convicted of an offence. The court is considering binding the parents over in the interests of preventing the commission by MOORE of further offences.

In relation to s. 376 of the Sentencing Code (Sentencing Act 2020) (binding over of parent or guardian), which of the following is correct?

A It shall be the duty of the court to exercise those powers if it is satisfied, having regard to the circumstances of the case, that their exercise would be desirable in the interests of preventing the commission of further offences.

B The court may exercise those powers if it is satisfied, having regard to the circumstances of the case, that their exercise would be desirable in the interests of preventing the commission of further offences.

C The court may exercise those powers unless there are compelling circumstances not to do so.

D The court cannot exercise these powers as MOORE is not aged under 16 years.

Question 7.18

Section 376 of the Sentencing Code (Sentencing Act 2020) provides for the binding over of a parent or guardian to order them to enter into a recognizance to take proper care of and exercise proper control over their child following conviction.

For how long can this recognizance be imposed?

A Three months.
B Six months.
C One year.
D Three years.

Question 7.19

The Education Act 1996 provides that penalty notices can be issued to parents or guardians who fail to ensure the regular attendance of their child who is registered at a State school or fail to ensure that their excluded child is not found in a public place during school hours without a justifiable reason.

Which of the following is correct in relation to children to whom this applies?
A Any child provided they are or have been in full-time education.
B A child of compulsory school age (5–16).
C A child of compulsory school age (5–16) or 17 if in sixth form.
D A child of school age (5–15).

Question 7.20

An authority to remove truants to designated premises under s. 16 of the Crime and Disorder Act 1998 is in effect and Constable McGIVERN found LAWRENCE, who is 14 years of age, at a time and in a public place covered by the s. 16 authorisation. Constable McGIVERN reasonably suspects that LAWRENCE is of a compulsory school age and absent from school with no lawful authority.

Can Constable McGIVERN use the power under s. 16 of the Act in this situation?
A Yes, and LAWRENCE should be returned to his own school.
B No, the officer only 'suspects' LAWRENCE is of a compulsory school age and is absent from school without authority.
C No, as s. 16 only applies to children who have been excluded by a school for a fixed period or permanently.
D Yes, and the officer may remove LAWRENCE to designated premises or the school from which he is absent.

ANSWERS

Answer 7.1

Answer **B** — Where a power of arrest is attached to a provision of an injunction under s. 34 of the Policing and Crime Act 2009, a constable may arrest without warrant a person whom the constable has reasonable cause to suspect to be in breach of the provision. This makes answer A incorrect. There is no requirement for the person suspected to be in breach of the provision to be in the company of other gang members, making answer C incorrect. Answer D is incorrect as the constable making the arrest must inform the person who applied for the injunction of the arrest, and the person arrested must be brought before a judge of the court that granted the injunction within 24 hours of the arrest (s. 43) (correct answer B).

General Police Duties, para 3.7.2

Answer 7.2

Answer **C** — Section 34 of the 2009 Act, as amended, states:

(1) A court may grant an injunction under this section against a respondent aged 14 or over if the first and second conditions are met.
(2) The first condition is that the court is satisfied on the balance of probabilities that the respondent has engaged in or has encouraged or assisted—
   (a) gang-related violence, or
   (b) gang-related drug-dealing activity.
(3) The second condition is that the court thinks it is necessary to grant the injunction for either or both of the following purposes—
   (a) to prevent the respondent from engaging in, or encouraging or assisting, gang-related violence or gang-related drug-dealing activity;
   (b) to protect the respondent from gang-related violence or gang-related drug-dealing activity.

An injunction could be granted against CURRY and STROUD (correct answer C).

General Police Duties, para 3.7.2

Answer 7.3

Answer **A** — Part 1 of the Anti-social Behaviour, Crime and Policing Act 2014 creates the power for a civil court to grant injunctions if it is satisfied, on the balance of probabilities, that the respondent has engaged or threatened to engage in anti-social behaviour and it is just and convenient to grant the injunction for the purpose of preventing the respondent from engaging in anti-social behaviour.

Section 2(1) of the 2014 Act defines 'anti-social behaviour' as:

(a) conduct that has caused, or is likely to cause, harassment, alarm or distress to any person, or
(b) conduct capable of causing nuisance or annoyance to a person in relation to that person's occupation of residential premises, or
(c) conduct capable of causing housing-related nuisance or annoyance to any person.

The 2014 Act requires the person to have engaged in conduct that has caused, or is likely to cause, harassment, alarm or distress to *any person* regardless of where they live. Answer D is therefore incorrect.

A court may only grant an injunction against a person aged 10 or over (s. 1(1)); therefore answers B and C are incorrect.

General Police Duties, paras 3.7.3, 3.7.3.2

Answer 7.4

Answer **D** — Part 1 of the Anti-social Behaviour, Crime and Policing Act 2014 creates the power for a civil court to grant injunctions if it is satisfied, on the balance of probabilities, that the respondent has engaged or threatened to engage in anti-social behaviour and it is just and convenient to grant the injunction for the purpose of preventing the respondent from engaging in anti-social behaviour.

The court may attach conditions to the injunction (such as attending a drug re-habilitation programme) and specify the person (an individual or an organisation) who is responsible for supervising compliance.

There is no minimum or maximum term for the injunction for adults, so the court may decide that the injunction should be for a specified period or an indefinite period (however, in the case of injunctions against under-18s, the maximum term is 12 months).

Answers A, B and C are therefore incorrect.

General Police Duties, para. 3.7.3.4

Answer 7.5

Answer **D** — An application for a civil injunction for dealing with anti-social behaviour must be made to a youth court where the respondent is under 18 years of age or to the High Court or County Court in any other case (s. 1(8)(a) and (b)). Such an application can only be made by the police, the local authority and other specified bodies (s. 5(1)).

A youth court may give permission for an application for an injunction against a person aged 18 or over to be made to the youth court if an application to the youth court has been made, or is to be made, for an injunction against a person aged under 18, and the youth court thinks that it would be in the interests of justice for the applications to be heard together (s. 18(2)).

General Police Duties, para. 3.7.3

Answer 7.6

Answer **C** — The Sentencing Code (Sentencing Act 2020, s. 330) states:

> In this Code 'criminal behaviour order' means an order which, for the purpose of preventing an offender from engaging in behaviour that is likely to cause harassment, alarm or distress to any person—
> (a) prohibits the offender from doing anything described in the order;
> (b) requires the offender to do anything described in the order.

The Crown Court, the magistrates' court and the youth court are able to make a criminal behaviour order (CBO) for the most serious and persistent offenders where they have been convicted of an offence (s. 331(1)).

The court cannot make a CBO of its own motion but only on the application of the prosecution (s. 331(1)(b)) which makes the correct answer C.

General Police Duties, para. 3.7.4.1

Answer 7.7

Answer **B** — The Sentencing Code (Sentencing Act 2020, s. 330) states:

> In this Code 'criminal behaviour order' means an order which, for the purpose of preventing an offender from engaging in behaviour that is likely to cause harassment, alarm or distress to any person—
> (a) prohibits the offender from doing anything described in the order;
> (b) requires the offender to do anything described in the order.

The order can include prohibitions and/or positive requirements that assist in preventing the offender from engaging in behaviour that could cause harassment, alarm or distress in the future (s. 333).

Whether they be prohibitions or requirements, the terms of the order must be 'reasonable, proportionate, realistic, practical, clear and enforceable' (*R v Bones* [2005] EWCA Crim 2395).

Before the court can impose a requirement, the person (whether an individual or an organisation) responsible for monitoring the offender's compliance with the requirement needs to be identified.

The order takes effect on the day it is made (s. 334(1)), and the period of the order must be set out in the order itself (s. 334(3)). For a person under 18 years of age, the order must be for not less than one year and for no more than three years (s. 334(4)). Therefore, answer B is correct.

General Police Duties, para. 3.7.4.3

Answer 7.8

Answer **D** — Part 3 of the Anti-social Behaviour, Crime and Policing Act 2014 provides a dispersal power that enables officers (constables in uniform and PCSOs) to direct a person who has committed, *or is likely to commit*, anti-social behaviour to leave a specified area and not return for a specified period of up to 48 hours (making answer C incorrect).

The dispersal power can only be used where an officer of at least the rank of inspector has authorised its use in a specified locality (s. 34(1)) and the inspector reasonably believes that the exercise of the dispersal powers may be required in order to remove or reduce the likelihood of the anti-social behaviour occurring. There is no requirement to consult with the local authority or publicise the dispersal notice in advance; the notice under the 2014 Act may be used spontaneously, provided the appropriate authorisation is given in writing.

There is no requirement for at least two people to be present before the power may be used to disperse people. A direction may be given to 'a person' to leave the area and not return.

Answers A and B are therefore incorrect.

General Police Duties, para. 3.7.5

Answer 7.9

Answer **A** — Part 3 of the Anti-social Behaviour, Crime and Policing Act 2014 contains a dispersal power that enables officers (constables in uniform and PCSOs) to direct a person who has committed, or is likely to commit, anti-social behaviour to leave a specified area and not return for a specified period of up to 48 hours.

The dispersal power can only be used where an officer of at least the rank of inspector has authorised its use in a specified locality (s. 34(1)) and the inspector reasonably believes that the exercise of the dispersal powers may be required in order to remove or reduce the likelihood of the anti-social behaviour occurring.

The officer must specify the area from which the person is excluded, and may specify when and by which route they must leave the area (s. 35(5)(b) and (c)). Where the officer believes that an individual is under the age of 16, an officer can remove that individual to a place where he/she lives or to a place of safety (s. 35(7)). There is no requirement to have warned an individual before utilising the power to take them home and, since this power only applies to those under the age of 16, answers C and D are incorrect.

No time restrictions apply under the 2014 Act, so answer B is incorrect.

General Police Duties, para. 3.7.5.2

Answer 7.10

Answer **D** — Part 4 of the Anti-social, Crime and Policing Act 2014 deals with Community Protection Notices (CPNs). The notice is intended to deal with unreasonable, ongoing problems or nuisances which negatively affect the community's quality of life by targeting those responsible (s. 43(1)). The notice imposes on an individual or a body a requirement to stop doing specified things, a requirement to do specified things or a requirement to take reasonable steps to achieve specified results (s. 43(3)). The only requirements that may be imposed are ones that are reasonable to impose in order (a) to prevent the detrimental effect referred to in s. 43(1) from continuing or recurring or (b) to reduce that detrimental effect or (c) to reduce the risk of its continuance or recurrence (s. 43(4)).

In many areas, councils already take the lead in dealing with these kinds of issues and they are able to issue the notice. However, the power to issue a notice is also available to the police and PCSOs, if designated by the chief constable (s. 53(5)). Answers A and B are incorrect.

There is no requirement for an officer of the rank of inspector to authorise notices under this section; therefore, answer C is incorrect.

General Police Duties, paras 3.7.6, 3.7.6.1

Answer 7.11

Answer **B** — When a closure notice is issued, the police or local authority must apply to the magistrates' court for a closure order (s. 80(1)). The magistrates' court must hear the application for the closure order within 48 hours of the closure notice being issued (excluding Christmas Day) unless the closure notice has been cancelled by a cancellation notice (s. 80(3)).

Answers A, C and D are therefore incorrect.

General Police Duties, para. 3.7.7.1

Answer 7.12

Answer **A** — Answer B is incorrect as the dispersal power can be authorised by an officer of the rank of inspector or above (s. 34(1)). Answer D is incorrect as the authorisation can only be given where the police officer of or above the rank of inspector reasonably believes that, in respect of any locality within their police area, the exercise of the dispersal powers in Part 3 of the Act may be required in order to remove or reduce the likelihood of the anti-social behaviour occurring. For instance, the inspector may have intelligence to indicate that there is likely to be anti-social behaviour on a particular housing estate during the weekend and authorise the use of the dispersal for 48 hours—this is a power to prevent as well as deal with ongoing antisocial behaviour. Answer C is incorrect as Part 3 of the Anti-social Behaviour, Crime and Policing Act 2014 provides a dispersal power that enables officers (constables in uniform and police community support officers (PCSOs)) to direct a person who has committed, or is likely to commit, anti-social behaviour to leave a specified area and not return for a specified period of up to 48 hours—so it is not limited to those who have actually carried out anti-social behaviour.

General Police Duties, paras 3.7.5, 3.7.5.1

Answer 7.13

Answer **D** — An officer would be able to require an individual to hand over items causing, or likely to cause, anti-social behaviour—for instance, alcohol or a can of spray paint (s. 37), meaning that answers A and C are incorrect. Answer B is incorrect as the officer does not have power under this provision to retain any seized item indefinitely. The officer must give the person information in writing about how and when they can recover the item, which must not be returned before the exclusion period is over (in the circumstances of the question, that exclusion period is 24 hours), meaning that answer D is correct.

General Police Duties, para. 3.7.5.2

Answer 7.14

Answer **B** — Parenting orders are defined by s. 8 of the Crime and Disorder Act 1998:

(4) A parenting order is an order which requires the parent—
    (a) to comply, for a period not exceeding twelve months, with such requirements as are specified in the order, and
    (b) subject to subsection (5) below, to attend, for a concurrent period not exceeding three months and not more than once in any week, such counselling or guidance sessions as may be specified in directions given by the responsible officer …

As can be seen, the period is three months; answers A, C and D are therefore incorrect.

General Police Duties, para. 3.7.8.1

Answer 7.15

Answer **B** — A parenting order may be made against:

- one or both biological parents (this could include an order against a father who may not be married to the mother);
- a person who is a guardian.

Therefore, answer C is incorrect.

A guardian is defined as any person who, *in the opinion of the court*, has for the time being the care of a child or young person (Children and Young Persons Act 1933, s. 107(1)), as it is the court that will decide who is *in fact* a 'guardian'; therefore, answers A and D are incorrect.

General Police Duties, para. 3.7.8.1

Answer 7.16

Answer **B** — The maximum permitted period is 12 months (answers A, C and D are incorrect).

General Police Duties, para. 3.7.9

Answer 7.17

Answer **B** — The Sentencing Code (Sentencing Act 2020, s. 376) provides for the binding over of a parent or guardian and states:

(1) This section applies where—
    (a) a person aged under 18 is convicted of an offence, and
    (b) a court is sentencing the offender for the offence.

(2) The court has the following powers—
    (a) the court may, with the consent of the offender's parent or guardian, order the parent or guardian to enter into a recognizance to take proper care of the offender and exercise proper control over the offender, and
    (b) if—
        (i)   the parent or guardian refuses consent, and
        (ii) the court considers the refusal unreasonable,
    the court may order the parent or guardian to pay a fine not exceeding £1,000.
(3) For the purposes of this section—
    (a) taking 'care' of a person includes giving the person protection and guidance, and
    (b) 'control' includes discipline.
(4) If the offender is aged under 16 when sentenced, the court must—
    (a) exercise its powers under subsection (2), if satisfied, having regard to the circumstances of the case, that doing so would be desirable in the interests of preventing the offender from committing further offences, or
    (b) state in open court that it is not so satisfied, and why not.

As MOORE is 17, these powers still apply; answer D is therefore incorrect. If MOORE were under 16 the court must exercise those powers but between 16 and 18 they are not mandated; answers A and C are therefore incorrect.

General Police Duties, para. 3.7.8.2

Answer 7.18

Answer **D** — The recognizance can be imposed on the parent or guardian for up to three years or until the offender is aged 18, whichever is the shorter (s. 376(7) of the Sentencing Code (Sentencing Act 2020)); answers A, B and C are therefore incorrect.

General Police Duties, para. 3.7.8.2

Answer 7.19

Answer **B** — The Education Act 1996 provides that penalty notices can be issued to parents or guardians who fail to ensure the regular attendance of their child of compulsory school age (5–16) who is registered at a State school, or fail to ensure that their excluded child is not found in a public place during school hours without a justifiable reason; answers A, C and D are therefore incorrect.

General Police Duties, para. 3.7.10

Answer 7.20

Answer **B** — A local authority is under an obligation by s. 16 of the Crime and Disorder Act 1998 to designate premises in a police area ('designated premises') as premises to which children and young persons of compulsory school age may be removed under this section, and they must notify the chief officer of police for that area of the designation. When an order to remove truants has been issued, if a constable has reasonable *cause to believe* that a child or young person found by him/her in a public place in a specified area during a specified period:

- is of compulsory school age; *and*
- is absent from a school without lawful authority;

the constable may remove the child or young person to designated premises, or to the school from which he/she is absent. The state of mind of the officer is all-important here and as Constable McGIVERN only 'suspects', the power is unavailable (correct answer B).

General Police Duties, para. 3.7.10

8 Processions and Assemblies

QUESTIONS

Question 8.1

A public assembly was taking place in a main thoroughfare in a city centre to demonstrate against student fees. The chief constable of the force had placed conditions in advance as to the location and the number of people who should be present. On the day of the event, road closures were in place and the demonstration went on for ten hours. The length of the assembly was not included in the original conditions and, although the demonstration was peaceful, the police had genuine concerns over the disproportionate disruption being caused to traffic and pedestrians. As a result, the chief constable issued a further notice authorising the demonstration to be terminated.

Were the chief constable's actions lawful in these circumstances?

A Yes, provided the chief constable was present at the assembly.
B Yes, regardless of whether the chief constable was present at the assembly.
C No, there were no conditions set as to the length of the demonstration in the original notice and the police should have allowed it to continue.
D No, there was no evidence that it was necessary to terminate the demonstration to prevent disorder, damage or intimidation.

Question 8.2

Constable JEFFERS is on uniform patrol and has been deployed to deal with a trespassory assembly, in respect of which an order under s. 14A of the Public Order Act 1986 has been obtained prohibiting it taking place. The officer is four-and-a-half miles from the historical monument where the assembly was due to take place, and is carrying out powers granted by s. 14C of the 1986 Act, preventing access to the site. Using s. 14C of the Act, the officer has stopped a vehicle, and has directed the occupants not to proceed in the direction of the assembly.

Are the officer's actions lawful?

A Yes, as the officer was in uniform the actions are lawful.

B Yes, the actions are lawful; it is immaterial that the officer was in uniform.

C No, the officer is outside the radius set by the Act at four miles.

D No, the officer has no power to stop vehicles under this section.

Question 8.3

A group of people have organised a procession demonstrating against pay cuts and working conditions at their workplace. Several people are involved in the organisation of different parts of the procession. One person organises the route and the time, another is organising people to be there, another is organising refreshments and another is organising marshals. On the day of the march, to avoid the police, the march takes place two hours prior to the notification originally given to the police.

In these circumstances, who has committed an offence contrary to s. 11(7) of the Public Order Act 1986?

A Only the person who organised the change of the time of the march.

B Only the person who originally organised the march and the person who organised the change of the time of the march.

C Only the person who gave the original notification to the police.

D Each of the persons taking any organisational part in the march would commit this offence.

Question 8.4

Section 12 of the Public Order Act 1986 allows for conditions to be imposed on public processions. THOMAS intends to hold a public procession in four weeks' time and the police are considering applying conditions.

How should these conditions be set?

A In advance of the day of the procession, by the chief constable and in writing.

B On the day of the procession, by the senior officer present and orally.

C On the day of the procession, by the senior officer present and in writing.

D On the day of the procession, by the chief officer of the police and orally.

Question 8.5

MARTIN has organised a peaceful march through a town centre to protest against public sector cutbacks. The march has been authorised by the chief officer of police for the area and the route has been agreed. The protesters are now gathered at the starting point. However, an hour ago, the senior police officer at the scene, Inspector CARROLL, received intelligence about a group of separate individuals planning to intercept the march with the intention of causing serious disorder. Inspector CARROLL is meeting with MARTIN to discuss rerouting the march to avoid a disturbance. MARTIN is against this, believing it will dilute the impact of the protest.

Which of the comments below is correct in relation to Inspector CARROLL's power to impose further conditions at this stage (such as rerouting the march) to prevent serious disorder?

A Inspector CARROLL cannot change the conditions of the procession because the procession has not commenced (the power to impose conditions rests with the chief officer of police for the area).

B As the senior officer at the scene, Inspector CARROLL may impose conditions in these circumstances.

C Inspector CARROLL must call a superintendent to the scene, who may impose conditions in these circumstances.

D As there is no intelligence to suggest MARTIN's group intends anything other than a peaceful march, Inspector CARROLL cannot impose further conditions.

Question 8.6

Constable MEREDITH has been called to a public meeting which is being held in relation to the building of a new trunk road. A person attending the meeting has been acting in a disorderly manner with the purpose of preventing the meeting taking place.

What action can the officer take under s. 1 of the Public Meeting Act 1908 (trying to break up a public meeting)?

A Require the person's name and address and report that person for summons.

B Require the person to leave.

C Require the person to leave if requested to do so by the chair of the meeting.

D Require the person's name and address if requested by the chair of the meeting.

Question 8.7

Sergeant FOULKES attended an appointment with the chair of the local town council. A public meeting is due to be held to discuss an application to build a new housing estate on a greenfield site on the outskirts of the town. The chair had heard that a number of people were going to attend to protest against the application and wanted to discuss the support the council could expect from the police during the meeting if the people attending became disorderly.

An offence may be committed under s. 1(1) of the Public Meeting Act 1908 if a person is disorderly at such a meeting. What powers would Sergeant FOULKES have to deal with such an offence at the meeting?

A Sergeant FOULKES may use the statutory power provided by the Act to arrest any person reasonably suspected of committing this offence.

B Sergeant FOULKES may, if requested by the chair, remove any person reasonably suspected of committing this offence.

C Sergeant FOULKES may, if requested by the chair, require any person reasonably suspected of committing this offence to declare his/her name and address.

D Sergeant FOULKES must, if requested by the chair, remove any person reasonably suspected of committing this offence.

ANSWERS

Answer 8.1

Answer **A** — Under s. 14(1) of the Public Order Act 1986, if the senior police officer, having regard to the time or place at which and the circumstances in which any public assembly is being held or is intended to be held, reasonably believes that:

- (a) it may result in serious public disorder, serious damage to property or serious disruption to the life of the community, or
  - (aa) in the case of an assembly in England and Wales, the noise generated by persons taking part in the assembly may result in serious disruption to the activities of an organisation which are carried on in the vicinity of the assembly,
  - (ab) in the case of an assembly in England and Wales—
    - (i) the noise generated by persons taking part in the assembly may have a relevant impact on persons in the vicinity of the assembly, and
    - (ii) that impact may be significant, or
- (b) the purpose of the persons organising it is the intimidation of others with a view to compelling them not to do an act they have a right to do, or to do an act they have a right not to do,
  - ((1A) The senior police officer may give directions imposing on the persons organising or taking part in the assembly—
    - (a) in the case of an assembly in England and Wales, such conditions as appear to the officer necessary to prevent the disorder, damage, disruption, impact or intimidation mentioned in subsection (1);
    - (b) in the case of an assembly in Scotland, such conditions as to the place at which the assembly may be (or continue to be) held, its maximum duration, or the maximum number of persons who may constitute it, as appear to the officer necessary to prevent the disorder, damage, disruption or intimidation mentioned in subsection (1)(a) or (b).
  - (1A) The senior police officer may give directions imposing on the persons organising or taking part in the assembly—
    - (a) in the case of an assembly in England and Wales, such conditions as appear to the officer necessary to prevent the disorder, damage, disruption, impact or intimidation mentioned in subsection (1);
    - (b) in the case of an assembly in Scotland, such conditions as to the place at which the assembly may be (or continue to be) held, its maximum duration, or the maximum number of persons who may constitute it, as appear to the officer necessary to prevent the disorder, damage, disruption or intimidation mentioned in subsection (1)(a) or (b).

Section 14(1) allows for the police to react to the prevailing circumstances during the assembly; therefore, even though no conditions were set in advance as to the length of the demonstration, provided it appeared necessary to prevent disorder, damage, disruption or intimidation, it was lawful to impose further conditions while the demonstration was being held. Answer C is therefore incorrect.

A direction under s. 14(1) was lawful where a senior police officer imposed a condition that a Climate Camp protest against the G20 Summit in London must stop. The demonstration had lasted the best part of 12 hours and the court held that this was quite long enough for the protesters to take advantage of their human rights under Art. 10 (Freedom of Expression) and Art. 11 (Freedom of Assembly and Association) and those wishing to remain were intent on continuing to block the highway, the main thoroughfare into and out of the City. There was no justification to prolong the demonstration and its continuation would cause serious disturbances and disruption to traffic and pedestrians wishing to use the highway. The police had a duty to clear the highway and that could not be done without removing the protesters by force if necessary (*R (On the Application of Moos)* v *Commissioner of Police of the Metropolis* [2011] EWHC 957 (Admin)). Serious disruption is included in this section and answer D is incorrect.

Finally, under s. 14(2), 'the senior police officer' means:

(a) in relation to an assembly being held, the most senior in rank of the police officers present at the scene, and
(b) in relation to an assembly intended to be held, the chief officer of police.

This means that in advance of the assembly, the chief constable was the appropriate officer to impose conditions; however, once it had commenced, any further conditions must be imposed by the senior police officer present at the scene (*R* v *Lucas* (2014) 17 April (not reported)), where the notice under s. 14 was signed by a chief officer who was not present at the scene, making it invalid). Answer B is therefore incorrect.

General Police Duties, para. 3.8.4.4

Answer 8.2

Answer **D** — Under s. 14A of the Public Order Act 1986, the chief officer of police has the power, if he/she reasonably believes that it is intended to hold a trespassory assembly which may result in serious disruption to the life of the community or significant damage to land or a building or monument which is of historical, archaeological or scientific importance, to apply to the district council for an order prohibiting for a specified period the holding of all trespassory assemblies in the district or part of it. The order must not last for more than four days and must not apply to an area greater than that represented by a circle of a five-mile radius from a specified centre, and therefore answer C is incorrect. A constable, who must be in uniform, has power to stop someone he/she reasonably believes to be on his/her way to an assembly prohibited by an order under s. 14A and to direct him/her not to proceed in the direction of the assembly, and therefore answer B is incorrect. This power, however, does not apply to vehicles and is restricted to 'stop that person', and answer A is therefore incorrect. Other powers exist to stop the vehicle, however.

General Police Duties, paras 3.8.4.6, 3.8.4.7

Answer 8.3

Answer **D** — The Public Order Act 1986 places certain obligations on the organisers of public processions that are intended:

- to demonstrate support for, or opposition to, the views or actions of any person or body;
- to publicise a cause or campaign; or
- to mark or commemorate an event.

If a public procession is to be held for any of these purposes, the organisers must give written notice—by delivering it to a police station in the relevant police area—unless it is not reasonably practicable to do so (s. 11(1) and (4)). Under s. 11(3), the notice must specify:

- the date and time of the proposed procession;
- the proposed route; and
- the name and address of the person(s) proposing to organise it.

If such a procession is held without compliance with these requirements, or if a procession takes place on a different date, time or route, each of the people organising it commits a summary offence (s. 11(7)); as answers A, B and C limit persons by use of the term 'only', they are all incorrect.

General Police Duties, para. 3.8.4.1

Answer 8.4

Answer **A** — There are two occasions when conditions can be imposed on a procession—in advance or during the procession—and there are differences between them. Where advance notice is given, as in this case, the senior officer designated to carry out the power is the chief officer of police and answers B and C are therefore incorrect. If the conditions are set in advance (as with the case in the question), they must be in writing and therefore answer D is incorrect. If the procession had begun, the power falls to the senior officer present, who may make the order orally. However, clearly formal, written notice would probably stave off future litigation.

General Police Duties, para. 3.8.4.2

Answer 8.5

Answer **B** — Under s. 12(1) of the Public Order Act 1986, if the senior police officer, having regard to the time or place at which and the circumstances in which any public procession is being held or is intended to be held and to its route or proposed route, reasonably believes that:

(a) it may result in serious public disorder, serious damage to property or disruption to the life of the community, or

  (aa) In the case of a procession in England and Wales, the noise generated by persons taking part in the procession may result in serious disruption to the activities of an organisation which are carried on in the vicinity of the procession,

  (ab) in the case of a procession in England and Wales—

    (i) the noise generated by persons taking part in the procession may have a relevant impact on persons in the vicinity of the procession, and

    (ii) that impact may be significant, or

(b) the purpose of the persons organising it is the intimidation of others with a view to compelling them not to do an act they have a right to do, or to do an act they have a right not to do,

he may give directions imposing on the persons organising or taking part in the procession such conditions as appear to him necessary to prevent such disorder, damage, disruption or intimidation, including conditions as to the route of the procession or prohibiting it from entering any public place specified in the directions.

Section 12(1)(a) covers situations where any serious disorder is anticipated, regardless of whether it is thought the source will be the persons attending the march or anyone else. Answer D is therefore incorrect.

Where a procession is being held, or a procession is intended to be held and persons are assembling with a view to taking part in it, the 'senior police officer' is the most senior in rank of the police officers present at the scene (s. 12(2)(a)) and the direction may be given orally. Inspector CARROLL, as the senior police officer at the scene, may impose these conditions and answers A and C are therefore incorrect.

For any other intended procession (i.e. pre-planned) the senior police officer is the chief officer of police (s. 12(2)(b)), whose direction must be given in writing (s. 12(3)).

General Police Duties, para. 3.8.4.2

Answer 8.6

Answer **D** — It is an offence, contrary to s. 1(1) of the Public Meeting Act 1908, for a person at a lawful public meeting to act in a disorderly manner for the purpose of preventing the transaction of the business for which the meeting was called. There is no power given by this Act to require a person to leave, even at the request of the chair, which makes answers B and C incorrect. However, following a request from the chair, the officer can demand the name and address of the person suspected of committing the offence under s. 1(1). A further offence is committed if the person fails to comply with this demand contrary to s. 1(3) of the 1908 Act. Note that it is only at the request of the chair that the person's name and address can be demanded; answer A is therefore incorrect.

General Police Duties, para. 3.8.5

Answer 8.7

Answer **C** — Section 1 of the Public Meeting Act 1908 states:

(1) Any person who at a lawful public meeting acts in a disorderly manner for the purpose of preventing the transaction of the business for which the meeting was called together shall be guilty of an offence.
(2) Any person who incites others to commit an offence under this section shall be guilty of a like offence.

If a constable reasonably suspects any person of committing this offence, he/she *may*, if requested by the person chairing the meeting, require the offender to *declare his/her name and address immediately*. Failing to comply with such a request or giving false details is a summary offence (s. 1(3)). Answers B and D are incorrect.

There is no statutory power of arrest provided by the 1908 Act; therefore, answer A is incorrect. Of course, if the person fails to give his/her name and address, the arrest may be necessary under s. 24 of the Police and Criminal Evidence Act 1984.

General Police Duties, para. 3.8.5

9 | **Public Order Offences**

QUESTIONS

Question 9.1

DENNIS owns an off-licence and had just closed the premises late at night, locking the door. HUDSON arrived at the premises in a drunken state demanding to be let in to buy a bottle of wine. DENNIS refused to allow HUDSON in and HUDSON began shouting, 'If you don't let me in, I'll smash all these windows.' HUDSON then sat on the wall waiting for DENNIS to open the shop door.

Assuming that an arrest may be necessary in these circumstances, does DENNIS have the power to arrest HUDSON for a breach of the peace, contrary to common law?

A No, the threats were made towards DENNIS's property not DENNIS.

B Yes, provided DENNIS reasonably believed HUDSON would carry out the threat.

C Yes, provided DENNIS reasonably believed HUDSON was capable of carrying out the threat.

D No, only a police officer has the power of arrest to prevent a breach of the peace that has not yet occurred.

Question 9.2

Constable CAREY attended a report of a violent domestic dispute taking place in a home. On arrival, the officer could hear sounds of a disturbance coming from inside the premises (shouting, screaming and glass breaking). The front door was locked and despite Constable CAREY knocking loudly several times, there was no reply.

Considering Constable CAREY's powers of entry, which of the following statements is correct?

A Constable CAREY may enter the premises to prevent a breach of the peace and remain there in order to do so.

B Constable CAREY may enter the premises only if s. 17 of the Police and Criminal Evidence Act 1984 applies; there are no additional powers to enter to prevent a breach of the peace.

C Constable CAREY may enter the premises provided the disturbance affected members of the public outside the property.

D Constable CAREY may enter the premises provided the disturbance could be heard by members of the public outside the property.

Question 9.3

A group of 20 people have been charged with the offence of riot following a serious incident of disorder on a housing estate. The Crown Prosecution Service intends introducing evidence that at least 15 of the defendants were threatening violence towards people from a minority ethnic group, while five defendants actually used violence towards them. Other evidence shows that at least ten other people were gathered near those charged. These people did not take part in the threats or violence but their presence added to the intimidation.

According to s. 1 of the Public Order Act 1986, who can be found guilty of riot in these circumstances?

A Any of the people present who were not victims of the incident.

B Any of the defendants who used or threatened to use unlawful violence.

C The five defendants who actually used unlawful violence.

D None of the people present, as only five defendants actually used violence.

Question 9.4

HOWLEY has been charged, along with a number of other people, with an offence of violent disorder under s. 2 of the Public Order Act 1986. HOWLEY intends to use the defence that he was intoxicated at the time of the incident and that he was not aware of his actions.

What does s. 6 of the Public Order Act 1986 state in relation to how intoxication will, if at all, impact on the charge?

A It cannot be used as a defence in relation to this offence (s. 2 violent disorder) or an offence under s. 1.

B HOWLEY may use this defence if he can show either that his intoxication was not self-induced or that it was caused solely by taking a substance in the course of medical treatment.

C HOWLEY may use this defence but only if he can show that his intoxication was not self-induced.

D HOWLEY may use this defence but only if he can show that his intoxication was caused solely by taking a substance in the course of medical treatment.

Question 9.5

WORTON, CAMERON and MAHROOF appeared in Crown Court for violent disorder, contrary to s. 2 of the Public Order Act 1986, following a large fight outside a pub which was captured on CCTV. After hearing the evidence, the jury acquitted WORTON of the offence.

How, if at all, does the acquittal of WORTON affect the case of violent disorder against CAMERON and MAHROOF?

A Only two people are required to have used or threatened unlawful violence during the incident for this offence to be complete and the acquittal of WORTON has no effect.

B When there are three defendants and one is acquitted of this offence, the other two defendants must also be acquitted.

C The other two defendants may still be convicted of the offence, provided it can be shown that there were three or more people using or threatening unlawful violence during the incident.

D CAMERON and MAHROOF can be convicted but only if it can be shown that they both actually used unlawful violence (as opposed to threatening unlawful violence) during the incident.

Question 9.6

Constable CARLISLE attended a report of a stolen vehicle being driven around a housing estate. On arrival, the officer saw SALTER getting out of the stolen vehicle. Constable CARLISLE arrested SALTER, who began violently to resist arrest. While the officer was waiting for back-up, a crowd of about eight people gathered around and each of them threatened violence towards Constable CARLISLE. Some of the people then started to punch and kick the officer to aid SALTER's escape.

Has an offence of violent disorder, under s. 2 of the Public Order Act 1986, been committed in these circumstances?

A Yes, if it can be shown that the people were present together, using or threatening unlawful violence.

B Yes, but only in respect of the people who were present together, using unlawful violence.

C Yes, if it can be shown that the people were present together, using or threatening unlawful violence simultaneously.

D Yes, if it can be shown that SALTER and the other people were deliberately acting together to use or threaten unlawful violence.

Question 9.7

WEBB and CAHILL were in dispute about a boundary between their gardens. One day, CAHILL returned from work as WEBB was about to cut down a tree which was in the disputed boundary area. CAHILL, who owned an Alsatian dog that lived in a kennel in the rear garden, saw what was happening and shouted at WEBB, 'Stop that or I'll set the dog on you and it will cause you serious injury.' The dog was still in the kennel and asleep, but WEBB was genuinely in fear that CAHILL would carry out the threat. At the time, WEBB was alone in one enclosed garden and CAHILL was alone in the other. There were no other people present at the scene.

Could CAHILL be guilty of an offence under s. 3 of the Public Order Act 1986 (causing an affray) in these circumstances?

A No, there was no likelihood of another person being present at the scene who would fear for their safety and the offence cannot be committed by the use of words alone.

B Yes, CAHILL threatened WEBB with immediate personal violence.

C No, CAHILL would have to threaten or use personal violence towards WEBB rather than making a verbal threat to set a dog on WEBB.

D Yes, had a person of reasonable firmness been at the scene, they would have feared for their safety.

Question 9.8

SADIQUE is a Ugandan Asian and has bought a product which has failed to work. He returns it to the shop and is dealt with by AKANJI, a shop assistant who is black and Nigerian by birth. Less than happy with the service, SADIQUE calls AKANJI 'an African twat' and 'an African bitch'. AKANJI is very distressed by this and contacts the police.

Has SADIQUE committed an offence contrary to s. 31(1)(b) of the Crime and Disorder Act 1998 (racially aggravated intentional harassment, alarm or distress)?

A No, as 'African' does not describe a racial group.
B No, as SADIQUE is from the same racial group as AKANJI.
C Yes, provided SADIQUE intended to distress AKANJI.
D Yes, there is no need to prove intent, provided distress is caused.

Question 9.9

Constable ROBINSON was on patrol in a shopping centre when she saw INCE walking along, shouting and swearing in a loud voice. There were a number of shoppers in the area and Constable ROBINSON approached INCE and advised him to stop swearing and annoying people. INCE ignored Constable ROBINSON and walked away, continuing to swear loudly at passers-by. Constable ROBINSON decided that it was necessary to issue INCE with a Disorder Penalty Notice for an offence contrary to s. 5 of the Public Order Act 1986.

What would have to be proved in relation to INCE's state of mind for the offence under s. 5 to be made out?
A That he intended his behaviour to be threatening or abusive or was aware that it was.
B Only that he actually intended his behaviour to be threatening or abusive.
C Only that he was aware that his behaviour was threatening or abusive.
D That he ought to have been aware that his behaviour was threatening or abusive.

Question 9.10

GROSS is walking his dog in a park and allows the dog to foul near some swings where a group of children are playing and being supervised by McGUINNESS and several other adults who are all sitting on bikes. McGUINNESS is disgusted by the behaviour of GROSS allowing his dog to foul so close to where children are playing and tells him how he feels. GROSS reacts by telling McGUINNESS to 'Mind your own fuckin' business or I'll kick your head in!' McGUINNESS tells GROSS to watch his language in front of the children to which GROSS responds, 'I'll set my dog on you, if you don't fuck off!' At this point, he pulls on the lead of his dog dragging it towards McGUINNESS and causing the dog to bark loudly at McGUINNESS. Several of the children start to cry and this action causes McGUINNESS and the other adults to fear for their personal safety. GROSS walks up to McGUINNESS and looks at the bike McGUINNESS is sitting on and kicks it, damaging the front wheel of the bike in the process. GROSS is thoroughly aware that his conduct from the outset is violent.

At what point, if at all, does GROSS first commit the offence of affray (contrary to s. 3 of the Public Order Act 1986)?

A When he tells McGUINNESS to 'Mind your own fuckin' business or I'll kick your head in!'

B When he says, 'I'll set my dog on you, if you don't fuck off!' and pulls the dog towards McGUINNESS.

C When he kicks the wheel of McGUINNESS's bike damaging the front wheel.

D The offence of affray has not been committed in these circumstances.

Question 9.11

In excess of 100 shoppers are waiting outside the front doors of an electrical store to get a bargain in a 'Black Friday' sale. PARKER and TURNER are right at the front of the queue as they had camped outside the shop overnight. As it gets closer to the store opening (at 9 am), the crowd become agitated after some pushing and shoving led to queue-jumping. At 8.50 am, several dozen people start chanting 'Let us in or we'll kick the door in!' At 8.55 am, PARKER starts violently kicking the front door of the shop shouting, 'Let us in, you fuckin' twats!' Moments later, TURNER joins in by violently kicking the glass in the door of the shop shouting, 'We've been here all night so open up or I'll kick the fuckin' door off the hinges!' The manager of the store becomes concerned about the situation and, fearing for the safety of the customers, his staff and himself, he opens the shop doors letting the customers rush inside.

When, if at all, is the offence of riot (contrary to s. 1 of the Public Order Act 1986) committed?

A The offence is first committed when several dozen people start chanting 'Let us in or we'll kick the door in!'

B The offence is first committed when PARKER starts violently kicking the door frame of the shop shouting 'Let us in, you fuckin' twats!'

C The offence is first committed when TURNER starts violently kicking the glass in the door shouting, 'We've been here all night so open up or I'll kick the fuckin' door off the hinges!'

D The offence of riot has not been committed in these circumstances.

ANSWERS

Answer 9.1

Answer **B** — A breach of the peace was defined specifically in *R v Howell* [1982] QB 416. A breach of the peace generally occurs when an act is done, or threatened to be done:

• which harms a person or, in his/her presence, his/her property; or
• which is likely to cause such harm; or
• which puts someone in fear of such harm.

Since DENNIS was in fear that harm would be done to the shop, answer A is incorrect. A constable or any other person may arrest without warrant any person:

• who is committing a breach of the peace;
• whom he/she reasonably believes will commit a breach of the peace in the immediate future; or
• who has committed a breach of the peace, where it is reasonably believed that a recurrence of the breach of the peace is threatened.

The power of arrest is given to a constable or any other person (answer D is therefore incorrect). There is no requirement for the person to reasonably believe that the other person is capable of carrying out the threat, merely that the threat may be carried out. Answer C is incorrect.

General Police Duties, paras 3.9.2, 3.9.2.4

Answer 9.2

Answer **A** — A breach of the peace may take place on private premises as well as in public places (*R v Chief Constable of Devon and Cornwall, ex parte Central Electricity Generating Board* [1982] QB 458) and the police are entitled to enter premises to prevent a breach of the peace and to remain there in order to do so (*Thomas v Sawkins* [1935] 2 KB 249). This power is not affected by the general powers of entry provided by s. 17 of the Police and Criminal Evidence Act 1984—it is an additional power and answer B is incorrect.

Although the courts have declared that the presence of a member (or members) of the public is a highly relevant factor when dealing with a breach of the peace (*McConnell v Chief Constable of Greater Manchester Police* [1990] 1 WLR 364), it has also been held that if a breach of the peace takes place on private property, there is no requirement to show that the resulting disturbance affected members of the public outside that property (*McQuade* v *Chief Constable of Humberside Police* [2001] EWCA Civ 1330). Answers C and D are therefore incorrect.

General Police Duties, para. 3.9.2.1

Answer 9.3

Answer **C** — Under s. 1(1) of the Public Order Act 1986:

> Where 12 or more persons who are present together use or threaten unlawful violence for a common purpose and the conduct of them (taken together) is such as would cause a person of reasonable firmness present at the scene to fear for his personal safety, each of the persons using unlawful violence for the common purpose is guilty of riot.

The offence of riot may be made out in these circumstances against the five defendants who actually used violence (answer D is therefore incorrect). However, only those defendants who actually used violence will be guilty, and therefore answers A and B are incorrect.

General Police Duties, para. 3.9.3

Answer 9.4

Answer **B** — Section 6(5) of the Public Order Act 1986 states:

> For the purposes of this section a person whose awareness is impaired by intoxication shall be taken to be aware of that of which he would be aware if not intoxicated, unless he shows either that his intoxication was not self-induced or that it was caused solely by the taking or administration of a substance in the course of medical treatment.

The defence under s. 6(5) applies to all of the general Public Order Act offences; therefore, answer A is incorrect.

The defence may be raised either when the defendant claims intoxication was not self-induced or that it was caused solely by the taking or administration of a substance in the course of medical treatment. Answers C and D are therefore incorrect.

General Police Duties, para. 3.9.3.2

Answer 9.5

Answer **C** — Section 2(1) of the Public Order Act 1986 states:

> Where 3 or more persons who are present together use or threaten unlawful violence and the conduct of them (taken together) is such as would cause a person of reasonable

firmness present at the scene to fear for his personal safety, each of the persons using or threatening unlawful violence is guilty of violent disorder.

Section 2(1) requires that *three* or more persons were present together who used or threatened unlawful violence, and therefore answer A is incorrect.

In order to convict any defendant of this offence, it must be shown that there were three or more people using or threatening violence. However, where two of the defendants are acquitted, the remaining defendant can still be convicted (*R* v *Mahroof* (1989) 88 Cr App R 317) as long as it can be proved that there *were* three or more people using or threatening violence (perhaps from CCTV evidence of the incident). If it cannot be proved that there were three or more people using or threatening unlawful violence, the court should acquit each defendant (*R* v *McGuigan* [1991] Crim LR 719). Therefore, answer B is incorrect.

For an offence of riot, under s. 1 of the Act, only the persons who actually used violence may be convicted. This is not the case for an offence under s. 2; therefore, answer D is incorrect.

General Police Duties, para. 3.9.4

Answer 9.6

Answer **A** — Under s. 2(1) of the Public Order Act 1986, where three or more persons who are present together use or threaten unlawful violence and the conduct of them (taken together) is such as would cause a person of reasonable firmness present at the scene to fear for their personal safety, each of the persons using or threatening unlawful violence is guilty of violent disorder. Unlike the offence of riot (under s. 1 of the Act), for this offence each of the persons using *or* threatening unlawful violence may be guilty of the offence; therefore, answer B is incorrect.

Under s. 2, there is no requirement to show that the persons using or threatening unlawful violence did so simultaneously (unlike the offence under s. 1), and therefore answer C is incorrect.

The circumstances in this question are similar to the case of *R* v *NW* [2010] EWCA Crim 404. In that case, a person was violently resisting arrest by a police officer, during which time a crowd gathered and various members of the crowd used or threatened violence. The Court of Appeal held that for the purposes of this section it was not necessary for a person to deliberately act in combination with at least two other people present at the scene, but that it is sufficient that at least three people be present, each separately using or threatening unlawful violence. Answer D is therefore incorrect.

General Police Duties, para. 3.9.4

Answer 9.7

Answer **A** — Under s. 3(1) of the Public Order Act 1986, a person is guilty of affray if he/she uses or threatens unlawful violence towards another and his/her conduct is such as would cause a person of reasonable firmness present at the scene to fear for his/her personal safety.

However, in order to prove this offence, the threat cannot be made by words alone (s. 3(3)). CAHILL has not committed an act of violence towards WEBB (either personally or with the dog) in these circumstances as the behaviour merely amounted to a verbal threat. Answer B is therefore incorrect.

The 'action' by the defendant may consist of utilising something else such as a dog to threaten the violence (*R v Dixon* [1993] Crim LR 579). Answer C is therefore incorrect.

Finally, for this offence to be complete, the House of Lords has held that in order to prove the offence of affray, the threat of unlawful violence has to be towards a person (or persons) present at the scene (*I v DPP* [2001] UKHL 10). This means that there does have to be *someone* other than the defendant at the scene.

Once this element has been proved, it will be necessary to prove the second element; namely, whether the defendant's conduct would have caused a hypothetical person present at the scene to fear for his/her personal safety (*R v Sanchez* (1996) 160 JP 321 and *R v Carey* [2006] EWCA Crim 17).

However, where the likelihood of a hypothetical person of reasonable firmness being present was low, this element of the offence was not satisfied. In *R (On the Application of Leeson) v DPP* [2010] EWHC 994 (Admin), a woman had issued a drunken threat to kill her long-term partner whilst holding a knife, in a bathroom, in an otherwise unoccupied house. In these circumstances, the court held that there was no possibility of a hypothetical bystander fearing for their safety.

The most recent case (*Leeson* noted previously) places a different perspective on the 'hypothetical' third person, and in the example given in this question, the two parties were in separate enclosed gardens, with very little likelihood of another person being affected by the behaviour (as opposed to a situation in a pub, for example, where several people could be injured). This makes answer A correct, and answer D incorrect.

General Police Duties, para. 3.9.5

Answer 9.8

Answer **C** — This question loosely follows the circumstances of *R v White (Anthony Delroy)* [2001] 1 WLR 1352, where the Court of Appeal upheld White's conviction for this offence. The court held that the words used are to be construed as they are generally used in England and Wales; and on that basis the word 'African' described a racial group defined by reference to race, and therefore answer A is incorrect. This offence can be committed towards people from the same racial group as the accused, and answer B is therefore incorrect. This is a crime of 'specific intent' and as such does require the intent to be proven, and therefore answer D is incorrect.

General Police Duties, paras 3.9.6, 3.9.7

Answer 9.9

Answer **A** — Section 6 of the Public Order Act 1986 states that a person is guilty of an offence under s. 5 only if:

> he intends his words or behaviour, or the writing, sign or other visible representation, to be threatening or abusive, or is aware that it may be threatening or abusive, or (as the case may be) he intends his behaviour to be or is aware that it may be disorderly.

This is not an offence which relies only on the intent of the person exhibiting the behaviour; it can also be committed if a person is simply aware that his/her behaviour is threatening or abusive. Answer B is therefore incorrect. This is also a case of either/or: INCE would either have to intend his behaviour to be threatening or abusive, or he would have to be aware that it was; therefore, answer C is incorrect.

The fact that a person ought to have known that his/her behaviour was threatening or abusive is immaterial, making answer D incorrect.

General Police Duties, para. 3.9.8

Answer 9.10

Answer **B** — Section 3 of the Public Order Act 1986 states:

> (1) A person is guilty of affray if he uses or threatens unlawful violence towards another and his conduct is such as would cause a person of reasonable firmness present at the scene to fear for his personal safety.

A threat cannot be made by the use of words alone (s. 3(3)) which means that answer A is incorrect. There must be some action by the defendant—even if that 'action' consists of utilising something else such as a dog to threaten the violence (*R* v *Dixon* [1993] Crim LR 579). So, in using the dog, the offence of affray has been committed, meaning that answer D is incorrect. 'Violence' does not include violence towards property so the offence would not be committed by the actions of GROSS at answer C.

General Police Duties, para. 3.9.5

Answer 9.11

Answer **B** — Section 1(1) of the Public Order Act 1986 states that where 12 or more persons who are present together use or threaten unlawful violence for a common purpose and the conduct of them (taken together) is such as would cause a person of reasonable firmness present at the scene to fear for his/her personal safety, each of the persons using unlawful violence for the common purpose is guilty of riot. An important point to note is that it is only the persons *using* violence who can be guilty of the offence of riot. 'Violence' is defined under s. 8 of the Public Order Act 1986 and at s. 8(a) it states that 'violence' will include violent conduct against property as well as violent conduct towards persons (except in the context of affray). So the first few ingredients for a potential riot situation would require 12 or more persons present together (you have that number and more outside the shop) using or threatening violence (the threats by the crowd and also the use of violence on property by PARKER and TURNER) for a common purpose (getting into the shop). However, only those using violence commit the offence and the point at which violence is *first* used is when PARKER violently kicks the door of the shop so the correct answer is B.

General Police Duties, paras 3.9.3 to 3.9.3.1

10 | Sporting Events

QUESTIONS

Question 10.1

The police were working at a designated football match when, at half time, a complaint was received that away fans had been engaged in racialist chanting during the first half. Stewards and the police viewed CCTV and played back images of away supporters shouting, 'You're just a town full of Pakis' at the home fans. They managed to identify the area of the ground where the chanting was coming from and extra stewards and officers were posted to take action if needed.

Considering the offence under s. 3(1) of the Football (Offences) Act 1991 ('racialist' chanting), which of the following statements is correct?

A The prosecution would need to show that the chanting might have been racialist in its nature.

B The prosecution would need to show that the chanting *was* racialist in its nature.

C The prosecution would need to show that the chanting may have been perceived as being racialist in its nature by the people it was directed at.

D The prosecution would need to show that the away fans intended the chanting to be racialist in its nature.

Question 10.2

The police have been looking for JENSEN to serve a notice on him prior to applying for a banning order against him, because of his violent behaviour at Premier League football matches. JENSEN has so far evaded the police; however, officers working at a home tie of a UEFA Champions League match have circulated his photograph. JENSEN is spotted outside the ground at the end of the game by Constable BARNETT and because the next game for the club is in two weeks' time, which is the return leg abroad, the officer is keen to detain JENSEN before he disappears again.

Would Constable BARNETT be entitled to detain JENSEN in these circumstances, using powers under s. 21A(2) of the Football Spectators Act 1989?

A No, there is no power of detention at this time because this is not within the control period.

B Yes, JENSEN could be detained for up to a maximum of six hours while a decision is being made whether to serve a notice on him.

C No, JENSEN has not yet been served with a notice outlining that a banning order is to be applied for.

D Yes, JENSEN could be detained for up to a maximum of ten hours while a decision is being made whether to serve a notice on him.

Question 10.3

HUNTER was driving a public service vehicle containing a number of passengers who support an English Premier League club. HUNTER was driving the supporters home from a match against another Premier League club. The vehicle was stopped on the motorway by the police, who found that many of the passengers were either in possession of alcohol or drunk. HUNTER admitted stopping at a shop, to allow the passengers to buy alcohol, which they brought onto the vehicle.

Who, if anyone, has committed an offence under s. 1 of the Sporting Events (Control of Alcohol etc.) Act 1985?

A No offences were committed under this Act as the supporters were not on their way to a designated sporting event.

B Only HUNTER commits an offence.

C Only HUNTER and anyone who was drunk in the vehicle.

D HUNTER along with anyone who was in possession of alcohol and anyone who was drunk in the vehicle commit an offence.

Question 10.4

GITTENS was involved in an accident while driving to a Premier League football match, which was due to commence in three hours. GITTENS had managed to obtain a distress flare, which was in the car at the time of the accident. Constable MAY attended the scene and, whilst dealing with the accident, saw the flare on the front passenger seat of the car. GITTENS admitted to Constable MAY that he was intending to smuggle it into the ground.

Would Constable MAY be able to deal with GITTENS in relation to the flare under s. 2A of the Sporting Events (Control of Alcohol etc.) Act 1985?

A No, it was outside the period of a designated sporting event.

B Yes, GITTENS was in possession of an article the main purpose of which is the emission of a flare.

C Yes, GITTENS had with him an article the main purpose of which is the emission of a flare.

D No, GITTENS was not at a designated sports ground or trying to enter one.

Question 10.5

WINGROVE supports a football team, which is a member of the English Premier League, that has qualified for the Champions League. WINGROVE has managed to buy 50 tickets for an away game in Germany (classed as a 'designated football match') and has advertised them for sale on a website. WINGROVE intends making a profit by selling the tickets at more than their market value.

Which of the statements below is correct in relation to the ticket touts offence under s. 166 of the Criminal Justice and Public Order Act 1994?

A The offence has not been committed as it does not apply to football matches abroad.

B The offence will only be committed if WINGROVE actually sells a ticket.

C No offence has been committed as the offence only applies to international football matches abroad.

D Provided WINGROVE is not authorised by the organisers of the match, the offence will be committed.

ANSWERS

Answer 10.1

Answer **B** — It is an offence under s. 3(1) of the Football (Offences) Act 1991 to engage or take part in chanting of an indecent or racialist nature at a designated football match.

Section 3(2) goes on to describe the meaning of 'chanting' and 'racialist':

(a) 'chanting' means the repeated uttering of any words or sounds (whether alone or in concert with one or more others); and
(b) 'of a racialist' nature means consisting of or including matter which is threatening, abusive or insulting to a person by reason of his colour, race, nationality (including citizenship) or ethnic or national origins.

The wording of s. 3(2)(b) requires that the chanting *is*, rather than *might be*, threatening, abusive or insulting. Answer A is therefore incorrect.

One way to prove this element of the offence would be the evidence of a person who was threatened, abused or insulted, but this is not expressly required in the Act (and answer C is incorrect). The court is able to make a judgment for itself, for example in *DPP* v *Stoke on Trent Magistrates' Court* [2003] EWHC 1593 (Admin) it was held that shouting 'You're just a town full of Pakis' at supporters from Oldham fell squarely within the definition.

There is no requirement for the prosecution to show that the defendants intended the chanting to be racialist in its nature; they would simply need to demonstrate that it was racialist. Answer D is therefore incorrect.

General Police Duties, para. 3.10.3

Answer 10.2

Answer **A** — The Football Spectators Act 1989, s. 21A states:

(1) This section and section 21B below apply during any control period in relation to a regulated football match outside the United Kingdom or an external tournament if a constable in uniform—
    (a) has reasonable grounds for suspecting that the condition in section 14B(2) above is met in the case of a person present before him, and
    (b) has reasonable grounds to believe that making a banning order in his case would help to prevent violence or disorder at or in connection with any regulated football matches ...

(2) The constable may detain the person in his custody (whether there or elsewhere) until he has decided whether or not to issue a notice under section 21B, and shall give the person his reasons for detaining him in writing.

The condition referred to in s. 21A(1)(a) is that the person has at any time caused or contributed to any violence or disorder in the United Kingdom or elsewhere.

Answer C is incorrect as there is no requirement to serve a notice on a person *before* detaining him/her under s. 21A(2). The actual purpose of the power is to detain a person in order to decide whether or not to serve a notice of a banning order on him/her.

A person may not be detained under subs. (2) for more than four hours (the initial period of detention) or, with the authority of an officer of at least the rank of inspector, six hours (s. 21A(3)). Therefore, the *maximum* period of detention while deciding whether or not to serve the notice is six hours and answer D is incorrect.

Finally, both answers B and D are also incorrect because the power under s. 21A(2) is only applicable during any control period in relation to a regulated football match outside the United Kingdom or an external tournament. 'Control period' means, in relation to a regulated football match outside England and Wales, the period:

• before the day of the match; and
• ending when the match is finished or cancelled.

This means there is no power to detain JENSEN at this time; however, the opportunity to do so will come before the next game for the club, in the five-day period leading up to the second leg.

General Police Duties, para. 3.10.4.4

Answer 10.3

Answer **D** — Section 1 of the Sporting Events (Control of Alcohol etc.) Act 1985 applies to people who are being conveyed in public service vehicles or railway passenger vehicles, which are being used for the principal purpose of carrying passengers to *or from* designated sporting events (s. 1(1)). Answer A is therefore incorrect.

Under s. 1(2), a person who knowingly causes or permits alcohol to be carried on a vehicle to which the section applies is guilty of an offence (which makes HUNTER guilty of the offence). Other offences are committed by any person who has alcohol in his/her possession while on a vehicle to which this section applies (s. 1(3)), or to a person who is drunk on such a vehicle (s. 1(3)), this makes answers B and C incorrect and answer D correct.

General Police Duties, para. 3.10.5.1

Answer 10.4

Answer **D** — Under s. 2A(1) of the Sporting Events (Control of Alcohol etc.) Act 1985, a person is guilty of an offence if he/she has an article or substance to which this section applies in his/her possession:

(a) at any time during the period of a designated sporting event when he is in any area of a designated sports ground from which the event may be directly viewed, or

(b) while entering or trying to enter a designated sports ground at any time during the period of a designated sporting event at the ground.

Articles include distress flares, smoke bombs, fumigators and fireworks.

However, the offence is not committed when the person is on his/her way to the ground (whether it is inside or outside the period of a designated sporting event). Answers A, B and C are therefore incorrect.

Note that the offence can be committed by being in 'possession' of the article, a broader concept than 'having with him'.

General Police Duties, para. 3.10.5.4

Answer 10.5

Answer **D** — It is an offence under s. 166(1) of the Criminal Justice and Public Order Act 1994 for an unauthorised person to sell a ticket for a designated football match, or otherwise to dispose of such a ticket to another person. A person is 'unauthorised' unless he/she is authorised in writing to sell or otherwise dispose of tickets for the match by the organisers of the match (s. 166(2)(a)).

Section 166(2)(aa) outlines the criteria for 'selling' a ticket, which include offering to sell a ticket, exposing a ticket for sale and advertising that a ticket is available for purchase. Answer B is therefore incorrect.

As the game concerned is a 'designated football match', answers A and C are incorrect.

General Police Duties, para. 3.10.6

11 | Domestic Abuse

QUESTIONS

Question 11.1

JENSON and AVERY have recently entered into a romantic relationship. They have a verbal argument over parking and a neighbour calls police. Constable FROUD attends to speak with them. Unknown to JENSON, AVERY has a history of offending against her ex-partners. In relation to a previous partner, a neighbour contacted the police control centre to state that they had seen AVERY hitting her in their garden. When patrols attended, no information was given to police and no prosecution took place. There was also another report from a local hospital which suspected that AVERY was responsible for breaking her ex-partner's ribs. After speaking to both JENSON and AVERY, Constable FROUD viewed police systems and identified these reports along with others. Constable FROUD believes that JENSON should be aware of the previous reports.

Which of the following statements is correct in relation to the Domestic Violence Disclosure Scheme (2016)?

A As Constable FROUD believes a disclosure is necessary to prevent further crime, he may disclose information.

B Constable FROUD may not disclose information, the scheme is only available when a request is made by a member of the public.

C Constable FROUD may disclose information, but this will be after a multi-agency meeting.

D Constable FROUD may not disclose information; the scheme relates to matters which are convicted only.

Question 11.2

DAWSON and BALL have been in an intimate relationship for six months. They attend a family party and DAWSON behaves in a way which BALL's uncle (KIMBER) perceives to be worrying. When BALL goes to the bar to get a drink, another guest approaches her and starts to talk. DAWSON sees this and marches over and insists that BALL goes back to the table. KIMBER is watching this and, when DAWSON leaves the table to get another drink, he speaks to BALL about what happened but BALL dismisses it as protective, loving behaviour. KIMBER is worried and is thinking of going to his local police station for information about DAWSON.

Which of the following statements is correct in relation to the Domestic Violence Disclosure Scheme (2016) 'Right to ask'?

A KIMBER has no 'Right to ask' as he is a third party; requests must only be accepted from partners.
B KIMBER as a third party has a 'Right to ask' but only if BALL consents.
C KIMBER has no 'Right to ask'; requests can be accepted from third parties but there must be a close family link—an uncle is not a close link within legislation.
D KIMBER as a third party has a 'Right to ask' without conditions.

Question 11.3

Chief Inspector GRIGGS has been presented with an application for a Domestic Violence Protection Notice (DVPN) by Constable AIDEN. The circumstances are that the victim, who resides with the suspected perpetrator, is believed to be at risk of future violence from them. Constable AIDEN wishes to approach the local magistrates' court to ask for it to issue a Domestic Violence Protection Order (DVPO). The aim of this is to prohibit any future violence against the victim, who agrees with the decision of Constable AIDEN.

Considering the powers under s. 24 of the Crime and Security Act 2010, which of the following statements is correct?

A Chief Inspector GRIGGS can issue a DVPN, he must then attend in person to a magistrates' court to apply for a DVPO.
B Chief Inspector GRIGGS cannot issue a DVPN as this power is conferred upon an officer of at least the rank of superintendent.
C Chief Inspector GRIGGS can issue a DVPN as the victim consents to it being issued.
D Chief Inspector GRIGGS cannot issue a DVPN as this power is conferred upon an officer of at least the rank of assistant chief constable.

Question 11.4

Constable BAKER is investigating a report of domestic abuse between two persons who are in an intimate personal relationship with each other. AIDEN is aged 17 and

FARTHING is 18 and they both live together in a flat which they jointly lease. Neighbours have reported hearing arguments and the sounds of loud noises and thuds coming from their flat. FARTHING is often heard screaming and pleading, 'Please stop, you're hurting me.' Constable BAKER is considering approaching Superintendent MALIK for a Domestic Violence Protection Notice (DVPN) in relation to AIDEN.

Considering the powers under s. 24 of the Crime and Security Act 2010, which of the following statements is correct?

A A DVPN would not be issued in these circumstances as they can only be issued to persons over the age of 18.

B A DVPN may be issued if Superintendent MALIK has reasonable grounds to suspect that AIDEN has been violent towards FARTHING and the DVPN is necessary to protect against violence or threats of violence.

C A DVPN would not be issued as the relationship does not fall into the statutory definition of domestic abuse as both persons must be over 18.

D A DVPN may be issued, but only if FARTHING consents.

Question 11.5

A Domestic Violence Protection Notice (DVPN) has been issued by Superintendent JONES. Constable PARKER is now applying to the magistrates' court for a Domestic Violence Protection Order (DVPO). At first, the victim consented to Constable PARKER applying for a DVPO but has since reconciled with the perpetrator and wishes for the application to be stopped.

Considering the powers under s. 24 of the Crime and Security Act 2010, which of the following statements is correct?

A Constable PARKER must apply to the magistrates' court for a DVPO within 48 hours of the DVPN being served for it to be heard within seven working days.

B Constable PARKER must apply to the magistrates' court for a DVPO which will hear the application no later than 48 hours after the DVPN was served.

C Constable PARKER must complete a further DVPN for Superintendent JONES to consider as the victim no longer consents.

D Constable PARKER must now withdraw the application as the victim no longer consents.

Question 11.6

DREW and CHAPMAN were in a relationship for 16 years and married for 14 years; the relationship ended abruptly and acrimoniously. During the years that they were married, they jointly purchased a family home and had two children who are aged 12 and 10. Matters are proceeding through the family court in relation to access to the children and to determine the division of assets accrued during the relationship. Currently, child contact is arranged through a third party, BILINGTON, who is the father of DREW. Recently, whilst collecting the children, CHAPMAN has become verbally abusive to BILINGTON in the presence of both children. Not wanting to make matters worse, DREW has not requested any action from the court in relation to this.

Considering the provisions under s. 42 of the Family Law Act 1996, could the court issue a non-molestation order?

A Yes, the court may decide to issue a non-molestation order in relation to the children only.

B No, the court would not issue a non-molestation order as DREW has not made an application.

C Yes, the court may decide to issue a non-molestation order in relation to both the children and BILINGTON.

D No, the purpose of non-molestation orders is to prevent future threats of violence only.

Question 11.7

SMITH and TAYLOR were in a relationship for four years and have recently separated. All matters were agreed in relation to child contact and division of assets. As such, there are no open family proceedings. SMITH has moved into the address of BRYANT which is in the same area as they are friends who met as neighbours. TAYLOR becomes incensed by this, believing them to be in a new relationship. TAYLOR begins to comment whenever BRYANT walks past and has started to prevent the children attending their contact time, telling them that SMITH has ruined everything.

Considering the provisions under s. 42 of the Family Law Act 1996, could the court issue a non-molestation order?

A No, the court will not consider an application as there are no other active family proceedings.

B Yes, the court may issue a non-molestation order in relation to SMITH only, as the former partner.

C No, the court will not consider an application at this time, but one can be made when family proceedings are instigated.

D Yes, the court may issue a non-molestation order in relation to the children, BRYANT and SMITH.

Question 11.8

JEPSEN and MILES met online; they both wanted a non-intimate relationship as nei-ther believed in intimacy with a partner before marriage. Their companionship over three months led to them agreeing to marry. The wedding is planned for 12 months' time, and they remain in a non-intimate relationship, living separately until they are married. MILES initially held the budget for the wedding, giving MILES power over the decisions JEPSON could make regarding the daily finances. MILES provides a weekly allowance, sometimes meaning that JEPSON's rental payments are late. When JEPSON asks to have his wages paid back into his own account, MILES be-comes defensive and accuses JEPSON of not trusting her, threatening to break off the engagement. Not wanting to upset MILES, JEPSON asks his landlord for flexi-bility and does not mention it again.

Considering s. 1 of the Domestic Abuse Act 2021 and the definition of domestic abuse, which of the following statements is correct?

A This behaviour would not fall under the definition of domestic abuse as JEPSON and MILES would not be considered personally connected.
B The behaviour is not abusive as the definition does not include economic abuse.
C The behaviour is abusive under the definition which includes economic abuse, and JEPSON and MILES are considered personally connected.
D The behaviour would not be considered abusive under the definition because JEPSON and MILES do not reside at the same address.

Question 11.9

CARR and RAINE have been in a relationship for six months and have recently moved in together. One evening, CARR has the television remote and wants to watch the early evening news, this is because she is aware of a local interest story where a friend has been interviewed. RAINE has just got home from work and has been looking forward to watching highlights of the previous day's rugby match whilst cooking dinner. They have a verbal disagreement over who will watch their preferred choice. RAINE is holding a large kitchen knife whilst chopping some vegetables and says, 'You're making me so angry, wonder what would happen if I came over and slipped' and he pointed the knife in the direction of CARR. This was intending CARR to think that she may be stabbed. This upsets CARR who puts the television remote down and goes upstairs. RAINE happily changes the channel and watches the rugby highlights.

Considering the definition of domestic abuse under s. 1 of the Domestic Abuse Act 2021, which of the following statements is correct in relation to 'behaviour'?

A To be considered abusive, behaviour must be violent; threatening behaviour is not included within the definition.

B A single incident is not enough to be considered abusive, there must be a course of conduct of two or more occasions.

C A single incident is not enough to be considered abusive, unless the levels of violence result in physical injury.

D To be considered abusive, behaviour can be a single incident and can include threatening behaviour.

Question 11.10

Superintendent CHAPMAN has issued a Domestic Violence Protection Notice (DVPN) which was presented by Constable FORD. Police have information that the victim who resides with the suspected perpetrator is believed to be at risk of future violence from them. Constable FORD is now preparing to attend the local court to ask for it to issue a Domestic Violence Protection Order (DVPO). The aim of this is to prohibit any future violence against the victim, who agrees with the application.

Considering the powers under s. 24 of the Crime and Security Act 2010, which of the following statements is correct?

A Constable FORD must apply to the Crown Court for a DVPO and the court will hear the application within 48 hours.

B The Crown Court may grant a DVPO for a duration of a maximum of 30 days.

C Constable FORD must apply to the local magistrates' court for a DVPO and the court will hear the application within seven working days.

D The magistrates' court may grant a DVPO for a period lasting 14–28 days.

ANSWERS

Answer 11.1

Answer **C** — The Domestic Violence Disclosure Scheme, also known as Clare's Law, gained momentum following the tragic case of Clare Wood, who was murdered by her former partner in 2009. Her partner had three previous convictions under the Protection from Harassment Act 1997. Explanation of the scheme is provided by the Home Office Domestic Violence Disclosure Scheme (DVDS) Guidance (2016). Answer C is correct as disclosures under the scheme are determined by local multi-agency forums consisting of police, probation services, social services and other agencies who decide whether any disclosure is lawful, necessary and proportionate. This therefore makes answer A incorrect as police must work with other agencies.

The DVDS recognises two procedures for disclosing information: 'Right to ask' is triggered by a member of the public applying to the police for a disclosure; 'Right to know' is triggered by the police making a proactive decision to disclose information to protect a potential victim. This means that answer B is incorrect.

Answer D is incorrect as there does not need to be a conviction for a disclosure to take place. The DVDS is focused on disclosure and risk management where person B is identified as having a conviction, caution, reprimand or final warning for violent or abusive offences; and/or information held about B's behaviour which reasonably leads the police and other safeguarding agencies to believe that B poses a risk of harm to A.

General Police Duties, para. 3.11.6

Answer 11.2

Answer **D** — The principal aim of the Domestic Violence Disclosure Scheme (DVDS) is to introduce recognised and consistent procedures, based on this common law power, for the police to consider the disclosure of information in order to protect a member of the public who may be at risk of harm from domestic violence or abuse. The DVDS recognises two procedures for disclosing information: 'Right to ask' is triggered by a member of the public applying to the police for a disclosure; 'Right to know' is triggered by the police making a proactive decision to disclose information to protect a potential victim. Under the 'Right to ask', individual members of the public, whether the partner (A) or a third party (C), can now proactively seek information. Therefore this makes both answer A incorrect and answer D correct. There are no conditions to a third party request for information and no requirement for the consent of the partner or close family links which makes both answers B and C incorrect.

General Police Duties, para. 3.11.6

Answer 11.3

Answer **B** — A Domestic Violence Protection Notice (DVPN) is the initial notice issued by the police to provide emergency protection to an individual believed to be the victim of domestic abuse and violence. The power to issue a DVPN is provided by s. 24 of the Crime and Security Act 2010 which states in subs. (1) that a member of a police force not below the rank of superintendent ('the authorising officer') may issue a DVPN. This makes both answer B correct and answer D incorrect.

Answers A and C are therefore also incorrect as the authorising must be by a superintendent or above. In addition to this, answer A is incorrect as *any* constable must apply to a magistrates' court for a DVPO—it does not need to be the officer who authorises the DVPN. Answer C is additionally incorrect as a DVPN will be issued in circumstances where the victim does not agree or consent.

General Police Duties, para. 3.11.5

Answer 11.4

Answer **A** — Answer A is correct because a DVPN may only be issued to a person who is aged 18 years or over.

Section 24 of the Crime and Security Act 2010 provides that:

(2) A DVPN may be issued to a person ('P') aged 18 years or over if the authorising officer has reasonable grounds for believing that—
  (a) P has been violent towards, or has threatened violence towards, an associated person, and
  (b) the issue of the DVPN is necessary to protect that person from violence or a threat of violence by P.

Therefore answer B is incorrect as the authorising officer must *believe* and not suspect. Whilst steps will be undertaken to ascertain the wishes of all involved, the person for whom the protection is sought need not consent to it which means that answer D is incorrect. The age of 18 is relevant for a DVPN to be issued but it is not the case within the definition of domestic abuse. The Domestic Abuse Act 2021 provides the first statutory definition of domestic abuse and states:

(1) This section defines 'domestic abuse' for the purposes of this Act.
(2) Behaviour of a person ('A') towards another person ('B') is 'domestic abuse' if—
    (a) A and B are each aged 16 or over and are personally connected to each other, and
    (b) the behaviour is abusive.

Therefore answer C is incorrect.

General Police Duties, paras 3.11.2, 3.11.5

Answer 11.5

Answer **B** — Answer B is correct and A incorrect as where a DVPN has been issued, a constable must apply to a magistrates' court for a Domestic Violence Protection Order (DVPO). The application must be heard by the magistrates' court not later than 48 hours after the DVPN was served (s. 27).

Whilst the wishes of all parties are considered at the point at which the DVPN is authorised, there is no requirement for any amendments to be made once the notice has been approved which means that both answers C and D are incorrect. In addition, answer D suggests that the application will only proceed if the victim consents; this is not true and applications are made in circumstances where there is no consent.

General Police Duties, para. 3.11.5

Answer 11.6

Answer **C** — The Family Law Act 1996, s. 42 states:

(1) In this Part a 'non-molestation order' means an order containing either or both of the following provisions—
    (a) provision prohibiting a person ('the respondent') from molesting another person who is associated with the respondent;
    (b) provision prohibiting the respondent from molesting a relevant child.

Therefore answer A is incorrect as both the children and BILINGTON are associated persons within this section. Non-molestation orders do not just relate to spouses or former partners but to anyone who is associated with the respondent. This makes answer C correct. The behaviours to be prohibited are *molesting* ones and therefore not restricted to violence which makes answer D incorrect.

Under s. 42, the court may make a non-molestation order in two circumstances:

(a) if an application for the order has been made (whether in other family proceedings or without any other family proceedings being instituted) by a person who is associated with the respondent; or

(b) if in any family proceedings to which the respondent is a party the court considers that the order should be made for the benefit of any other party to the proceedings or any relevant child even though no such application has been made.

Therefore answer B is incorrect.

General Police Duties, para. 3.11.7.1

Answer 11.7

Answer **D** — The Family Law Act 1996, s. 42 states:

(1) In this Part a 'non-molestation order' means an order containing either or both of the following provisions—
   (a) provision prohibiting a person ('the respondent') from molesting another person who is associated with the respondent;
   (b) provision prohibiting the respondent from molesting a relevant child.

Non-molestation orders do not just relate to spouses or former partners but to anyone who is associated with the respondent. This makes answer B incorrect and, for the same reason, answer D correct.

Under s. 42, the court may make a non-molestation order in two circumstances:

(a) if an application for the order has been made (whether in other family proceedings or without any other family proceedings being instituted) by a person who is associated with the respondent; or

(b) if in any family proceedings to which the respondent is a party the court considers that the order should be made for the benefit of any other party to the proceedings or any relevant child even though no such application has been made.

Therefore both answers A and C are incorrect.

General Police Duties, para. 3.11.7.1

Answer 11.8

Answer **C** — The Domestic Abuse Act 2021 provides the first statutory definition of domestic abuse and s. 1 states:

(1) This section defines 'domestic abuse' for the purposes of this Act.

(2) Behaviour of a person ('A') towards another person ('B') is 'domestic abuse' if—

(a) A and B are each aged 16 or over and are personally connected to each other, and

(b) the behaviour is abusive.

(3) Behaviour is 'abusive' if it consists of any of the following—

(a) physical or sexual abuse;

(b) violent or threatening behaviour;

(c) controlling or coercive behaviour;

(d) economic abuse (see subsection (4));

(e) psychological, emotional or other abuse;

and it does not matter whether the behaviour consists of a single incident or a course of conduct.

The economic element to this scenario is covered by the definition which means that answer B is incorrect. 'Economic abuse' means any behaviour that has a substantial adverse effect on a person's ability to acquire, use or maintain money or other property, or obtain goods or services (s. 1(4)). This behaviour may be behaviour consisting of conduct directed at another person, for example the complainant's child (s. 1(5)).

The question now is to consider whether they are personally connected; this is covered in s. 2 which states:

(1) For the purposes of this Act, two people are 'personally connected' to each other if any of the following applies—

(a) they are, or have been, married to each other;

(b) they are, or have been, civil partners of each other;

(c) they have agreed to marry one another (whether or not the agreement has been terminated);

(d) they have entered into a civil partnership agreement (whether or not the agreement has been terminated);

(e) they are, or have been, in an intimate personal relationship with each other;

(f) they each have, or there has been a time when they each have had, a parental relationship in relation to the same child (see subsection (2));

(g) they are relatives.

Therefore answer A is incorrect and answer C is correct as MILES and JEPSON are considered personally connected. Nothing within the sections adds any criteria to live at the same address which makes answer D incorrect.

General Police Duties, paras 3.11.2, 3.11.3

Answer 11.9

Answer **D** — The Domestic Abuse Act 2021, s. 1 states:

(3) Behaviour is 'abusive' if it consists of any of the following—

(a) physical or sexual abuse;

(b) violent or threatening behaviour;

(c) controlling or coercive behaviour;

(d) economic abuse (see subsection (4));

(e) psychological, emotional or other abuse;

and it does not matter whether the behaviour consists of a single incident or a course of conduct.

Therefore the correct answer is D. Answer A is incorrect as threatening behaviour is included. Answers B and C are both incorrect as there is no requirement for a course of conduct or injury.

General Police Duties, para. 3.11.2

Answer 11.10

Answer **D** — DVPNs are covered by the Crime and Security Act 2010. The purpose of a DVPN is to secure the immediate protection of a victim of domestic violence and abuse (V) from future violence or a threat of violence from a suspected perpetrator (P). A DVPN prohibits P from molesting V and, where they cohabit, may require P to leave those premises.

Where a DVPN has been issued, a constable must apply to a magistrates' court for a Domestic Violence Protection Order (DVPO). The application must be heard by the magistrates' court not later than 48 hours after the DVPN was served (s. 27(3)). The DVPO is an order lasting between 14 and 28 days, which prohibits P from molesting V and may also make provision about access to shared accommodation (s. 28(8)). A person who breaches a DVPN may be arrested without warrant (s. 25(1)(b)) and must be held in custody to appear before a magistrates' court within 24 hours when an application for a DVPO can be heard (s. 26).

General Police Duties, para. 3.11.5

12 | Hatred and Harassment Offences

QUESTIONS

Question 12.1

MEREDITH holds racist opinions about black people. One day he was at home with several friends who share his beliefs, when COWANS, who is black, knocked on his door collecting money on behalf of charity. MEREDITH invited COWANS into his house on the pretext of looking for money. When they were in the living room of the house, MEREDITH began racially abusing COWANS in front of his friends. His intention all along was to stir up racial hatred. When COWANS eventually left the house, he contacted the police to report the incident.

Considering offences under s. 18 of the Public Order Act 1986 (using words or behaviour or displaying written material stirring up racial hatred), does the fact that the incident took place in a dwelling affect whether or not the police can take any action?

A No, the offence may be committed anywhere.

B Yes, the offence may only be committed in a public place.

C No, the offence may be committed in a public or private place.

D Yes, the offence may not be committed when both persons are in a dwelling.

Question 12.2

WADE lives in a small cul-de-sac and is openly homophobic. WADE became aware that two people of the same sex had bought a house in the street and the rumours amongst the neighbours were that the people were in a homosexual relationship. One day, neighbours noticed several posters in the front windows of WADE's house, on which were written, 'Sign my petition to get rid of sexual deviants from this street'. WADE's intention was to make the new neighbours uncomfortable about living in the area, so that they would move out.

Could WADE be guilty of an offence, under s. 29B of the Public Order Act 1986, of stirring up hatred against the neighbours on the grounds of sexual orientation?

A No, WADE has not used threatening words or behaviour or displayed any written materials, intending to stir up hatred on the grounds of their sexual orientation.

B Yes, WADE has used threatening, abusive or insulting words or behaviour about a person's sexual orientation.

C No, this offence can only be committed where a person uses words or behaviour and does not include the use of written materials.

D Yes, WADE has used threatening, abusive or insulting words or behaviour intending to stir up hatred on the grounds of sexual orientation, or where hatred was likely to be stirred up.

Question 12.3

CRUTCHER and BOYCE are members of an animal rights extremist group and were targeting two companies which CRUTCHER and BOYCE believed were suppliers to a third company which tested its products on animals. Following a discussion between the two, CRUTCHER sent a threatening letter to the chief executive of one company supplying the goods and BOYCE sent a threatening email to the chief executive of the other company supplying the goods. Their intention was to persuade both companies to stop supplying the third company with their products by causing alarm and distress to the recipients of the letter and email.

Which of the following comments is correct in relation to a 'course of conduct' in respect of an offence under s. 1(1A) of the Protection from Harassment Act 1997?

A Their conduct would be sufficient to amount to a 'course of conduct' in these circumstances.

B This would not amount to a 'course of conduct' as each person would have to send communications to at least two people.

C For a 'course of conduct' to be established, each person would have to send communications to at least two people from each company.

D As the communications they sent to each person were in a different form, this would not amount to a 'course of conduct'.

Question 12.4

REEVES has sent two threatening letters to his probation officer. However, the second letter was not received until four-and-a-half months after the first.

Could REEVES be guilty of harassment contrary to ss. 1 and 2 of the Protection from Harassment Act 1997?

A No, as probation officers are unlikely to feel distress.

B No, owing to the length of time between the letters.

C Yes, but only if the probation officer is likely to feel alarmed and distressed.

D Yes, but only if the probation officer is likely to feel alarmed or distressed.

Question 12.5

Following the break-up of a long-term relationship with FRAMPTON, CLARKSON moved away to live with friends in Scotland. Before leaving, CLARKSON was convicted of harassment against FRAMPTON, contrary to s. 2 of the Protection from Harassment Act 1997. FRAMPTON has heard that CLARKSON intends returning to live nearby and has also been told by friends that CLARKSON is still angry about the break-up and will try to resume contact. FRAMPTON intends seeking a County Court injunction against CLARKSON to avoid being subjected to further harassment.

Which of the statements below is correct in respect of an injunction issued under ss. 3 and 3A of the Protection from Harassment Act 1997?

A Only the High Court may issue an injunction in respect of an apprehended breach of the 1997 Act.

B An injunction may not be issued in respect of an apprehended breach of the 1997 Act.

C An injunction could only be issued in these circumstances if CLARKSON had previously been convicted of an offence contrary to s. 4 of the 1997 Act.

D The County Court could issue an injunction even for an apprehended breach of the 1997 Act.

Question 12.6

HEMMING and MAYOR own 'Oak Farm' where they breed guinea pigs. These guinea pigs are sold to a pharmaceutical company which researches the nervous and immune systems. As a result of this, over the past few years Oak Farm and its employees have been subject to activities from an animal rights activist group. The activists will regularly park near to the farm and chant at the workers who enter and try to encourage the workers to quit and seek employment elsewhere. MURRAY and WALTON are two new employees and the activists have been targeting both of them repeatedly over the past two weeks in the hope that they will quit.

Which of the following statements is correct in respect of an injunction under ss. 3 and 3A of the Protection from Harassment Act 1997?

A The activists' behaviour must amount to an offence for an injunction to be sought.

B Only HEMMING and MAYOR can apply for an injunction on behalf of Oak Farm as a company.

C Either MURRAY or WALTON or Oak Farm can apply for an injunction.

D Only MURRAY or WALTON can apply for an injunction directly.

Question 12.7

OLTON has been arrested for an offence of harassment, under s. 4 of the Protection from Harassment Act 1997, over a dispute about money owed to him by LOVE. It is alleged that OLTON made three phone calls to LOVE during which he threatened to injure his family if the money was not paid within a week. OLTON intended LOVE to fear that he would carry out the threat.

Given that OLTON has engaged in a course of conduct, what would have to be shown in relation to LOVE's state of mind in order for the offence to be complete?

A That OLTON's course of conduct caused LOVE to fear that violence will be used against him.

B That OLTON's course of conduct caused LOVE to fear that violence may be used against him.

C That OLTON's course of conduct caused LOVE to fear that violence will be used against him or his family.

D That OLTON's course of conduct caused LOVE to fear that immediate violence will be used against him.

Question 12.8

BERTRAND worked in the Information Department of a police force and specialised in computer programming. BERTRAND had previously been in a relationship with ROSS, a work colleague, which had ended recently. BERTRAND was upset at the break-up and became convinced that ROSS was now in a relationship with another colleague. BERTRAND managed to access ROSS's emails and monitored them remotely every day for about a month to obtain information about the new relationship. ROSS suspected this was happening and asked BERTRAND to stop. BERTRAND was aware that ROSS was upset but carried on accessing the emails.

Would BERTRAND's behaviour amount to stalking under s. 2A(1) of the Protection from Harassment Act 1997?

A Yes, provided a course of conduct can be proved.

B No, this offence requires some positive action by the defendant and BERTRAND has not actually used the information for anything.

C Yes, regardless of whether a course of conduct can be proved.

D No, this offence requires some form of act or omission by the defendant, which has not occurred in these circumstances.

Question 12.9

When BERRY split up from her boyfriend, TROTT, he began posting abusive messages on his Facebook account, calling her a 'slut' and 'whore'. The abuse got worse and TROTT posted a number of photographs on his account of BERRY with no clothes on. Eventually, TROTT posted explicit photographs of the pair having sex. After each Facebook message or photograph, TROTT sent BERRY a message telling her to look at his account. BERRY was not concerned about her safety and initially ignored the abuse and photographs of her with no clothes on; however, she became extremely distressed because of the explicit photographs. Eventually, BERRY moved away from the area and changed her telephone number to avoid receiving messages from TROTT. She also stopped all contact with her family and friends because of the Facebook account.

Which of the following statements is correct in relation to the offence of stalking under s. 4A of the Protection from Harassment Act 1997?

A The offence has not been committed as TROTT has not threatened BERRY with violence.

B As BERRY was not in fear that TROTT would use violence against her, this would not amount to an offence of stalking.

C BERRY only became extremely distressed when TROTT posted the explicit photographs; this was a single act and did not amount to a course of conduct and would not amount to stalking.

D TROTT has pursued a course of conduct which has had a substantial adverse effect on BERRY's day-to-day activities and this amounts to an offence of stalking.

Question 12.10

DONOVAN works in a laboratory where a number of experiments are carried out in relation to genetically modified crops. WARBRICK is opposed to the use and sale of genetically modified crops and follows DONOVAN home from the laboratory one evening. DONOVAN is inside her house when she sees WARBRICK standing on the pavement outside her house holding a sign with 'You are Murdering the Future of Our Children!' written on it. WARBRICK is also repeatedly shouting, 'Stop going to work! Stop playing God!' DONOVAN contacts the police and states how distressed she is and, as a result, PS PURCELL and PC TANSILL (on uniform mobile patrol) arrive at the scene. PS PURCELL speaks to WARBRICK who states that he only wants DONOVAN to stop her 'evil work', causing PS PURCELL to believe WARBRICK is at the house to persuade DONOVAN that she should not do something that she is entitled to do.

Could a direction under s. 42 of the Criminal Justice and Police Act 2001 be given to WARBRICK in these circumstances?

A Yes, the direction can be given to WARBRICK by PS PURCELL or PC TANSILL.

B No, a direction under s. 42 must be given by an officer of the rank of inspector or above.

C Yes, but the direction must be given to WARBRICK by PS PURCELL.

D No, a direction under s. 42 must be given by an officer of the rank of superintendent or above.

Question 12.11

LITTLEWOOD, RYAN and PERCY are peacefully protesting outside the offices of a financial institution which has business links to Saudi Arabia. The three are protesting about alleged human rights violations in Saudi Arabia and are trying to persuade the workers at the financial institution not to go into work. Inspector HOWSON attends the scene with PC SNETHAM (both officers are on uniform patrol) where they speak to a supervisor at the financial institution. Whilst there have been no allegations that what LITTLEWOOD, RYAN and PERCY are doing involves any unlawful activity, several members of staff at the financial institution have told their supervisor that a number of their clients have cancelled business appointments that day because they have seen the protest reported on a local TV station and consequently the financial institution is losing money.

Is it possible for Inspector HOWSON to give the three protesters a direction to leave the vicinity of the financial institution (using the discretionary power under s. 42 of the Criminal Justice and Police Act 2001)?

A No, because there are no reports that the protesters have caused any workers at the financial institution any harassment, alarm or distress.

B Yes, but this is only possible because Inspector HOWSON is in uniform.

C No, because the power is only available when the person(s) concerned is/are outside (or in the vicinity of) any premises that are used by any individual as his/her dwelling.

D Yes, but any direction given to the protesters must be given in writing.

Question 12.12

LEACH believes that all Muslims are a deadly threat to national security and that they should be forcibly removed from the United Kingdom. Intending to stir up religious hatred, he writes a pamphlet titled 'Muslim Menace' in which he expresses his views on the subject in a very threatening manner. LEACH approaches BRYANT, a publisher, and asks him to publish 1,000 copies of the pamphlet. BRYANT reads the pamphlet and agrees to publish it as he is sympathetic to LEACH's views and also wishes to stir up religious hatred. Once the copies have been made, LEACH picks them up and takes them back to his house. LEACH then asks his friend, PERRY, to stand on a street corner and hand out the pamphlets. PERRY asks what is in the pamphlets as he cannot read. LEACH states that they are in protest about the closure of a local factory and the resulting lost jobs. PERRY agrees to hand out the leaflets and goes out and distributes them to the public on a street near LEACH's house.

Only taking into account the offence of publishing or distributing written material (under s. 29C of the Public Order Act 1986), which of the following comments is true?

A LEACH, BRYANT and PERRY have all committed the offence in these circumstances.

B Only BRYANT has committed the offence in these circumstances.

C Only BRYANT and PERRY commit the offence in these circumstances.

D The offence is not committed in these circumstances.

ANSWERS

Answer 12.1

Answer **D** — An offence is committed contrary to s. 18(1) of the Public Order Act 1986, where a person uses threatening, abusive or insulting words or behaviour, intending to stir up racial hatred (or where it is likely to be stirred up). Certainly, the behaviour of the person in the question would meet these criteria. However, s. 18(2) states that the offence may be committed in a public or private place but not when the words or behaviour used are not heard by persons other than those in that or another dwelling. The requirement is similar to those under ss. 4 and 5 of the same Act and, since both persons were in the same dwelling, no offence is committed, whatever MEREDITH's intentions! Answers A, B and C are incorrect for this reason.

General Police Duties, para. 3.12.2.1

Answer 12.2

Answer **A** — Section 29B of the 1986 Act deals with 'hatred on the grounds of sexual orientation'. This covers hatred against a group of persons defined by reference to their sexual orientation, be they heterosexual, homosexual or bisexual. The offence may involve the use of words or behaviour or *display of written material* (s. 29B). Therefore, answer C is incorrect.

However, the offences differ from the offences of stirring up racial hatred in two respects. First, the offences apply only to 'threatening' words or behaviour, rather than 'threatening, abusive or insulting' words or behaviour. The second difference is that in this section, the offences apply only to words or behaviour if the accused 'intends' to stir up hatred on grounds of sexual orientation. They do not apply in circumstances where a person displays a sign about an individual's sexual orientation that is threatening, abusive or insulting or which is 'likely' to stir up hatred without the relevant intention so answers B and D are incorrect.

General Police Duties, paras 3.12.2, 3.12.2.5

Answer 12.3

Answer **A** — Under s. 1(1A) of the Protection from Harassment Act 1997, a person commits an offence if he/she pursues a course of conduct which involves harassment

of two or more persons and which he/she knows or ought to know involves harassment of those persons and by which he/she intends to persuade any person not to
do something which that person is entitled or required to do or to do something
that he/she is not under any obligation to do.

Under s. 7(3)(b) of the Act, a course of conduct for this offence must involve, in
the case of conduct in relation to two or more people, conduct on at least one occasion to each of those people. The fact that the letters were sent by two different
people is irrelevant, because under s. 7(3A) a person's conduct may be aided and
abetted by another, and both would commit this offence provided it can be shown
that they were acting together. Answer B is therefore incorrect.

Home Office Circular 34/2005 provides examples of offences which might be
committed under s. 1(1A). In this guidance, it cites the example of an animal rights
extremist sending a threatening email on one occasion to an individual working
for one company and another similar letter to a different individual working for
another company, with the intention of persuading them to stop supplying a third
company with their products (similar to the circumstances in this question). Since
the offence may be committed by sending different forms of communication to
only one person from each company, answers C and D are incorrect (this is true even
though the communications were sent by two different people).

General Police Duties, para. 3.12.4.4

Answer 12.4

Answer **D** — Section 1 of the Protection from Harassment Act 1997 states that a
person must not pursue a course of conduct:

(a) which amounts to harassment of another, and
(b) which he knows or ought to know amounts to harassment of the other.

Course of conduct has been considered by the courts. In *Lau* v *DPP* [2000] 1 FLR 799,
the Divisional Court held that although only two incidents are necessary, the fewer
the number of incidents and the further apart they are, the less likely it is that there
will be a finding of harassment. In *Baron* v *CPS* (2000) 13 June, unreported, the court
accepted that the more spread out and limited in number the incidents and the
more indirect their means of delivery (in this case by letter), the less likely it is that
a course of conduct amounting to harassment will be found. However, there is no
rule and it will depend upon the facts of each individual case. In *Baron*, two letters
sent some four-and-a-half months apart could be a course of conduct amounting to
harassment, and therefore answer B is incorrect.

Note that it is alarm *or* distress; the court need only be satisfied that the behaviour involved one or the other (*DPP* v *Ramsdale* [2001] EWHC 106 (Admin)), and therefore answer C is incorrect.

Finally, the court in *Baron* refused to endorse the view that public service employees are less likely to be caused distress by threatening letters, and therefore answer A is incorrect.

General Police Duties, paras 3.12.4, 3.12.4.2, 3.12.4.3

Answer 12.5

Answer **D** — Under ss. 3 and 3A of the Protection from Harassment Act 1997, the High Court *or* County Court may issue an injunction in respect of civil proceedings brought with regard to an actual *or* apprehended breach of s. 1(1) and (1A). Answers A and B are therefore incorrect.

The effect of this is that a defendant may be made the subject of an injunction even though his/her behaviour has not amounted to an offence under the 1997 Act, or regardless of whether he/she were previously convicted of a s. 4 offence. Answer C is therefore incorrect.

General Police Duties, para. 3.12.4.8

Answer 12.6

Answer **C** — Answer A is incorrect as under ss. 3 and 3A of the Protection from Harassment Act 1997, the High Court or a County Court may issue an injunction in respect of civil proceedings brought in respect of an actual or apprehended breach of s. 1(1) and (1A). The effect of this is that a defendant may be made the subject of an injunction even though his/her behaviour has not amounted to an offence under the 1997 Act.

Answer C is correct, making answers B and D incorrect because the person who is the victim of the offence under s. 1(1A), or any person at whom the persuasion is aimed, may apply for an injunction. Whilst a company cannot be the 'direct' victim of harassment, a company could apply for an injunction on behalf of the employees of the company as an 'indirect' victim of the harassment. For example, where people who work for a life science or fur company are being harassed in order to persuade them not to work for that company, or in order to persuade the company not to supply another company, either the employees themselves (the 'direct' victim) or the company in question (the 'indirect' victim) could apply for an injunction.

General Police Duties, para. 3.12.4.8

Answer 12.7

Answer **A** — Under s. 4(1) of the Protection from Harassment Act 1997:

A person whose course of conduct causes another to fear, on at least two occasions, that violence will be used against him is guilty of an offence if he knows or ought to know that his course of conduct will cause the other so to fear on each of those occasions.

The course of conduct is proved because threats were made by OLTON on three occasions; however, the defendant's course of conduct must cause the victim to fear that violence *will* be used against him/her, rather than *might*. This is a strict requirement and showing that the conduct caused the victim to be seriously frightened of what might happen in the future is not enough (*R v Henley* [2000] Crim LR 582). Answer B is therefore incorrect.

On the other hand, s. 4 does not state that the victim must fear that *immediate* violence will be used against him/her. Answer D is therefore incorrect.

Finally, answer A is correct and answer C is incorrect because the course of conduct for the purpose of s. 4 has to cause a person to fear, on at least two occasions, that violence would be used against *him/her*, rather than against a member of their family (*Mohammed Ali Caurti* v *DPP* [2001] EWHC Admin 867).

General Police Duties, para. 3.12.5

Answer 12.8

Answer **A** — Under s. 2A(1) of the Protection from Harassment Act 1997, a person is guilty of an offence if:

- the person pursues a course of conduct in breach of s. 1(1) of the 1997 Act (i.e. a course of conduct which amounts to harassment); and
- the course of conduct amounts to stalking.

There are two matters, therefore, which need to be proved. Has the person pursued a course of conduct which amounts to harassment? Does the conduct amount to stalking? Answer C is incorrect because a course of conduct must be proved.

Section 2A(2) states that a course of conduct amounts to stalking of another person if it amounts to harassment and the person knows or ought to know that the course of conduct amounts to harassment of the other person. This section also states that the acts or omissions involved must be those that are associated with stalking; therefore, answer B is incorrect.

Section 2A(3) lists examples of behaviours associated with stalking, which include:

(a) following a person,
(b) contacting, or attempting to contact, a person by any means,

(c) publishing any statement or other material—
  (i) relating or purporting to relate to a person, or
  (ii) purporting to originate from a person,
(d) monitoring the use by a person of the internet, email or any other form of electronic communication,
(e) loitering in any place (whether public or private),
(f) interfering with any property in the possession of a person,
(g) watching or spying on a person.

Since simply monitoring a person's email amounts to an offence, answers B and D are incorrect.

General Police Duties, para. 3.12.6.1

Answer 12.9

Answer **D** — Section 4A of the Protection from Harassment Act 1997 prohibits a course of conduct relating to the offence of stalking involving fear of violence or serious alarm or distress. The first arm of the offence prohibits a course of conduct that causes the victim to fear, on at least two occasions, that violence will be used against him/her (which is similar to the existing s. 4 offence).

The second arm of the offence prohibits a course of conduct which causes 'serious alarm or distress' which has a 'substantial adverse effect on the day-to-day activities of the victim', which will include the victim moving home and changing the way he/she socialises. This is designed to recognise the serious impact that stalking may have on victims, even where an explicit fear of violence is not created by each incident of stalking behaviour. Answers A and B are incorrect as the offence may be committed when *either* of these outcomes is present and BERRY has most certainly changed her lifestyle as a result of TROTT's behaviour.

The issue of a 'course of conduct' relating to the s. 4 offence was addressed in *R (On the Application of A)* v *DPP* [2004] EWHC 2454 (Admin). In this case, the defendant's conduct on the first occasion (e.g. a threat to burn the victim's house down) did not cause the victim undue concern, but a second threat some time later to do the same thing *did* put the victim in fear of violence, partly because this was the second time the threat had been made. The defendant argued that the victim had only been put in fear of violence by his threats to burn her house down on the second occasion, and therefore there had been no course of conduct (i.e. the victim had only feared violence on one occasion, as opposed to the two occasions that were required by the section). The Divisional Court disagreed and held that the magistrates were entitled to find as a matter of fact that the two incidents had put the victim in fear of violence, notwithstanding her admission that, on the first occasion, she had not been too concerned. While this case relates to a different offence, the elements for a course of conduct will be the same for s. 4 and s. 4A, and therefore answer C is incorrect.

General Police Duties, paras 3.12.5, 3.12.6.2

Answer 12.10

Answer **C** — Section 42 of the Criminal Justice and Police Act 2001 provides a discretionary power to give directions to people in the vicinity. The power arises where:

- the person is outside (or in the vicinity of) any premises that are used by any individual as his/her dwelling; and
- the constable believes, on reasonable grounds, that the person is there for the purpose of representing or persuading the resident (or anyone else):
  – that he/she should not do something he/she is entitled or required to do; or
  – that he/she should do something that he/she is under no obligation to do; and
- the constable also believes, on reasonable grounds, that the person's presence amounts to, or is likely to result in, the harassment of the resident or is likely to cause alarm or distress to the resident.

The discretionary power is available to the most senior ranking police officer at the scene (PS PURCELL), making answers A, B and D incorrect.

General Police Duties, para. 3.12.6

Answer 12.11

Answer **C** — There is no requirement that the officer giving a direction using the power under s. 42 of the Criminal Justice and Police Act 2001 be in uniform (making answer B incorrect), nor is there any requirement that the direction be given in writing (it can be given orally), making answer D incorrect. Answer A is incorrect as the power is available when the person to whom the direction is going to be given is outside (or in the vicinity of) any premises that are used by any individual as his/her dwelling (correct answer C). Even if the protesters were acting in a way that caused workers at the financial institution harassment, alarm or distress, the power would still not be available.

General Police Duties, para. 3.12.7

Answer 12.12

Answer **B** — Section 29C of the Public Order Act 1986 deals with the publication and distribution of written material which is threatening and the person publishing or distributing the material *intends* thereby to stir up religious hatred. Unlike the similar offence under s. 19 of the Act (publishing or distributing material in respect of *racial* hatred), this offence does not contain the proviso which states that having regard to all the circumstances the publication or distribution of the material is likely to stir up such hatred. Therefore, the only way this can be committed is with that intention to stir up religious hatred. This means PERRY does not commit the offence and so answers A and C are incorrect. Clearly, the offence is committed by BRYANT (the publisher), meaning that answer D is incorrect.

General Police Duties, para. 3.12.2.6

13 | Offences and Powers Relating to Information and Communications

QUESTIONS

Question 13.1

STOCKWELL works for a shipping company in the post room. The company specialises in the procurement and shipping of specialist ingredients and supplies these to many of the top restaurants across the world. JOYE has decided to set up a company to work in competition with STOCKWELL's company. He knows that STOCKWELL is paid a low wage and is in significant debt. He approaches STOCKWELL and asks him to access the accounts held on the company computer system; with these JOYE would contact the suppliers and undercut STOCKWELL's company resulting in JOYE gaining the contracts. In return, JOYE offers STOCKWELL a large sum of money. STOCKWELL agrees to do this as he is permitted to use the computers on his break. When at work next, he accesses the accounts and sends them to JOYE.

Considering the offence under s. 1 of the Computer Misuse Act 1990, which of the following statements is correct?

A   As an employee of the company, STOCKWELL has legitimate access to the system and has not committed an offence.

B   STOCKWELL has not committed an offence under this section as there is a requirement for fraudulent activity to take place.

C   STOCKWELL has committed an offence because he is making a gain from accessing the information.

D   STOCKWELL has committed an offence because accessing the accounts falls outside his normal scope of work.

Question 13.2

BAKER works as a computer software engineer for a pharmaceutical company. Unbeknown to the company, BAKER does not agree with the development of vaccines to prevent illness and disease. The company is starting medical trials for a new vaccine which has the potential to counter a number of the symptoms felt by sufferers of migraine. BAKER has been tasked to create a system which will record any adverse reactions, symptom improvement and other information of note from the sample trial group. BAKER deliberately codes the software so that the wrong data will populate the fields and will not be relevant to the participant against whom it is recorded. He hopes to ruin the reputation of the company, forcing it to focus on other areas of research.

Considering the offence under s. 3 of the Computer Misuse Act 1990, which of the following statements is correct?

A This Act does not prevent or hinder access to any program held by the computer; therefore, this offence is incomplete.

B The offence is committed as the Act has impaired the reliability of the data.

C The offence would be complete if his intent was to cause financial loss for the company.

D The offence is committed because BAKER intends to damage the company's reputation.

Question 13.3

MILES is an electronics designer and has significant knowledge, expertise and skill in understanding how to develop programs to be placed onto computers to obtain information from them. He does this as a hobby as his job is very well paid, but he likes to spend time decoding other programs and understanding how to disable them. COOPER knows that MILES likes to do this and asks him to create a code which would hack into the local car factory systems. MILES agrees as COOPER states that this is so that he can see how the code works and MILES provides it to COOPER on a USB stick. Unbeknown to MILES, COOPER is part of an organised crime group and intends to give this to the leader of the group to improve his status as he believes that the group can use this to obtain money from client accounts.

Considering the offences under s. 1, 3 or 3ZA of the Computer Misuse Act 1990, which of the following statements is correct?

A Both MILES and COOPER commit offences.

B Neither MILES nor COOPER commit offences.

C Only MILES is guilty of an offence.

D Only COOPER is guilty of an offence.

Question 13.4

Inspector DEACON has been called to attend the scene of a sudden death. BILLINGS, aged 78, appears to have suffered a cardiac arrest and died in the dining room of his house. Inspector DEACON is attending to ensure that he is satisfied that there are no suspicious circumstances. During his attendance, an amount of data is collected in relation to BILLINGS.

Considering the requirements under s. 2 of the Data Protection Act 2018, which of the following statements is correct in relation to the data collected?

A There are no restrictions on the data collected; personal data under this section relates only to identifiable living individuals.

B Inspector DEACON will need to obtain the permission of BILLINGS's next of kin to continue to process the data.

C Inspector DEACON can collect the data which can be processed, but only for six months from the date of BILLINGS's death.

D Inspector DEACON cannot process the data under this section.

Question 13.5

BURTON was undergoing an acrimonious separation from his partner, HASTINGS, who had started seeing another person, GRANT. BURTON managed to find out where GRANT was working and left a message (written on a piece of paper in an envelope) with a receptionist at the office building that GRANT works in. BURTON asked the receptionist to pass the envelope to GRANT. The message stated that HASTINGS was in hospital after a car crash and had suffered life-threatening injuries. The story was completely false. The receptionist forgot to pass the envelope to GRANT.

Considering the offence under s. 1 of the Malicious Communications Act 1988, which of the following statements is correct?

A This was not a threatening or indecent message; therefore, this offence is incomplete.

B The offence has not been committed as it was not an electronic communication.

C The offence would be complete if it was BURTON's intention to cause GRANT or any other person anxiety or distress.

D The message was not seen by GRANT so the offence is not committed.

Question 13.6

POOLE owns a property which he is renting out privately to REECE. REECE has failed to pay the rent for the last three months and, despite calling at the premises several times in the last month, POOLE has been unable to collect the money owed to him. In desperation, POOLE sent a text message to REECE which said, 'I'm coming to re-claim my property Monday and if you're there, I'm going to personally throw you into the street.' REECE was fearful because of the contents of the text and contacted the police.

Section 1(2) of the Malicious Communications Act 1988 outlines a defence for someone who sends a message which amounts to a threat. In respect of this defence, what would POOLE have to show in order to avoid prosecution for this offence?

A POOLE would have to show that he did not intend the message to be threatening.

B POOLE would have to show that an ordinary person would think the demands were reasonable.

C POOLE would have to show that he reasonably believed that the threat was a proper means of enforcing the demand.

D POOLE would have to show that there were reasonable grounds for making the demand, that he believed the threat was a proper means of enforcing the de-mand and that reasonable grounds existed for that belief.

Question 13.7

HEALD was infatuated with his neighbour, FARR, and continually asked her out on dates. FARR was flattered and not at all threatened by this, but refused to go out with him. HEALD then made an indecent phone call to FARR in an effort to 'turn her on'. HEALD did not, however, intend FARR to be distressed by these calls. She was not threatened and found it all mildly amusing.

Does HEALD commit the offence outlined in s. 127 of the Communications Act 2003 of improper use of a public electronic communications network?

A Yes, but only if it can be proved the phone call was grossly offensive.

B Yes, even though HEALD did not intend to cause distress and FARR was not dis-tressed by the call.

C No, HEALD did not make persistent use of a public electronic communications network.

D No, FARR was not caused annoyance, inconvenience or needless anxiety by the call.

Question 13.8

GOODHEW is a Member of Parliament. An important vote has taken place where, if agreed, a bill will be passed which will place restrictions on photography near areas of interest for aviation. MOORE is an aviation enthusiastic who has spent many years researching and perfecting the best locations to take photographs of aeroplanes in flight. The proposed changes will mean that MOORE will lose most of these places and he therefore believes that the photographs he takes will be impacted. After hearing that GOODHEW voted in favour of the bill, MOORE loads his social media page and records himself threatening to go to the MP's office and hit him. He posts this and after receiving some comments of encouragement he then writes a letter to GOODHEW in which he makes further threats to him intending to cause him distress.

Has MOORE committed an offence under s. 1(1) of the Malicious Communications Act 1988?

A Yes, the offence has been committed in respect of both the letter and the social media video.

B No, because he has made threats, the message conveyed must be indecent or grossly offensive.

C Yes, but only in relation to the letter that he sent to GOODHEW.

D No, because he must have a course of conduct of at least three occasions.

Question 13.9

HIND, who is aged 16, has been arrested for possession of a Class A drug, amphetamine. During interview, he has told Constable SCOPE that there is significant drug possession and dealing at his school. HIND tells him that all the teachers are aware and no one does anything to stop it as the school is being controlled by a local gang. HIND states that he and another pupil would be willing to pass information to police so that they can act to put a stop to it as he would like to focus on his education.

Which statement as prescribed by the Regulation of Investigatory Powers (Directed Surveillance and Covert Human Intelligence Sources) Order 2010 is correct?

A An assistant chief constable or commander can give the relevant authority for a period of four months beginning on the day after the authorisation is granted.

B An assistant chief constable or commander can give the relevant authority for a period of four months beginning on the day the authorisation is granted.

C In the case of a juvenile, the authority must come from the chief constable or commissioner for a period of four months beginning on the day after the authorisation is granted.

D In the case of a juvenile, the authority must come from the chief constable or commissioner for a period of six months beginning on the day after the authorisation is granted.

Question 13.10

WALDER has worked for the Rainbow Centre for the past 12 months as a call handler. His job is to process information from clients who are making insurance claims. On several occasions, he has felt bad for the customers as he knows the matrix used to assess their claims. The information that these clients have provided does not meet the threshold to be accepted, but he feels that they are genuine claims and so he adds additional information to the claim forms. His employers become suspicious because he starts to have a higher claim rate than his co-workers. So, one evening his manager, SIMM, listens to the calls and realises that WALDER has been adding additional information to increase the likelihood of those claims being accepted. The next day, WALDER is fired. The weekend after, when the office is closed, WALDER calls SIMM at home and tells him that he has just walked past the office and seen that it is on fire. This is untrue. Distressed, SIMM calls the fire and rescue authority to report a fire and rushes to the scene.

Considering the offence under s. 49 of the Fire and Rescue Services Act 2004, which of the following statements is correct?

A SIMM has committed an offence when he calls to report the fire.

B WALDER may have committed an offence.

C SIMM and WALDER have both committed an offence when SIMM calls to report the fire.

D WALDER commits an offence in relation to SIMM by causing him distress.

Question 13.11

MORTON is a well-known public figure and is taking legal advice about bringing a case against the police under Article 8 of the European Convention on Human Rights (respect for private and family life). The circumstances were that MORTON reported to the police her suspicion that someone was trying to hack into her emails. MORTON alleges that the police failed to act and, as a result, the hacker subsequently managed to download several photographs of her with no clothes on, from emails sent by a friend. The photographs were displayed on the internet and MORTON claims this was potentially ruinous to her career.

Which of the following statements is correct in relation to MORTON's potential claim?

A The aim of Article 8 is to protect a person's life from interference by 'public authorities': it therefore does not apply in these circumstances.

B The State has a positive obligation to prevent others from interfering with an individual's right to private and family life; therefore, Article 8 may apply in these circumstances.

C The State has a positive obligation to prevent others from interfering with an individual's right to private and family life, but this does not extend to a person's correspondence; therefore, Article 8 would not apply in these circumstances.

D The State has a positive obligation to prevent others from interfering with an individual's right to private and family life, but this duty only extends to maintaining public safety; therefore, Article 8 would not apply in these circumstances.

Question 13.12

PETERSON is at work on NHS premises; he is a kitchen assistant and has no authorised access to computer systems. One day whilst at work, he walks past AHERN and can see his computer screen. He notices that AHERN is looking at a file of NAPIER with whom he attended college. He subtly looks over AHERN's shoulder to try and read what the notes say. AHERN looks around but PETERSON pretends that he had stopped to pick something up and he then goes back to the kitchen. PETERSON cannot stop thinking about what he has seen. He had romantic feelings towards NAPIER and would like to try and find his address. That evening when AHERN has gone home, PETERSON looks in his desk and believes that he has found the password to the system. He begins to attempt to log on, and is successful. He pulls up the relevant program and just as he is about to get NAPIER's address, AHERN returns to his desk causing PETERSON to run away. Section 1 of the Computer Misuse Act 1990 makes provision in relation to unauthorised access to computer material.

Where a person is not authorised and they have the required intent and knowledge, at which point would an offence under this section first be committed?

A Looking at material on a computer screen.

B Attempting to log on to a computer.

C When they are successfully logged on to the system.

D When the actual program is accessed.

Question 13.13

POWDRILL was a computer software engineer who worked for a company which distributed electronic equipment bought by customers online. POWDRILL was sacked by the company for allegedly stealing. Seeking revenge, POWDRILL devised a program which sent three million emails to the company's inbox in one day. POWDRILL hoped that the volume of emails would cause the company's online computer package to crash. However, another software engineer working for the company realised what was happening and implemented a program which intercepted the emails. In the end, no damage was done to the company.

If POWDRILL were to be prosecuted for an offence under s. 3 of the Computer Misuse Act 1990, which of the following statements would be correct in respect of the 'intent' required for this offence?

A The prosecution would have to show that POWDRILL intended causing an economic loss to the company.

B The prosecution must show that POWDRILL intended to impair the operation of the company's software program.

C The prosecution would have to show that POWDRILL intended to impair the operation of the company's software program, or was reckless as to whether it would be impaired.

D The prosecution would have to show that POWDRILL intended causing permanent damage to the company's computer program.

Question 13.14

Constable PETERS is a member of a Neighbourhood Policing Team on a housing estate which suffers from a significant drug problem. The officer has formed a good relationship with young people in the area and has been approached by GAMLIN who lives on the estate and is aged 14. GAMLIN has disclosed to the officer that her older brother (who is 23 years old), whom she lives with but does not get on with, is actively dealing heroin. She told Constable PETERS that she would like to give regular information about her brother's activities. The officer has returned to the station and has sought advice from the specialists in this area of policing.

In these circumstances, could officers seek authority to recruit GAMLIN as a CHIS?

A No, on no occasion should the use or conduct of a CHIS be authorised when he/she is under 16 years of age.

B Yes, but any authorisation would be limited to a time frame of four months beginning on the day authorisation was granted.

C No, on no occasion should the use or conduct of a CHIS under 16 years of age be authorised to give information against someone in the same household as that person.

D Yes, but any authorisation would be limited to a time frame of one month beginning on the day authorisation was granted.

Question 13.15

Detective Inspector GREEN has been telephoned by DC CALDWELL, an officer working in the Drug Squad. The officer has received information that a large quantity of drugs is due to be moved into the area within the next hour to an address well known to the team. DC CALDWELL is at court applying for a warrant to search the premises but wishes to set up a directed surveillance operation urgently to monitor the address.

Is Detective Inspector GREEN able to give an urgent authority for directed surveillance?

A No, inspectors are only able to give urgent authorities for CHIS activity.

B Yes, Detective Inspector GREEN may give an urgent authority if it is not reasonably practicable to have the application considered by a superintendent.

C Yes, inspectors are able to give authorities for directed surveillance in any situation; the restrictions relating to urgent authorities apply to CHIS activity.

D No, only a superintendent is able to give urgent authorities.

Question 13.16

Superintendent MILLER has given an urgent authorisation for CHIS activity by GOUGH, who has passed on information to the police about a potential bomb-making 'factory' in a house in the neighbourhood. GOUGH has been tasked, within strict parameters, to find out more information while the police organise an armed response.

Given that the CHIS has been authorised orally, which of the following statements is correct as to how long the authorisation should last?

A The authorisation will last for 24 hours unless renewed.

B The authorisation will last for 48 hours unless renewed.

C The authorisation will last for 72 hours unless renewed.

D The authorisation will last for 96 hours unless renewed.

Question 13.17

DAWSON was arrested for a series of frauds against elderly people. The police believed that SHELLEY, a solicitor, had been passing information to DAWSON about clients and their bank accounts in a conspiracy to commit fraud. DAWSON asked for SHELLEY to represent him while he was in custody. The officer in charge, Detective Chief Inspector PATTERSON, considered making an application to place covert listening devices in the police station interview room to listen in on their legal consultation.

Which of the following statements is correct in relation to the police being allowed to use such surveillance methods?

A This is permissible and will be treated as directed surveillance.

B This is permissible and will be treated as intrusive surveillance.

C This is not permissible; surveillance carried out on premises used for legal consultations would only be authorised where there is a risk to life.

D This is not permissible; all communications between lawyers and their clients are subject to legal privilege.

Question 13.18

PLUNKETT and FERRIS had been arrested by the police for conspiracy to commit murder. They had been interviewed over several days in the police station and neither person made any comment during interview. They were charged with the offence and were being taken to court in the back of a police van. Unknown to the pair, a directed surveillance authority had been obtained to place a covert listening device in the vehicle which recorded crucial evidence pointing to their guilt.

In relation to the authority obtained, which of the following statements is correct?

A This authority was incorrectly given; this amounted to intrusive surveillance because PLUNKETT and FERRIS were in a vehicle.

B This authority was correctly given; the regulations relating to intrusive surveillance apply only on residential premises.

C This authority was incorrectly given; this amounted to intrusive surveillance because information was obtained using a covert listening device.

D This authority was correctly given; this amounted to directed surveillance because PLUNKETT and FERRIS were not inside a private vehicle.

Question 13.19

The police are investigating an organised crime group suspected of committing a series of armed robberies. Intelligence has been received that key members of the group have arranged to meet in a remote hotel in a week's time. Consideration is being given to applying for an authorisation to conduct surveillance at the hotel with audio and visual devices (microphones and cameras). The investigating officers are planning to place devices in common areas, such as the communal bar and dining room, and in private hotel bedrooms.

The Covert Surveillance and Property Interference Code of Practice provides guidance on what is intrusive surveillance. Which of the following is correct in relation to the type of surveillance authorisation the officers would require?

A A directed surveillance authorisation for the common areas and an intrusive surveillance authorisation for the private hotel bedrooms.

B An intrusive surveillance authorisation for the common areas and private hotel bedrooms; a hotel is a 'residential premises' according to the Code.

C A directed surveillance authorisation for the common areas and private hotel bedrooms; a hotel is not a 'residential premises' according to the Code.

D A directed surveillance authorisation for the common areas and an intrusive surveillance authorisation for the private hotel bedrooms; however, if they only plan to use listening devices in the private hotel bedrooms, this would also amount to directed surveillance.

ANSWERS

Answer 13.1

Answer **D** — The Computer Misuse Act 1990, s. 1 states:

(1) A person is guilty of an offence if—
  (a) he causes a computer to perform any function with intent to secure access to any program or data held in any computer or to enable any such access to be secured;
  (b) the access he intends to secure, or enable to be secured, is unauthorised; and
  (c) he knows at the time when he causes the computer to perform the function that that is the case.
(2) The intent a person has to have to commit an offence under this section need not be directed at—
  (a) any particular program or data;
  (b) a program or data of any particular kind; or
  (c) a program or data held in any particular computer.

There is nothing contained in the definition which states that fraudulent activity must take place, or that a gain must be made which makes both answers B and C incorrect.

Any access must be 'unauthorised'. If the defendant is authorised to access a computer, albeit for restricted purposes, then it was originally held that he/she did not commit this offence if he/she then used any information for some other unauthorised purpose (e.g. police officers using data from the Police National Computer (PNC) for private gain (*DPP* v *Bignell* [1998] 1 Cr App R 1)). However, in *R* v *Bow Street Metropolitan Stipendiary Magistrate, ex parte Government of the USA* [2000] 2 AC 216, it was held that where an employee accessed accounts that fell outside his normal scope of work and passed on the information, in this instance to credit-card forgers, he was not authorised to access the specific data involved. This makes answer A incorrect, as whilst there is legitimate access it has been used outside the normal scope of work. For the same reason, answer D is the correct answer.

General Police Duties, para. 3.13.5

Answer 13.2

Answer **B** — The Computer Misuse Act 1990, s. 3 states:

(1) A person is guilty of an offence if—
  (a) he does any unauthorised act in relation to a computer;
  (b) at the time when he does the act he knows that it is unauthorised; and
  (c) either subsection (2) or subsection (3) below applies.

(2) This subsection applies if the person intends by doing the act—
- (a) to impair the operation of any computer;
- (b) to prevent or hinder access to any program or data held in any computer; or
- (c) to impair the operation of any such program or the reliability of any such data.

(3) This subsection applies if the person is reckless as to whether the act will do any of the things mentioned in paragraphs (a) to (c) of subsection (2) above.

The correct answer is B because causing a computer to record information that came from one source when it in fact came from another clearly affects the reliability of that information for the purposes of s. 3(2)(c) (*Zezev* v *USA*; *Yarimaka* v *Governor of HM Prison Brixton* [2002] EWHC 589 (Admin)). Answer A is incorrect as the intent was not to prevent or hinder access to any program but instead to impair the reliability of the information. Answer C is incorrect as there is no requirement within this section for financial loss, in the same way answer D is incorrect as there is no requirement to damage a reputation of a company.

General Police Duties, para. 3.13.5.4

Answer 13.3

Answer **A** — The Computer Misuse Act 1990, s. 3A states:

(1) A person is guilty of an offence if he makes, adapts, supplies or offers to supply any article intending it to be used to commit, or to assist in the commission of, an offence under section 1, 3 or 3ZA.

(2) A person is guilty of an offence if he supplies or offers to supply any article believing that it is likely to be used to commit, or to assist in the commission of, an offence under section 1, 3 or 3ZA.

(3) A person is guilty of an offence if he obtains any article—
- (a) intending to use it to commit, or to assist in the commission of, an offence under section 1, 3 or 3ZA, or
- (b) with a view to its being supplied for use to commit, or to assist in the commission, of, an offence under section 1, 3 or 3ZA.

(4) In this section 'article' includes any program or data held in electronic form.

To commit the offence under s. 3A(1), MILES must have intended the USB and program to be used in the commission of offences. This makes both answers B and C incorrect.

In s. 3A(2), an offence is committed if a person supplies or offers to supply any article *believing* that it is likely to be used to commit, or assist in the commission of, an offence. MILES again does not commit an offence as he does not hold this belief. COOPER commits the offence in these circumstances.

General Police Duties, para. 3.13.5.6

Answer 13.4

Answer **A** — The Data Protection Act 2018 is intended to provide a comprehensive legal framework for data protection in the United Kingdom, setting standards for protecting personal data, in accordance with the General Data Protection Regulation (EU) 2016/679 ('GDPR'). The GDPR forms part of the data protection regime alongside the 2018 Act.

The Data Protection Act 2018, s. 2, as amended by the Data Protection, Privacy and Electronic Communications (Amendments etc) (EU Exit) Regulations 2019 (SI 2019/419) states:

(1) The UK GDPR and this Act protect individuals with regard to the processing of personal data, in particular by—
  (a) requiring personal data to be processed lawfully and fairly, on the basis of the data subject's consent or another specified basis,
  (b) conferring rights on the data subject to obtain information about the processing of personal data and to require inaccurate personal data to be rectified, and
  (c) conferring functions on the Commissioner, giving the holder of that office responsibility for monitoring and enforcing their provisions.

Personal data shall be processed lawfully, fairly and in a transparent manner in relation to the data subject (Article 6).

'Personal data' means any information relating to an identified or identifiable living individual.

'Identifiable living individual' means a living individual who can be identified, directly or indirectly, in particular by reference to—

(a) an identifier such as a name, an identification number, location data or an online identifier, or
(b) one or more factors specific to the physical, physiological, genetic, mental, economic, cultural or social identity of the individual.

(Article 2a of the GDPR.)

General Police Duties, paras 3.13.6, 3.13.6.1

Answer 13.5

Answer **C** — Under s. 1(1)(a) of the Malicious Communications Act 1988, a person commits an offence if he/she sends to another person a letter, electronic communication or article of any description which conveys:

(i)   a message which is indecent or grossly offensive;
(ii) a threat; or
(iii) information which is false and known or believed to be false by the sender; ...

The offence is not restricted to threatening or indecent communications and can include giving false information therefore answer A is incorrect. Answer B is incorrect as the offence is not restricted to electronic communications.

It must be shown that one of the sender's purposes in so doing is to cause distress or anxiety, which may be intended towards the recipient or any other person (correct answer C).

The offence can be committed by using someone else unconnected to the situation to send, deliver or transmit a message and is complete when the message is 'sent'—it does not need to be received by the victim so answer D is incorrect.

General Police Duties, para. 3.13.9

Answer 13.6

Answer **D** — The wording of the statutory defence has been changed (by the Criminal Justice and Police Act 2001) to make the relevant test objective. It will no longer be enough that the person claiming the defence under s. 1(2) believed that he/she had reasonable grounds; the defendant will have to show that:

- there were in fact reasonable grounds for making the demand;
- he/she believed that the accompanying threat was a proper means of enforcing the demand; and
- reasonable grounds existed for that belief.

Answer D contains the only correct combination; therefore, answers A, B and C are incorrect.

General Police Duties, para. 3.13.9.1

Answer 13.7

Answer **B** — Section 127 of the Communications Act 2003 contains two separate offences. Under s. 127(1), a person is guilty of an offence if he/she:

  (a) sends by means of a public electronic communications network a message or other matter that is grossly offensive or of an indecent, obscene or menacing character; or
  (b) causes any such message or matter to be so sent.

Since the offence may be committed by sending a message that is grossly offensive *or* of an indecent character, answer A is incorrect.

The offence under subs. (1) is designed to deal with nuisance calls, and the offence is complete when the defendant sends the relevant message or other matter that is, as a matter of fact, indecent, obscene or menacing. There is no need to show intention on the part of the defendant or any resultant distress caused (answer D is therefore incorrect). The offence is complete by simply making an indecent phone call.

The separate offence under s. 127(2) of the Act *does* deal with causing annoyance, inconvenience or needless anxiety to another. Under this section, a person is guilty of an offence when he/she sends or causes a message to be sent by means of a public electronic communications network that he/she knows to be false, or persistently makes use of such a network. However, since the behaviour of the person in this scenario is covered by s. 127(1), the offence is complete and answer C is incorrect.

General Police Duties, para. 3.13.10

Answer 13.8

Answer **A** — The Malicious Communications Act 1988, s. 1 states:

(1) Any person who sends to another person—
   (a) a letter, electronic communication or article of any description which conveys—
      (i) a message which is indecent or grossly offensive;
      (ii) a threat; or
      (iii) information which is false and known or believed to be false by the sender; or
   (b) any article or electronic communication which is, in whole or part, of an indecent or grossly offensive nature,
   is guilty of an offence if his purpose, or one of his purposes, in sending it is that it should, so far as falling within paragraph (a) or (b) above, cause distress or anxiety to the recipient or to any other person to whom he intends that it or its contents or nature should be communicated.

In addition to letters, the above offence also covers any article; it also covers electronic communications which include any oral or other communication by means of an electronic communications network. This will extend to communications in electronic form such as emails, text messages, pager messages, social media etc. (s. 1(2A)).

Answer B is incorrect as whilst there is a provision for the message to be indecent or grossly offensive, it is not the only provision. The message can be a threat or false. Answer D is incorrect as there is no requirement for a course of conduct to be carried out. Answer A is correct and C incorrect as the threats can be conveyed either by article (the letter) or by electronic communication, which includes the use of social media.

General Police Duties, para. 3.13.9

Answer 13.9

Answer **B** — The Regulation of Investigatory Powers (Directed Surveillance and Covert Human Intelligence Sources) Order 2010 (SI 2010/521, as amended by SI

2013/2788) prescribes the ranks of those within the police service in England and Wales who can authorise a CHIS. In most cases, the relevant rank of an authorising officer for a CHIS is a superintendent and above. However, in urgent cases where it is not reasonably practicable to have the application considered by someone of that rank in the same organisation, an inspector may generally give the relevant authorisation (sch. 1, part 1 of the 2010 Order).

In the case of a juvenile CHIS, the authorisation must come from an assistant chief constable or commander who will give the authority in writing for a maximum of four months beginning on the day the authorisation is granted which makes B the correct answer.

General Police Duties, para. 3.13.7.4

Answer 13.10

Answer **B** — The Fire and Rescue Services Act 2004, s. 49 states:

(1) A person commits an offence if he knowingly gives or causes to be given a false alarm of fire to a person acting on behalf of a fire and rescue authority.

The offence requires proof that the defendant acted 'knowingly' (as opposed to e.g. mistakenly). The offence clearly applies where someone makes a malicious call to a fire and rescue authority. However, the wording 'causes to be given' potentially covers the making of a false report to a body other than a fire and rescue authority, for example the police, if the person knew that this would result in the police passing that call to the relevant fire and rescue authority.

Therefore the correct answer is B. WALDER may have committed an offence as the wording allows for a circumstance whereby the person knows that a report will be made to the relevant fire and rescue authority. Answers A and C are incorrect as SIMM would be reporting the fire in the belief that a fire was in fact alight in the office. SIMM would therefore not believe that he was making a false report. Answer D is incorrect as for this offence there is no requirement to cause distress.

General Police Duties, para. 3.13.10.1

Answer 13.11

Answer **B** — Article 8 of the European Convention on Human Rights states:

1. Everyone has the right to respect for his private and family life, his home and his correspondence.
2. There shall be no interference by a public authority with the exercise of this right except such as is in accordance with the law and is necessary in a democratic society

in the interests of national security, public safety or the economic wellbeing of the country, for the prevention of disorder or crime, for the protection of health or morals, or for the protection of the rights and freedoms of others.

The provisions of Article 8 extend a right to respect for a person's correspondence (as well as their private life, family life and home). Answer C is therefore incorrect.

Whilst the main aim of the Article is to protect these features of a person's life from arbitrary interference by 'public authorities', the State *does* have a positive obligation to prevent others from interfering with an individual's right to his/her private and family life (*Stjerna* v *Finland* (1994) 24 EHRR 194), and this duty extends beyond simply maintaining public safety. Answers A and D are therefore incorrect.

General Police Duties, para. 3.13.2

Answer 13.12

Answer **B** — An offence under s. 1 of the Computer Misuse Act 1990 is committed by causing a computer to perform a function, which means more than simply looking at material on a screen (answer A is incorrect). Any attempt to log on would involve getting the computer to perform a function (correct answer B as that is when the offence is first committed).

General Police Duties, para. 3.13.5.1

Answer 13.13

Answer **C** — Under s. 3(1) of the Computer Misuse Act 1990, a person is guilty of an offence if they do any unauthorised act in relation to a computer and at the time they do the act they know that it is unauthorised; and either subs. (2) or subs. (3) applies.

Under subs. (2), the person must *intend* by doing the act:

(a) to impair the operation of any computer;
(b) to prevent or hinder access to any program or data held in any computer; or
(c) to impair the operation of any such program or the reliability of any such data.

This section is designed to ensure that adequate provision is made to criminalise all forms of denial-of-service attacks in which the attacker denies the victim(s) access to a particular resource, typically by preventing legitimate users of a service accessing that service. An example of this is where a former employee, acting on a grudge, impaired the operation of a company's computer by using a program to generate and send five million emails to the company (*DPP* v *Lennon* [2006] EWHC 1201 (Admin)).

Section 3(3) of the Act states that this subsection also applies if the person is *reckless* as to whether the act will do any of the things mentioned in paras (a) to (c) of subs. (2) above. Therefore, the offence can be committed by a person who intends or is reckless as to whether the program is impaired and answer B is incorrect.

There is no requirement to prove an intent to cause an economic loss to the company, and therefore answer A is incorrect.

An 'unauthorised act' can include a series of acts, and a reference to impairing, preventing or hindering something includes a reference to doing so temporarily (s. 3(5)), and therefore answer D is incorrect.

General Police Duties, para. 3.13.5.4

Answer 13.14

Answer **B** — Special safeguards apply in relation to juveniles and vulnerable individuals. Juveniles are those under 18 years of age (making answer A incorrect). On no occasion should the use or conduct of a CHIS under 16 years of age be authorised to give information against *his/her parents or any person who has parental responsibility for him/her*. In other cases, authorisations should not be granted unless the special provisions contained in the Regulation of Investigatory Powers (Juveniles) (Amendment) Order 2018 (SI 2018/715) are satisfied. However, there would be nothing preventing the juvenile in this question providing information about her brother (making answer C incorrect). The time frame for a juvenile CHIS authorisation is four months (making answer D incorrect).

General Police Duties, para. 3.13.7.4

Answer 13.15

Answer **B** — The Regulation of Investigatory Powers (Directed Surveillance and Covert Human Intelligence Sources) Order 2003 (SI 2003/3171), as amended, sets out the relevant roles and ranks of those who can authorise directed surveillance. In the case of the police, the relevant rank will generally be at superintendent level and above, and the authorisation must be in writing except in urgent cases where oral authorisation may be given (s. 43(1)(a)).

Where it is not reasonably practicable to have the application considered by a superintendent or above, having regard to the urgency of the case, then an *inspector may give the relevant authorisation* which will only last 72 hours unless renewed by a superintendent.

Answers A, C and D are therefore incorrect.

General Police Duties, para. 3.13.7.4

Answer 13.16

Answer **C** — If a CHIS authorisation is given orally by a superintendent in an urgent case, it will only last for 72 hours unless renewed.

Answers A, B and D are therefore incorrect.

General Police Duties, para. 3.13.7.4

Answer 13.17

Answer **B** — Surveillance can be carried out in this situation (answers C and D are incorrect) as the Regulation of Investigatory Powers (Extension of Authorisation Provisions: Legal Consultations) Order 2010 (SI 2010/461) provides that directed surveillance carried out in relation to anything taking place on any premises specified in the Order that are being used for the purpose of legal consultations shall be treated as 'intrusive surveillance' (making answer A incorrect). 'Any premises' includes prisons, police stations, high-security psychiatric hospitals, the place of business of any professional legal adviser and any place used for the sittings and business of any court, tribunal, inquest or inquiry.

General Police Duties, para. 3.13.7.9

Answer 13.18

Answer **D** — The Covert Surveillance and Property Interference Code of Practice, Chapter 2, provides guidance on what is intrusive surveillance. Intrusive surveillance is covert surveillance that is carried out in relation to anything taking place on residential premises or in any private vehicle, and that involves the presence of an individual on the premises or in the vehicle, or is carried out by means of a surveillance device. Intrusive surveillance applies to vehicles as well as premises and answer B is therefore incorrect.

In *R v Plunkett* [2013] EWCA Crim 261, in admitting evidence of statements and admissions by the accused in a police van which were covertly recorded, it was held that a police van is not a private vehicle for the purposes of s. 26(3) and that the authorisation given by a superintendent under s. 28 of the Regulation of Investigatory Powers Act 2000 (RIPA) for directed surveillance was appropriate. Answer A is therefore incorrect.

The definition of surveillance as intrusive relates to the location of the surveillance and not any other consideration of the nature of the information that is expected to be obtained (see Code para. 2.12) or the method of obtaining the information. Answer C is therefore incorrect.

General Police Duties, para. 3.13.7.9

Answer 13.19

Answer **A** — The Covert Surveillance and Property Interference Code of Practice, Chapter 2, provides guidance on what is intrusive surveillance and states:

> 2.11 Intrusive surveillance is covert surveillance that is carried out in relation to anything taking place on residential premises or in any private vehicle, and that involves the presence of an individual on the premises or in the vehicle or is carried out by means of a surveillance device.

'Residential premises' are considered to be so much of any premises as is for the time being occupied or used by any person, however temporarily, for residential purposes or otherwise as living accommodation. This specifically includes hotel or prison accommodation that is so occupied or used (s. 48(1)). Answer C is therefore incorrect.

However, common areas (such as hotel dining areas) to which a person has access in connection with their use or occupation of accommodation are specifically excluded (s. 48(7)). Answer B is incorrect.

It is irrelevant for these purposes what kind of device the police intend to use to gather evidence; it is either intrusive surveillance according to the guidelines or it is not. Answer D is therefore incorrect.

General Police Duties, para. 3.13.7.9

14 | Offences Against the Administration of Justice and Public Interest

---

QUESTIONS

Question 14.1

REYNOLDS is an expert witness employed by a defence team in relation to a charge of causing death by dangerous driving. He is asked by the prosecution, whilst giving evidence, whether in his expert opinion the damage caused to the bottom of the car could have been caused by the vehicle being driven too quickly along the rough unmade road. He states that in his opinion it could not have been caused by driving too quickly; although he does actually believe it could have been caused by excess speed, he did not want to affect the defence as he was called as a defence witness.

In these circumstances, has REYNOLDS committed perjury?

A Yes, he has made a statement he knows to be false or believes not to be true.

B Yes, he has made a statement he knows to be false or believes not to be true and did so with the intent of misleading the court.

C No, as he was asked for an opinion and as an expert witness he is entitled to give an opinion.

D No, as the damage to the car would not be a material fact as the cause of the damage could only be a matter of opinion.

Question 14.2

CLANCY has been charged with committing a robbery which he denies; he asks his sister to provide an alibi for him stating that he was with her at the time of the offence. His sister is very suspicious about whether CLANCY did commit the robbery or not but does not believe he actually did it. She provides an alibi for him; however, she is not believed and the prosecution goes ahead.

Has CLANCY's sister committed an offence of assisting an offender contrary to s. 4 of the Criminal Law Act 1967?

A Yes, as she has committed an act with intent to impede his prosecution.

B Yes, as she has committed an act with intent to impede his prosecution and she has suspicion that he did actually commit the offence.

C No, as she did not know or believe him to be guilty of the offence; mere suspicion is not enough.

D No, as an offence has to have been committed and CLANCY denies committing the offence.

Question 14.3

PARLING has been giving alibi evidence in court on behalf of the defendant, AMOS, who is a very close friend of his. AMOS is on trial for an offence of aggravated burglary and states that he was not the offender. PARLING has been lawfully sworn and states that AMOS was with him in a different county on a fishing trip on the date of the offence. PARLING knows that if police make checks in relation to ANPR that his vehicle will be in the area he states, this is because he was there fishing. PARLING, however, was along. The police believe he is not telling the truth and saying the defendant was with him when he was not. The police believe PARLING is committing perjury.

Which of the following is correct in relation to the offence of perjury?

A The statement must be false and the defendant must know it is false but no further corroboration is required.

B The statement must be false and the defendant must intend it to be false; no further corroboration is required.

C The statement must be false and corroboration that the defendant knew it to be false is required.

D The statement must be false and corroboration that the statement is false is required.

Question 14.4

SCHUMANN contacts police to state that he is a witness to a murder. He did see the suspect in the area but he makes up several facts that cause the police to make inquiries that are not necessary. However, whilst engaged on one of these unnecessary inquiries, they actually obtain definitive evidence against the suspect.

Which of the following statements is true in relation to wasting police time?

A SCHUMANN is guilty of wasting police time as he caused several hours of wasted time.

B SCHUMANN is guilty of wasting police time as he caused wasteful employment of the police.

C SCHUMANN is not guilty of wasting police time as he did provide some useful information, i.e. seeing the suspect in the area.

D SCHUMANN is not guilty of wasting police time; as a result of information he gave, actual evidence was obtained.

Question 14.5

MILLIGAN has been charged with robbery and his brother believes that FRANKS has been a witness against him. In fact this is incorrect as, although he was interviewed, FRANKS could provide no material evidence. MILLIGAN's brother sends an email to FRANKS stating that he and his family will be in danger as he gave evidence against MILLIGAN.

Has an offence of harming witnesses contrary to s. 40 of the Criminal Justice and Police Act 2001 been committed?

A Yes, provided MILLIGAN's brother believes that FRANKS has been a witness against MILLIGAN.

B Yes, provided MILLIGAN's brother suspects that FRANKS has been a witness against MILLIGAN.

C No, as FRANKS has not in fact been a witness against MILLIGAN.

D No, no actual harm has been caused; as this is a threat, it will amount to witness intimidation contrary to s. 39 of the 2001 Act.

Question 14.6

SUMMERS is an accredited Police Community Support Officer (PCSO) and is dealing with ARTHURS for a fixed penalty offence. He requires ARTHURS to provide his name and address. ARTHURS refuses and SUMMERS exercises his power of detention as provided by sch. 4 to the Police Reform Act 2002. ARTHURS is less than impressed at this, and pushes the PCSO over and makes good his escape.

Consider the offence at common law of escaping. Which of the following is correct?

A ARTHURS has committed this offence; the offence is complete.
B ARTHURS has committed this offence provided he remains at liberty for at least 24 hours.
C ARTHURS has not committed this offence as it relates to escaping from prisons etc.
D ARTHURS has not committed this offence as it relates to lawful custody, i.e. by a police officer.

Question 14.7

RUDDOCK picks up a hammer and uses it to assault O'CONNELL. He then runs out of the shop where the assault took place and bumps into a neighbour who knows who RUDDOCK is. Thinking he will be able to identify him, he tells the neighbour to 'Keep your nose out if your missus wants to keep her good looks'. The neighbour is confused as he has no idea what has happened, but he is worried nevertheless.

In relation to witness intimidation (under s. 51 of the Criminal Justice and Public Order Act 1994), which of the following is correct?
A This is witness intimidation as it is intended that the investigation be obstructed.
B This is witness intimidation as an offence has taken place and the neighbour may well be a witness.
C This is not witness intimidation as an investigation has not commenced.
D This is not witness intimidation as the neighbour is unaware what the threat is about.

Question 14.8

HAZELL attended a police station and made an allegation of rape against a taxi driver, whom she stated had driven her home the previous evening. HAZELL said that she did not know the identity of the person who raped her and could not describe the taxi or the driver as she had been extremely intoxicated at the time. The police spent the next two days investigating the incident, but HAZELL later told them that she had made up the story because she had been late going home that night and she had a jealous boyfriend.

Would HAZELL's actions amount to an offence against the administration of justice and public interest in these circumstances?
A No, because a course of justice had not commenced before HAZELL made the allegation.

B No, because HAZELL did not identify any individual who may have been arrested or inconvenienced by her statement.

C Yes, HAZELL's conduct could amount to perverting the course of justice as there were possible consequences of detention, arrest, charge or prosecution.

D Yes, this could amount to an offence of wasting police time as over 24 hours' police time had been used, but it could never be perverting the course of justice.

Question 14.9

LEGG has been convicted of theft at Crown Court and given a custodial sentence. A private security company is responsible for transporting detainees to the local prison. Whilst en route to the prison, BRANDRICK rams the prison van with his Transit van and then overpowers the guards. Subsequently he assists LEGG to escape by unlocking his cell on the prison van.

In relation to the offence of assisting escape contrary to s. 39 of the Prison Act 1952, which of the following is true in respect of BRANDRICK's actions?

A He commits the offence when he rams the prison van with the intention of assisting the escape.

B He commits the offence only where he physically assisted the escape by unlocking the cell.

C He does not commit the offence as it relates only to escape from police or prison transport not from a private security company.

D He does not commit this offence as it does not relate to prisoners in transit to or from prison.

Question 14.10

ALBON has committed an armed robbery and is looking to avoid detection by the police. ALBON asks his friend to help him avoid arrest, telling him that he is wanted for theft. His friend agrees to hide him for a few days, and does so.

Has an offence of assisting an offender been committed by the friend in these circumstances?

A Yes, provided the friend's action actually delayed the arrest of ALBON.

B Yes, as his friend's actions were intended to hinder the arrest of ALBON.

C No, as the friend did not know or believe that ALBON was wanted for the more serious offence.

D No, as the friend has not lied to the police or taken any positive steps to impede his arrest.

Question 14.11

DEXTER had his motorbike stolen and reported it to the police. A short time later he received information that John GRIMES was riding round on the motorbike. DEXTER went to see John GRIMES. When he attended at the house he saw the motorbike in the front garden, undamaged. Alan GRIMES (the father of John GRIMES) walks out of the house and when confronted about the fact that his son had stolen the motorbike, offers to give DEXTER some free parts for the bike if he doesn't report it to the police. DEXTER accepts the free parts and only tells the police that he has found his motorbike and it was undamaged.

Has DEXTER committed an offence of concealing a relevant offence contrary to s. 5 of the Criminal Law Act 1967?

A Yes, as he has agreed to accept free parts for his silence.

B Yes, as he has agreed to accept the free parts for his silence which goes beyond reasonable compensation.

C No, as the agreement he reached was not with the person who stole the motorbike.

D No, as free parts for the bike would be seen as reasonable consideration.

ANSWERS

Answer 14.1

Answer **A** — Section 1(1) of the Perjury Act 1911 states:

> If any person lawfully sworn as a witness or as an interpreter in a judicial proceeding wilfully makes a statement material in that proceeding, which he knows to be false or does not believe to be true, he shall be guilty of perjury ...

To prove perjury, you must also show that the defendant knew the statement to be false or did not believe it to be true. There is no intent with this offence and it is committed in the conditions described; answer B is therefore incorrect.

Evidence of an opinion provided by a witness who does not genuinely hold such an opinion may also be perjury. This is true even where it is 'expert opinion'. It would be perjury if that opinion was one he/she knew to be false or did not believe to be true; answer C is therefore incorrect. 'Wilful' means deliberate or intentional (*R v Senior* [1899] 1 QB 283) and it must be proved that any alleged perjury was not the result of a misunderstanding or an accidental slip of the tongue (*R v Millward* [1985] QB 519). It could also involve being reckless as to whether or not the statement was true (*R (On the Application of Purvis) v DPP* [2020] EWHC 3573 (Admin)).

A 'statement material in that proceeding' means that the content of the evidence tendered in that case must have some importance to it and not just be of passing relevance. Would damage caused by excessive speed be material in a driving offence? Answer D is therefore incorrect.

General Police Duties, para. 3.14.2

Answer 14.2

Answer **C** — Section 4 of the Criminal Law Act 1967 states:

> (1) Where a person has committed a relevant offence, any other person who, knowing or believing him to be guilty of the offence or of some other relevant offence, does without lawful authority or reasonable excuse any act with intent to impede his apprehension or prosecution shall be guilty of an offence.
>
> (1A) In this section and section 5 below, 'relevant offence' means—
>   (a) an offence for which the sentence is fixed by law,
>   (b) an offence for which a person of 18 years or over (not previously convicted) may be sentenced to imprisonment for a term of five years (or might be so

sentenced but for the restrictions imposed by section 33 of the Magistrates' Courts Act 1980).

It must be shown that the defendant knew or believed the person to be guilty of that, or some other relevant, offence. Mere suspicion, however strong, that the 'assisted' person had committed a relevant offence will not be enough; answers A and B are therefore incorrect.

Merely denying an offence has been committed is not enough to say it has not; once charged, the offence would be said to have been committed. If this were not the case, then this offence would be ineffective as everyone would deny the offence! Answer D is therefore incorrect.

General Police Duties, para. 3.14.7

Answer 14.3

Answer **D** — Section 1 of the Perjury Act 1911 states:

(1) If any person lawfully sworn as a witness or as an interpreter in a judicial proceeding wilfully makes a statement material in that proceeding, which he knows to be false or does not believe to be true, he shall be guilty of perjury ...

(2) The expression 'judicial proceeding' includes a proceeding before any court, tribunal, or person having by law power to hear, receive, and examine evidence on oath.

(3) Where a statement made for the purposes of a judicial proceeding is not made before the tribunal itself, but is made on oath before a person authorised by law to administer an oath to the person who makes the statement, and to record or authenticate the statement, it shall, for the purposes of this section, be treated as having been made in a judicial proceeding.

Perjury requires a statement to be made that the defendant knew to be false or did not believe it to be true and to make the statement deliberately or intentionally. Corroboration is required in cases of perjury (Perjury Act 1911, s. 13); answers A and B are therefore incorrect. It is required solely in relation to the falsity of the defendant's statement. There is no requirement under s. 13 for corroboration of the fact that the defendant actually made the alleged statement or that he/she knew or believed it to be untrue; answer C is therefore incorrect. However, that corroboration can be documentary and may even come from the defendant's earlier conduct (*R* v *Threlfall* (1914) 10 Cr App R 112).

General Police Duties, para. 3.14.2

Answer 14.4

Answer **B** — Section 5 of the Criminal Law Act 1967 states:

(2) Where a person causes any wasteful employment of the police by knowingly making to any person a false report tending to show that an offence has been committed, or to give rise to apprehension for the safety of any persons or property, or tending to show that he has information material to any police inquiry, he shall be liable ...

It is widely thought that there is a minimum number of hours which must be wasted before a prosecution can be brought for this offence. There is no reliable authority on this point; answer A is therefore incorrect.

The fact that SCHUMANN gave some evidence, or by luck the police actually obtained evidence, is immaterial to the fact that he wasted police time by giving a false report; answers C and D are therefore incorrect.

General Police Duties, para. 3.14.10

Answer 14.5

Answer **A** — Section 40 of the Criminal Justice and Police Act 2001 deals with acts which harm or threaten to harm a potential witness; answer D is therefore incorrect. This offence refers to someone who has been (or is believed to have been) a witness in relevant proceedings—'believes' not 'suspects'; answer B is therefore incorrect.

As it relates to witnesses and those believed to have been witnesses it is irrelevant whether they were a witness or not; answer C is therefore incorrect.

General Police Duties, para. 3.14.6

Answer 14.6

Answer **A** — This offence applies to persons in lawful custody, anywhere. It is not restricted to custody units, prison etc. Answer C is therefore incorrect. Whether a person is 'in custody' or not is a question of fact and the word 'custody' is to be given its ordinary meaning (*E v DPP* [2002] EWHC 433 (Admin)). This could be shown by providing evidence that the person's liberty was restricted (as it is in the question) and that it was lawful (sch. 4 to the 2002 Act provides this). This custody is not restricted to sworn police officers and would include police community support officers (PCSOs), investigating officers or escort officers (who are given powers by the 2002 Act); answer D is therefore incorrect. The offence of escaping is completed immediately that liberty is obtained and is not subject to time restrictions on such liberty; therefore, answer B is incorrect.

General Police Duties, para. 3.14.9

Answer 14.7

Answer **C** — Section 51 of the Criminal Justice and Public Order Act 1994 states:

(1) A person commits an offence if—
    (a) he does an act which intimidates, and is intended to intimidate, another person ('the victim'),
    (b) he does the act knowing or believing that the victim is assisting in the investigation of an offence or is a witness or potential witness or a juror or potential juror in proceedings for an offence, and
    (c) he does it intending thereby to cause the investigation or the course of justice to be obstructed, perverted or interfered with.

(2) A person commits an offence if—
    (a) he does an act which harms, and is intended to harm, another person or, intending to cause another person to fear harm, he threatens to do an act which would harm that other person,
    (b) he does or threatens to do the act knowing or believing that the person harmed or threatened to be harmed ('the victim'), or some other person, has assisted in an investigation into an offence or has given evidence or particular evidence in proceedings for an offence, or has acted as a juror or concurred in a particular verdict in proceedings for an offence, and
    (c) he does or threatens to do it because of that knowledge or belief.

What is important, then, is the knowledge and belief that the person threatened is assisting in the investigation of an offence or is a witness or potential witness or a juror or potential juror in proceedings for an offence, and that the belief must have some substance to it. In this particular scenario, a threat has been made; however, it would not fit within the criteria for this offence; answers A and B are therefore incorrect.

It is immaterial what the victim feels. The offence could be made out even if the victim was not actually in fear; answer D is therefore incorrect.

General Police Duties, para. 3.14.5.1

Answer 14.8

Answer **C** — It is an offence at common law to do an act tending and intended to pervert the course of public justice. 'The course of public justice' includes the process of criminal investigation (*R v Rowell* [1978] 1 WLR 132)—it is not necessary that an investigation has commenced before the person makes a false complaint, such as the one previously. Answer A is therefore incorrect.

The conduct referred to in the scenario *may* amount to an offence of wasting police time (contrary to s. 5 of the Criminal Law Act 1967), although contrary to popular belief there is no minimum number of hours which must be wasted before a prosecution can be brought for this offence. However, it has also been held to amount to perverting the course of justice (*R v Goodwin* (1989) 11 Cr App R (S) 194, where a false allegation of rape was made to the police). Answer D is therefore incorrect.

Where a person makes a false allegation to the police justifying a criminal investigation with the possible consequences of detention, arrest, charge or prosecution, and that person intends that the allegation be taken seriously, the offence of perverting the course of justice is *prima facie* made out. This will be the case whether or not the allegation is capable of identifying specific individuals (*R v Cotter* [2002] 2 Cr App R 29, a case involving the boyfriend of a well-known black Olympic athlete who falsely claimed to have been attacked as part of a racist campaign). Answer B is therefore incorrect.

General Police Duties, para. 3.14.4

Answer 14.9

Answer **D** — Section 39 of the Prison Act 1952 states:

(1) A person who—
    (a) assists a prisoner in escaping or attempting to escape from a prison, or
    (b) intending to facilitate the escape of a prisoner—
        (i) brings, throws or otherwise conveys anything into a prison,
        (ii) causes another person to bring, throw or otherwise convey anything into a prison, or
        (iii) gives anything to a prisoner or leaves anything in any place (whether inside or outside a prison),
    is guilty of an offence.

The wording of the section seems to indicate that it only relates to 'escaping' from a prison, and this was verified by the Court of Appeal in *R v Moss and Harte* (1986) 82 Cr App R 116, where it was held that the offence under s. 39 of the 1952 Act does not apply to a prisoner who escapes while in transit to or from prison; answers A, B and C are therefore incorrect.

General Police Duties, para. 3.14.9

Answer 14.10

Answer **B** — For there to be an offence under s. 4 of the Criminal Law Act 1967 (assisting offenders), there must first have been a relevant offence committed by someone. That relevant offence must, in the case of this offence, have been committed by the 'assisted' person, in this case armed robbery.

The defendant can commit the offence before the person he/she has assisted is convicted of committing the relevant offence.

It must be shown that the defendant knew or believed the person to be guilty of that, or some other relevant, offence. Therefore, if the defendant believed that the 'assisted' person had committed a robbery when in fact he/she had committed a theft, that mistaken part of the defendant's belief will not prevent a conviction for this offence; answer C is therefore incorrect.

The relevant offences are:

(a) an offence for which the sentence is fixed by law,
(b) an offence for which a person of 18 years or over (not previously convicted) may be sentenced to imprisonment for a term of five years (or might be so sentenced but for the restrictions imposed by s. 33 of the Magistrates' Courts Act 1980).

This offence must involve some positive act by the defendant; simply doing or saying nothing will not suffice. In this case, the positive act of hiding the accused would be enough, irrespective of whether that actually delayed that person's arrest; answers A and D are therefore incorrect.

General Police Duties, para. 3.14.7

Answer 14.11

Answer **B** — Section 5 of the Criminal Law Act 1967 states:

(1) Where a person has committed a relevant offence, any other person who, knowing or believing that the offence or some other relevant offence has been committed, and that he has information which might be of material assistance in securing the prosecution or conviction of an offender for it, accepts or agrees to accept for not disclosing that information any consideration other than the making good of loss or injury caused by the offence, or the making of reasonable compensation for that loss or injury, shall be liable …

The main focus of this offence is:

• the acceptance of, or agreement to accept 'consideration' (i.e. anything of value);
• beyond reasonable compensation for loss/injury caused by the relevant offence;
• in exchange for not disclosing material information.

In this scenario, all three points are present so the offence is complete.

The legislation does not state that the agreement has to be with the person who committed the offence, only that one was committed; answer C is therefore incorrect. Had any part on the motorbike been broken or damaged, then the replacement parts may well have been reasonable compensation; however, as this is not the case answer D is therefore incorrect.

There has to be more than just an agreement of silence for the 'consideration', it must go beyond any consideration other than the making good of loss or injury caused by the offence, or the making of reasonable compensation for that loss or injury; answer A is therefore incorrect.

General Police Duties, para. 3.14.8

15 Terrorism and Associated Offences

Question 15.1

The police are investigating MARTINEZ, a member of an extreme animal rights group which, because of its suspected terrorist connections, has recently become a proscribed organisation in the United Kingdom.

Under s. 11 of the Terrorism Act 2000, a person commits an offence if they belong to a proscribed organisation; however, are there any circumstances under which MARTINEZ may claim a defence to this offence?

A Yes, MARTINEZ could claim that the organisation was not proscribed when she became a member.

B Yes, MARTINEZ would have to demonstrate visible evidence that she ceased to be a member of the organisation as soon as it was proscribed.

C Yes, MARTINEZ could claim that the organisation was not proscribed when she became a member *or* she has not taken part in the activities of the organisation at any time since it was proscribed.

D Yes, MARTINEZ could claim that the organisation was not proscribed when she became a member *and* she has not taken part in the activities of the organisation at any time since it was proscribed.

Question 15.2

CHARTERIS lived in a flat in London and believed that the person living in the opposite flat was a wanted terrorist. CHARTERIS's belief was based on a picture released by the police of a person who escaped after attempting to blow up a bus. CHARTERIS is too scared to contact the authorities.

Could CHARTERIS commit an offence under s. 38B(2) of the Terrorism Act 2000, by failing to disclose information about the person living in the opposite flat?

A Yes, CHARTERIS must disclose this information to a police officer as soon as reasonably practicable.

B Yes, CHARTERIS must disclose this information to a police officer or a member of Her Majesty's Forces as soon as reasonably practicable.

C No, CHARTERIS did not come into possession of the information through work or employment.

D No, this offence is only committed if a person fails to disclose information about an offence involving the commission, preparation or instigation of an act of terrorism.

Question 15.3

BAY is appearing in the Divisional Court having appealed against a conviction for encouraging acts of terrorism under s. 1(2) of the Terrorism Act 2006. The circumstances of the case were that BAY was accused of uploading videos on YouTube of scenes showing attacks on soldiers of the NATO 'Resolute Support Mission' (RSM) in Afghanistan by members of the Taliban. BAY did not deny posting the videos, but argued that there had been no 'encouragement' in the form of words or a statement and that the videos were not depicting scenes of terrorism since they were showing scenes of a war.

Which of the following statements is correct in relation to the term 'encouragement' in regard to an offence under s. 1(2) of the Terrorism Act 2006?

A Communication without words or any other statement (such as posting a video) would amount to 'encouragement' under the Act and the conviction should be upheld.

B Communication without words or any other statement would amount to 'encouragement'; however, the scenes shown were not depicting scenes of terrorism.

C The defendant has not made an oral 'statement', therefore, this does not amount to 'encouragement'.

D The defendant has not made a 'statement', whether written or otherwise; therefore, this does not amount to 'encouragement'.

Question 15.4

An authorisation is in place under s. 47A of the Terrorism Act 2000. Specific intelligence has been received that a terrorist suspect is going to leave an explosive package in a busy shopping area some time today. The police have decided to evacuate the centre, but an instruction has been given to search every person on their way out of the building.

Which of the following statements is correct in relation to the utilisation of this search power by the police?

A A constable in uniform may only use this power for the purpose of discovering whether the person concerned is a terrorist.

B A constable in uniform may only use this power if he/she reasonably suspects the person concerned is a terrorist.

C A constable in uniform may only use this power if he/she reasonably suspects the search will identify evidence that the person concerned is a terrorist.

D The purpose of the search is irrelevant; once an authorisation is in place under this section, the constable in uniform may simply search any person in the area.

Question 15.5

The police have been investigating five individuals suspected of preparing for acts of terrorism, and intelligence has been received that they are in possession of bomb-making equipment. In the early hours of the morning, their address is cordoned off, following a designation under s. 33 of the Terrorism Act 2000. Officers entered the address and arrested four of the five suspects. Intelligence is received that the fifth suspect is at an address—a nearby block of four flats—which was previously unknown to the investigation team. While an arrest team is en route to the address, further intelligence is received that the fifth person is in possession of the bomb-making equipment. Inspector BENSON has contacted the operational commander, Chief Inspector CAWLEY, and asked for authorisation to cordon off the new location immediately. Inspector BENSON has asked that the block of flats be included in the authorisation so that other residents may be removed from any danger presented by the bomb-making equipment.

Which of the following statements is correct in relation to an urgent authorisation under s. 33 of the Terrorism Act 2000?

A Chief Inspector CAWLEY does not have the power to make such a designation urgently, only a superintendent may do so in these circumstances.

B Inspector BENSON could make such a designation if it is required as a matter of urgency.

C The designation must be made by a superintendent unless there are reasonable grounds to suspect that an act of terrorism is about to take place in the locality.

D Inspector BENSON could make such a designation if it is required as a matter of urgency. However, the power relates to the removal of vehicles or pedestrians and not to people in dwellings.

Question 15.6

Information is received that there is a suspicious unattended bag left at the gateway to a park. PC HITCH (an officer in uniform) attends the scene and examines the bag from a safe distance. She is concerned about the contents of the bag and so specialist officers and equipment are called to establish its contents. Inspector SUTHERLAND (PC HITCH's supervisor) makes her way to the scene and, after being briefed by PC HITCH, considers that it would be expedient for the purposes of a terrorist investigation to designate a cordon (under the Terrorism Act 2000).

Which of the following statements is correct in respect of any such designation (under s. 34) and use of the power (under s. 36 of the Act)?

A PC HITCH would not be able to designate a cordon under any circumstances.

B Inspector SUTHERLAND may make a designation if she considers it necessary by reason of urgency.

C The powers available under s. 36 can be exercised by police officers in plain clothes.

D The maximum duration of such a designation will be 72 hours.

ANSWERS

Answer 15.1

Answer **D** — Under s. 11(1) of the Terrorism Act 2000, a person commits an offence if they belong to a proscribed organisation. It is a defence for a person charged with an offence under subs. (1) to prove:

(a) that the organisation was not proscribed on the last (or only) occasion on which he became a member or began to profess to be a member, *and*
(b) that he has not taken part in the activities of the organisation at any time while it was proscribed.

The defence is available for a person who can demonstrate *both* elements (a) and (b); therefore, answers A, B and C are incorrect.

General Police Duties, para. 3.15.2.1

Answer 15.2

Answer **A** — Section 38B of the Terrorism Act 2000 states:

(1) This section applies where a person has information which he knows or believes might be of material assistance—
   (a) in preventing the commission by another person of an act of terrorism, or
   (b) in securing the apprehension, prosecution or conviction of another person, in the United Kingdom, for an offence involving the commission, preparation or instigation of an act of terrorism.

A person commits an offence if he/she does not disclose the information as soon as reasonably practicable (s. 38B(2)). This would include disclosing information which would lead to the arrest of a person for an offence involving the commission, preparation or instigation of an act of terrorism, and therefore answer D is incorrect.

In England, Wales or Scotland, disclosure must be made to a constable, whereas in Northern Ireland, disclosure must be made to a constable or a member of Her Majesty's Forces (s. 38B(3)). Answer B is therefore incorrect.

Section 19 of the Act places a statutory duty on people who form a suspicion about terrorism offences, based on information that comes to their attention in the course of their employment. However, this is not the case for disclosure under s. 38B. Answer C is therefore incorrect.

Note that it is a defence for a person charged with an offence under s. 38B(2) to prove that they had a reasonable excuse for not making the disclosure (s. 38B(4)).

General Police Duties, para. 3.15.4.3

Answer 15.3

Answer **A** — An offence may be committed under s. 1(2) of the Terrorism Act 2006 when a person publishes a statement to encourage the commission, preparation or instigation of acts of terrorism or Convention offences ('Convention offences' include those in relation to explosives, biological weapons, chemical weapons, nuclear weapons, hostage-taking, hijacking, terrorist funds etc.).

Section 3(1) provides that the offence can be committed by publishing a statement electronically, i.e. via the internet and 'statement' includes a communication of any description, including a communication without words consisting of sounds or images or both (s. 20(6)). Answers C and D are therefore incorrect.

In *R v Gul* [2013] UKSC 64, the defendant's conviction was upheld by the Divisional Court after he had uploaded videos to the internet of scenes showing attacks on soldiers of the Coalition forces in Iraq and Afghanistan by insurgents. The court held that the videos *were* depicting scenes of terrorism within the definition of s. 1 of the Terrorism Act 2000, and therefore answer B is incorrect.

General Police Duties, para. 3.15.5.1

Answer 15.4

Answer **A** — Under s. 47A of the Terrorism Act 2000, a senior police officer may give an authorisation for searches to take place in a specified area or place. An authorisation under this section authorises any constable in uniform to stop and search vehicles and pedestrians.

A constable in uniform may exercise the power conferred by an authorisation only for the purpose of discovering whether there is anything which may constitute evidence that the vehicle concerned is being used for the purposes of terrorism or (as the case may be) that the person concerned is a terrorist within the meaning of s. 40 (s. 47A(4)). Answer D is incorrect—the purpose of the search *is* relevant, it must be to discover if the person is a terrorist or the vehicle is being used for terrorist activities.

However, the power conferred by such an authorisation may be exercised whether or not the constable reasonably suspects that there is such evidence on the person (s. 47A(5)). Answers B and C are therefore incorrect.

General Police Duties, para. 3.15.6.4

Answer 15.5

Answer **B** — Section 33 of the Terrorism Act 2000 provides the power to cordon off areas. Generally, the power to make such a designation is limited to a police officer who is of at least the rank of superintendent (s. 34(1)). However, s. 34(2) states that a constable who is not of the rank required by subs. (1) may make a designation if he/she considers it necessary by reason of urgency. Answer A is therefore incorrect.

Section 33(2) states that a designation may be made only if the person making it considers it expedient for the purposes of a terrorist investigation. Neither of these sections requires the authorising officer to have reasonable grounds to believe that an act of terrorism is about to take place in the locality, even if the matter is urgent, and therefore answer C is incorrect.

Section 36(1) of the Act outlines the actions a constable in uniform (or PCSO) may take in a cordoned area. He/she may order a person in a cordoned area to leave it immediately, order the driver or person in charge of a vehicle to move it from the area immediately, remove a vehicle in such an area or prohibit or restrict access to a cordoned area by pedestrians or vehicles. Under s. 36(1)(b), a power is given to order a person *immediately to leave premises which are wholly or partly in or adjacent to a cordoned area*. Answer D is therefore incorrect.

General Police Duties, paras 3.15.7.1 to 3.15.7.3

Answer 15.6

Answer **B** — Section 34(1)(a) of the Terrorism Act 2000 states that a designation under s. 33 (to create a cordon) may only be made by an officer of the rank of at least superintendent. However, s. 34(2) states that a constable who is not of that rank may make a designation if he/she considers it necessary by reason of urgency (making answer A incorrect and answer B correct). Section 34 provides police powers in respect of cordons but these are only available to officers in uniform, making answer C incorrect. Answer D is incorrect as the period of designation begins at the time the order is made and ends on the date specified in the order. The initial designation cannot extend beyond 14 days (s. 35(2)). However, the period during which a designation has effect may be extended in writing from time to time by the person who made it, or an officer of at least superintendent rank (s. 35(3)). There is a time limit of 28 days on extended designations and this appears to mean an overall time limit of 28 days beginning with the day on which the order is made (s. 35(5)).

General Police Duties, paras 3.15.7.1 to 3.15.7.2

16 | Diversity, Equality and Inclusion

QUESTIONS

Question 16.1

Constable LATTON was born female but has since childhood identified as being male. For the past three years, Constable LATTON has self-identified with the pronoun He and has now decided to investigate the options for gender reassignment surgery. He has approached his sergeant and disclosed that he is considering undergoing gender reassignment surgery. However, he is concerned about discrimination and how the operation would affect his work.

In relation to Constable LATTON's concerns, at what point would he be protected by s. 7(1) of the Equality Act 2010 (protected characteristics of gender reassignment)?

A Constable LATTON would be protected by s. 7 when he has undergone the process and returned to work.

B Constable LATTON would be protected by s. 7 when he has undergone the process but before he returns to work.

C Constable LATTON would be protected by s. 7 when he is undergoing or has undergone the process.

D Constable LATTON would be protected by s. 7 when he is proposing to undergo, is undergoing or has undergone the process.

Question 16.2

Constable JONES is a response officer and is the sole carer of his elderly parent, who is 94 years of age. Constable JONES has submitted a flexible working request to the senior management team, which would mean working fewer night shifts but would assist the officer financially due to the cost of carers. The senior management team has rejected the application for operational reasons. Constable JONES is considering taking action against the force for discrimination, citing that the decision of the senior management team is unreasonable.

Which of the following statements would be correct in relation to Constable JONES's potential claim of discrimination?

A Constable JONES would only have to demonstrate that the senior management team's decision was unreasonable in order to succeed with the claim.

B Constable JONES could succeed with the claim by showing that some other hypothetical person would have been treated more favourably.

C Constable JONES would have to demonstrate that some other person was treated more favourably in order to succeed with the claim.

D Constable JONES would have to demonstrate that there would be a tangible or material loss as a result of the decision.

Question 16.3

GRAVETT is a police staff member working in the force Control Room. GRAVETT has been receiving counselling and treatment for depression for a number of years. His GP has recommended a course of medicine which would improve GRAVETT's condition but would mean that he would need a full night's sleep every night. As a shift worker, this would prove difficult for GRAVETT and he has submitted a request to adjust his shifts to finish at 2 am on night shifts instead of 6 am. The request for reasonable adjustments has been rejected due to operational capacity and GRAVETT has now spoken to a solicitor to discuss a claim of discrimination under the Equality Act 2010.

Which of the following statements would be correct in relation to the level of disadvantage GRAVETT must have suffered in order for a claim like this to be successful?

A A tribunal would have to conclude that GRAVETT had been placed at a substantial disadvantage by a failure to make reasonable adjustments.

B A tribunal would conclude that even the slightest disadvantage caused to GRAVETT by a failure to make reasonable adjustments would amount to discrimination.

C The threshold for any disadvantage in such a case is that by a failure to make reasonable adjustments, GRAVETT had been caused some disadvantage.

D A tribunal should not have a specific level of disadvantage in mind when deciding whether or not GRAVETT had suffered discrimination; it should make a decision based on the facts presented.

Question 16.4

LEWIN was profoundly deaf and was a suspect in a drug dealing case. Officers executed a warrant at LEWIN's house and found controlled drugs, for which he was arrested. The team had taken Constable SPEARING with them—a Neighbourhood officer who had had numerous previous dealings with LEWIN and who was confident of being able to communicate the purpose of the search. LEWIN later sued the police for a breach of the Equality Act 2010, on the grounds that they had not provided an interpreter which put him at a substantial disadvantage during the search.

Which of the following statements is correct in relation to LEWIN's claim against the police?

A The claim is out of context; if officers have breached the terms of the Police and Criminal Evidence Act 1984, this is an evidential matter and not an equality issue.

B The Equality Act 2010 applies to operational matters; however, there is no disadvantage if the officers and LEWIN were able to communicate without an interpreter.

C The claim is out of context; the Equality Act 2010 does not apply as this is an operational matter and not an employment issue.

D This is a clear breach of the Equality Act 2010 and LEWIN should succeed with his claim against the police.

Question 16.5

Constable DODD has approached her inspector and disclosed that she believes she is suffering sexual harassment from her sergeant. Constable DODD reported that the sergeant often made remarks about her body in front of other members of the team. In private, he would talk about his sex life and would ask Constable DODD about sexual relationships with her partner. Constable DODD said she had confronted the sergeant about the behaviour and that he had told her that it did not amount to harassment.

What matters should be taken into account in relation to Constable DODD's perception of what had happened during any investigation?

A The investigating officer may take into account Constable DODD's perception of what had happened and compare this to the perception of other members of the team.

B The investigating officer may take into account Constable DODD's perception of what had happened and compare this to the perception of the sergeant.

C The investigating officer must take into account Constable DODD's perception of what had happened, regardless of the perception of other people.

D The investigating officer must take into account Constable DODD's perception of what had happened, depending on the evidence disclosed.

Question 16.6

Constable MELROSE has just started work on a response team in a new area. Officers are aware that before moving to the team, Constable MELROSE had made a complaint of racial discrimination against colleagues on another team and that the complaint had been unsubstantiated. Some officers on Constable MELROSE's new team decided to record problems they encountered with the officer, in fear that they may be the subject of a race discrimination claim at some future date.

Would the officers' behaviour amount to victimisation because of Constable MELROSE's previous complaint?

A Yes, even though the previous complaint was unsubstantiated, this amounts to victimisation.

B Yes, because Constable MELROSE had carried out a 'protected act'.

C No, however, the officers' behaviour could amount to direct discrimination.

D No, the behaviour of the officers concerned would not amount to victimisation in these circumstances.

Question 16.7

Constable AMIR is suing his police force. The claim relates to a failure by the force to allow Constable AMIR time off to attend a number of religious festivals throughout the year. Constable AMIR's line managers have not been cited as the officer understands the pressures of delivering operational policing; however, the claim is made against the force for failing to have policies and procedures in place to account for the religious beliefs of its staff.

Which of the following statements is correct in relation to the liability of the police force under s. 42 of the Equality Act 2010?

A Constable AMIR's line managers and the chief constable may be liable; the responsible authority is only liable for discrimination by members of staff towards people outside the force.

B The chief constable alone may be liable in these circumstances; the responsible authority has no liability under this Act.

C The chief constable and the responsible authority may be liable in these circumstances.
D Constable AMIR's line managers may be liable; the chief constable and the responsible authority are only liable for discrimination by members of staff towards people outside the force.

Question 16.8

MARLER has made a claim of discrimination under the Equality Act 2010 against her local police force. MARLER applied for a post as a PCSO and passed what amounted to a national selection process. However, she was told that although she had passed, there were insufficient posts to take her on at this time and that she would be contacted at a later time should any further vacancies arise. However, MARLER has been told by someone working in the recruitment department that the force had appointed three people from black and minority ethnic backgrounds who had also passed the process but who had scored fewer marks than she had. She had been told this had happened because the force was under-represented in this department by people from black and ethnic minority communities.

Would the behaviour of the force amount to discrimination in employment in these circumstances?
A No, the force can select whom it wants from a pool of people who have passed the process.
B Yes, provided MARLER's performance in the process was better than the people selected ahead of her.
C No, if the force is under-represented by people from black and ethnic minority communities, they can be selected ahead of other candidates provided they passed the process.
D No, provided each candidate was given a fair opportunity to pass the assessment; this is an example of positive action which the force is entitled to undertake.

Question 16.9

Constable STUBBS is currently suing her employers for discrimination in the workplace. She has cited several instances of inappropriate sexual behaviour towards her by her line managers in work. Constable STUBBS has also included evidence in her statement of inappropriate sexual behaviour towards her by work colleagues while they were at a social Christmas function in a nearby public house.

Would Constable STUBBS be able to rely on all of this evidence in her claim of discrimination against her employers?

A Yes, she may be able to rely on this evidence because the function was an extension of the workplace.

B No, but she would have been able to if the behaviour had taken place at an off-duty function at her actual workplace.

C Yes, she may rely on evidence of any inappropriate behaviour, inside or outside the workplace.

D No, her employers cannot be held liable for the behaviour of her colleagues outside the workplace.

ANSWERS

Answer 16.1

Answer **D** — Under s. 7(1) of the Equality Act 2010:

> A person has the protected characteristic of gender reassignment if the person is proposing to undergo, is undergoing or has undergone a process (or part of a process) for the purpose of re-assigning the person's sex by changing physiological or other attributes of sex.

A reference to a transsexual person is a reference to a person who has the protected characteristic of gender reassignment (s. 7(2)).

Since the officer is protected by the Act from the time he is proposing to undergo the operation (effectively now), answers A, B and C are incorrect.

General Police Duties, para. 3.16.3.3

Answer 16.2

Answer **B** — Section 13(1) of the Equality Act 2010 states:

> A person (A) discriminates against another (B) if, because of a protected characteristic, A treats B less favourably than A treats or would treat others.

Less favourable treatment of a person because that person is associated with a protected characteristic, for example because the person has a friend or partner with a particular protected characteristic, or carries out work related to a protected characteristic, is within the scope of this section. This might include carers of disabled people and elderly relatives, who can claim they were treated unfairly because of duties that they had to carry out at home relating to their care work. For example, the non-disabled mother of a disabled child can be discriminated against because of the child's disability (*Coleman* v *Attridge Law* (Case C-303/06) [2008] IRLR 722). This is known as 'associative discrimination'.

To constitute direct discrimination, the treatment experienced by B must be different from that of another person. This difference is often referred to as a 'comparator'. The treatment of B must be less favourable than the treatment afforded to a comparator. The comparator can be hypothetical where B can establish direct discrimination by showing that if there was another person in similar circumstances, but without B's protected characteristic, that person would be treated more favourably (for an explanation of hypothetical comparators, see *Shamoon* v *Chief Constable of the Royal Ulster Constabulary* [2003] UKHL 11). This is why answer B is correct, and answer C is incorrect.

Less favourable treatment is a broad concept and any disadvantage to which B has been subject will constitute such treatment. B need not have suffered a tangible or material loss (*Chief Constable of West Yorkshire Police* v *Khan* [2001] UKHL 48), and therefore answer D is incorrect.

However, it is not enough merely to show unreasonable treatment (*Bahl* v *The Law Society* [2004] IRLR 799). Answer A is therefore incorrect.

General Police Duties, para. 3.16.4.1

Answer 16.3

Answer **A** — Under s. 20 of the Equality Act 2010, where this Act imposes a duty to make reasonable adjustments, the requirement is that where a provision, criterion or practice puts a disabled person at a *substantial disadvantage* in relation to a relevant matter in comparison with persons who are not disabled, such steps should be taken as it is reasonable to have to take to avoid the disadvantage.

The section contains only one threshold for the reasonable adjustment duty, that of 'substantial disadvantage'; s. 212(1) defines 'substantial' as more than minor or trivial.

Answers B, C and D are therefore incorrect.

General Police Duties, para. 3.16.4.3

Answer 16.4

Answer **B** — Section 13(1) of the Equality Act 2010 states:

A person (A) discriminates against another (B) if, because of a protected characteristic, A treats B less favourably than A treats or would treat others.

Disability is one of the protected characteristics covered by the 2010 Act and the police service has a general 'public sector duty' as a public authority to eliminate discrimination and promote equality (see s. 149).

Section 20 of the Act outlines what is meant by the duty to make reasonable adjustments for the purposes of the Act and, under s. 20(5), the requirement is:

where a disabled person would, but for the provision of an auxiliary aid, be put at a substantial disadvantage in relation to a relevant matter in comparison with persons who are not disabled, to take such steps as it is reasonable to have to take to provide the auxiliary aid.

Section 21 provides that a failure to comply with any one of the reasonable adjustment requirements amounts to discrimination against a disabled person to whom the duty is owed.

The requirement to comply with the 2010 Act applies as much in an operational context as it does in employment legislation; the fact that the officers may have breached PACE is irrelevant in some ways; a discrimination case, if brought about, would be treated as a separate matter and could bring punishment on the force regardless of whether LEWIN is found guilty of supplying drugs. Answers A and C are therefore incorrect.

However, it was held that police officers lawfully searching the home of a man whom they knew to be profoundly deaf did *not* have any effect on the ability of the man and the officers to communicate with each other effectively without a British Sign Language interpreter being present. Officers who had had previous dealings with the man were satisfied on the basis of these dealings that they could achieve a basic level of communication with him without the benefit of an interpreter (*Finnegan* v *Chief Constable of Northumbria* [2013] EWCA Civ 1191). This case demonstrates that the circumstances in the question were not a *clear* breach of the Equality Act 2010 and answer D is therefore incorrect.

General Police Duties, para. 3.16.4.3

Answer 16.5

Answer **C** — Under s. 26 of the Equality Act 2010:

(1) A person (A) harasses another (B) if—
  (a) A engages in unwanted conduct related to a relevant protected characteristic, and
  (b) the conduct has the purpose or effect of—
    (i) violating B's dignity, or
    (ii) creating an intimidating, hostile, degrading, humiliating or offensive environment for B.
(2) A also harasses B if—
  (a) A engages in unwanted conduct of a sexual nature, and
  (b) the conduct has the purpose or effect referred to in subsection (1)(b).

The behaviour referred to involves unwanted conduct which is related to a relevant characteristic and has the purpose or effect of creating an intimidating, hostile, degrading, humiliating or offensive environment for the complainant or of violating the complainant's dignity (which is described clearly in this question).

In deciding whether conduct has the effect referred to in s. 26(1)(b), the perception of B, the other circumstances of the case and whether it is reasonable for the conduct to have that effect must be taken into account (s. 26(4)).

Therefore, while the investigating officer *may* take into account the perception of other members of the team in weighing up the evidence against the sergeant, he/she must take into account the victim's perception of what happened.

Answers A, B and D are therefore incorrect.

General Police Duties, para. 3.16.4.8

Answer 16.6

Answer **D** — Section 27 of the Equality Act 2010 states:

(1) A person (A) victimises another person (B) if A subjects B to a detriment because—
  (a) B does a protected act, or
  (b) A believes that B has done, or may do, a protected act.
(2) Each of the following is a protected act—
  (a) bringing proceedings under this Act;
  (b) giving evidence or information in connection with proceedings under this Act;
  (c) doing any other thing for the purposes of or in connection with this Act;
  (d) making an allegation (whether or not express) that A or another person has contravened this Act.

In *Bayode* v *Chief Constable of Derbyshire* [2008] UKEAT 0499 07 2205, the tribunal held that the complainant, a police constable who was a black African and Nigerian by national origin, had *not* been victimised where his colleagues recorded any problems they encountered with him in their PNBs for fear that he might make a race discrimination claim at some future date. Previous unsubstantiated discrimination claims had been made by the complainant. Answers A and B are therefore incorrect.

Direct discrimination is an entirely different matter to victimisation, and generally involves employers treating one group of people less favourably than others based on protected grounds, such as their racial origin, marital status, sex, religion or belief or sexual orientation. It is out of context in this scenario, and for that reason answer C is incorrect.

General Police Duties, para. 3.16.4.10

Answer 16.7

Answer **C** — Section 42 of the Equality Act 2010 states:

(1) For the purposes of this Part, holding the office of constable is to be treated as employment—
  (a) by the chief officer, in respect of any act done by the chief officer in relation to a constable or appointment to the office of constable;

(b) by the responsible authority, in respect of any act done by the authority in relation to a constable or appointment to the office of constable.

The Equality Act 2010 makes provisions for chief officers *and* 'responsible' authorities to be liable for acts done by them towards their staff. Answer B is therefore incorrect.

This liability is not limited to discrimination by members of staff towards people outside the force; it can include discrimination by members of staff towards people within the force, and therefore answers A and D are incorrect.

The chief officer of police is also vicariously liable for acts of race discrimination by staff under his/her direction and control. The statutory defence that an employer took all reasonable steps to prevent the acts of discrimination complained of is also available to chief officers (s. 109(4)).

General Police Duties, paras 3.16.5, 3.16.7

Answer 16.8

Answer **B** — Under s. 39 of the Equality Act 2010, it is unlawful for an employer to discriminate against or victimise employees and people seeking work. It applies where the employer is making arrangements to fill a job and in respect of anything done in the course of a person's employment.

There are a number of exceptions and defences to the provisions of the Act, but two of the more relevant defences in relation to discrimination or victimisation in employment are 'genuine occupational requirement' and 'positive action'.

'Positive action' refers to measures to alleviate disadvantage experienced by people who share a protected characteristic, reduce their under-representation in relation to particular activities and meet their particular needs (s. 158). It allows for measures to be targeted to particular groups, including training to enable them to gain employment, but any such measures must be a proportionate way of achieving the relevant aim.

An employer may also take a protected characteristic into consideration when deciding whom to recruit or promote, where people having the protected characteristic are at a disadvantage or are under-represented (s. 159).

However, this can be done only where the candidates are as qualified as each other. Therefore, if the three people with black or minority ethnic backgrounds had scored the same as MARLER in the assessment centre, the force has used positive action correctly, but if they had scored fewer marks, the force has not. The aim is to help employers achieve a more diverse workforce by giving them the option, when faced with candidates of *equal merit*, to choose a candidate from an under-represented group.

Answers A, C and D are therefore incorrect.

General Police Duties, para. 3.16.6

Answer 16.9

Answer **A** — Section 109 of the Equality Act 2010 states:

(1) Anything done by a person (A) in the course of A's employment must be treated as also done by the employer.
(2) ...
(3) It does not matter whether that thing is done with the employer's or principal's knowledge or approval.

Where acts amounting to discrimination take place outside the workplace, the employer and employees may still be caught within the framework of the legislation. So, for instance, where police officers engage in inappropriate sexual behaviour towards a colleague at a work-related social function, a tribunal may be entitled to hold that the function was an extension of the workplace and so hold the chief officer liable for the acts of his/her officers at that function (*Chief Constable of Lincolnshire* v *Stubbs* [1999] IRLR 81). Answer D is therefore incorrect.

This case deals with a specific example of behaviour where the officers were at a work-related function, which was an 'extension of the workplace'. The decision does not, therefore, mean that any behaviour can be included in such a claim (although it is worth noting that discrimination and victimisation are included in the Code of Conduct for police officers, which may include the conduct of an off-duty officer). Answer C is therefore incorrect. Lastly, this case did not specify that the location of the function was important, merely that it was an off-duty function and an extension of the workplace. Answer B is therefore incorrect.

General Police Duties, para. 3.16.7

17 | Complaints and Misconduct

QUESTIONS

Question 17.1

PC FOX has had a number of arguments with her supervisors and has refused to obey lawful orders on numerous occasions. Despite engaging in the Reflective Practice Review Process, the situation is still wholly unsatisfactory and this has resulted in an assessment that PC FOX's behaviour amounts to misconduct and will be dealt with by way of a misconduct meeting.

In relation to that misconduct meeting, which of the following comments is correct?

A As a result of the misconduct meeting, PC FOX could be dismissed with notice.

B An outcome of the misconduct meeting could be that PC FOX could be given a final written warning regarding her behaviour.

C The misconduct meeting panel could decide that PC FOX could be dismissed without notice.

D A variety of sanctions are available as a result of the misconduct meeting but this would not include an option to take no further action against PC FOX.

Question 17.2

Assistant Chief Constable MOREL was on suspension from duty, having been accused of a criminal offence under s. 2 of the Computer Misuse Act 1990. The officer was being investigated for accessing and using confidential information from a police computer system. Whilst on suspension, Assistant Chief Constable MOREL gave an interview to a national newspaper claiming to be innocent, that he was being harassed by the force investigating the incident and that he was being accused of attempting to discredit the force.

Could Assistant Chief Constable MOREL have breached the Standards of Professional Behaviour, under the Police (Conduct) Regulations 2020 (Discreditable Conduct), by giving the interview to the press?

A No, the Regulations only apply to police officers up to and including the rank of chief superintendent.

B Yes, the Regulations apply to all police officers up to and including the rank of assistant chief constable.

C No, the Regulations do not apply to police officers who are suspended, regardless of their rank.

D Yes, the Regulations apply to all police officers whether they are suspended or not.

Question 17.3

A complaint has been made about the behaviour of PC LLOYD, alleging that she has breached the Standards of Professional Behaviour which results in a misconduct hearing taking place. PC LLOYD wishes to be accompanied by a police friend during the misconduct hearing and asks TAYABALI (a police staff member) if he would act as her police friend during the proceedings.

Considering the role of a 'police friend', which of the following comments is correct?

A TAYABALI cannot act as a police friend as he is not a police officer.

B A person cannot be a police friend unless they are nominated to act as such by a police officer's staff association.

C TAYABALI can act as a police friend and ask questions of any witness at the misconduct hearing (subject to the discretion of the person(s) conducting that hearing).

D TAYABALI can act as a police friend but cannot do so in 'duty' time.

Question 17.4

An allegation of misconduct has been made against Sergeant LAKE. A temporary move to a new role and working location has been considered but it is not appropriate in the circumstances and consequently consideration is being given to suspending the officer from duty.

In relation to such a suspension from duty, which of the following comments is correct?

A The suspension must be authorised by a senior officer (which is an officer holding a rank above that of a chief superintendent).

B If Sergeant LAKE is suspended from duty, the Standards of Professional Behaviour will not apply to him whilst he is suspended.

C Any use of suspension from duty must be reviewed every three months.

D It is not an option as the decision to suspend an officer may only be taken where there is an allegation of gross misconduct.

Question 17.5

Constable MURPHY is being investigated for a misconduct matter but is currently on certificated sick leave, having had a back operation. The officer is not expected to return to work for several months; however, the investigating officer is keen to progress the complaint as soon as possible and wishes to interview Constable MURPHY. The officer's Police Federation representative has emailed the investigating officer claiming that it would be unfair to conduct an interview while the member is on sick leave.

Which of the following is correct in relation to whether an interview could be conducted while Constable MURPHY is on sick leave?

A Constable MURPHY may be interviewed or, alternatively, the investigating officer may send questions to the officer requesting a written response.

B Police officers may be interviewed while on certified sick leave if the allegation against them is considered to be serious enough.

C Police officers may not be interviewed while on certified sick leave; this would amount to a breach of the Conduct Regulations.

D Constable MURPHY may be interviewed while on certified sick leave but the interview must be conducted in person.

Question 17.6

A written notification is sent to Inspector O'KANE stating that his conduct is under investigation under reg. 17 of the Police (Conduct) Regulations 2020 as an allegation has been made about a breach of the Standards of Professional Behaviour.

Which of the following comments is correct in relation to how that written notification is given to Inspector O'KANE?

A The notification must be served on Inspector O'KANE in person.

B The notification cannot be sent by email to Inspector O'KANE.

C The notification must be sent by recorded delivery to Inspector O'KANE's last known address.

D It can be given to Inspector O'KANE in person by his police friend where the police friend has agreed to this.

Question 17.7

Constable WOODS is attending a misconduct hearing, having been accused of passing information to a member of the public, which was stored on the force intelligence system. The officer is accused of breaching the 'Confidentiality' standard included in the ten Standards of Professional Behaviour.

Which of the following is correct in relation to the panel who will hear the misconduct matter?

A It will be a three-person panel, chaired by an officer of at least the rank of superintendent and two independent members.

B It will be a five-person panel, chaired by a legally qualified person, assisted by an officer of at least the rank of superintendent and three independent members.

C It will be a five-person panel, chaired by an officer of at least the rank of superintendent, assisted by a human resources professional and three independent members.

D It will be a three-person panel, chaired by a legally qualified person and assisted by an officer of at least the rank of superintendent and an independent member.

Question 17.8

An allegation has been made that PC BUSHELL has breached the Standards of Professional Behaviour and an investigation into the matter has commenced.

How often should the investigator notify PC BUSHELL of the progress of the investigation?

A At least every four weeks from the start of the investigation.

B At least every six weeks from the start of the investigation.

C At least every eight weeks from the start of the investigation.

D At least every 12 weeks from the start of the investigation.

Question 17.9

Constable POWDRILL is being investigated for a breach of the Standards of Professional Behaviour. The matter is going to be heard in a misconduct hearing and the person chairing the misconduct hearing has decided to hold a misconduct pre-hearing under reg. 33 of the Police (Conduct) Regulations 2020.

Which of the following statements is correct in relation to that pre-hearing?

A The pre-hearing cannot be held in private.

B Constable POWDRILL is entitled to attend the pre-hearing.

C The pre-hearing cannot be held by telephone.

D The pre-hearing has to be recorded.

Question 17.10

Constable GRIFFITHS was subject to a complaint resulting in a misconduct meeting taking place where the allegation against the officer was proved. The sanction imposed on Constable GRIFFITHS at the misconduct meeting was a written warning. Constable GRIFFITHS wants to appeal against the finding at the misconduct meeting on the ground that there is evidence that could not reasonably have been considered at the time of the misconduct meeting which could have materially affected the finding.

Can the officer appeal against the finding at the misconduct meeting?

A No, as an appeal can only be made against the outcome of the meeting rather than the finding of the meeting.

B No, an appeal can only be made in relation to a misconduct hearing rather than a misconduct meeting.

C Yes, and if the person determining the appeal decides that the original disciplinary action imposed was too lenient, he/she may increase the outcome up to a maximum of a final written warning.

D Yes, and such an appeal will normally be heard within ten working days beginning with the working day after the determination that the officer concerned has arguable grounds of appeal.

Question 17.11

Assistant Chief Constable WALL has attended a misconduct meeting with the deputy chief constable. Assistant Chief Constable WALL was given a written warning at the meeting and is now seeking advice about making an appeal against the finding to a Police Appeals Tribunal.

Is Assistant Chief Constable WALL entitled to make such an appeal in these circumstances?

A No, the Police Appeals Tribunal does not hear appeals against the findings or outcomes of a misconduct meeting.

B Yes, as an appeal may be made to a Police Appeals Tribunal against any misconduct finding.

C Yes, an appeal may be made by an assistant chief constable against the finding or outcome of a misconduct meeting.

D No, the Police Appeals Tribunal only hears appeals against the findings or outcomes of an accelerated misconduct hearing.

Question 17.12

PC OWEN's abusive behaviour towards several members of the public has been cause for complaint. The assessment of PC OWEN's behaviour determined that he did not meet the Standards of Professional Behaviour and this eventually led to a misconduct meeting. At the misconduct meeting, PC OWEN was given a written warning regarding his behaviour and was told that the written warning will be put on his personal file.

For how long will that written warning remain 'live' on PC OWEN's file?

A Six months from the date the warning was given.

B Twelve months from the date the warning was given.

C Eighteen months from the date the warning was given.

D Twenty-four months from the date the warning was given.

Question 17.13

Constable TROOP breaches the Standards of Professional Behaviour by behaving in an overtly racist way to FRASER. The behaviour of the officer was recorded and seen live on a national television station and is incontrovertible evidence of a breach of the Standards of Professional Behaviour amounting to gross misconduct. As a result, the chief constable (the appropriate authority) of Constable TROOP's police force certifies the case as one where the 'special conditions' are satisfied and accelerated misconduct procedures are engaged.

In relation to such accelerated misconduct procedures (set out in Pt 5 of the Police (Conduct) Regulations 2020), which of the following comments is correct?

A PC TROOP's case will be heard by a chief constable of a different police force.

B Such an accelerated misconduct hearing will be held in private.

C There will be no live witness evidence at this accelerated misconduct hearing other than from PC TROOP.

D PC TROOP could not be represented by a police friend at this hearing.

Question 17.14

PC GROGAN breaches the Standards of Professional Behaviour; however, this is a low-level breach so the matter is referred to the Reflective Practice Review Process.

In relation to that process, which of the following comments is correct?

A The reviewer who conducts the process must be a police officer of or above the rank of inspector.

B PC GROGAN can apply for promotion even though he is participating in the process.

C PC GROGAN may be represented by a lawyer during the process.

D PC GROGAN may be represented by a police friend during the process.

ANSWERS

Answer 17.1

Answer **B** — The meeting may record a finding that the conduct of the police officer concerned amounted to misconduct and take no further action (making answer D incorrect) or impose one of the following outcomes:

- *Written warning*—the police officer will be told the reason for the warning, that they have a right to appeal, the name of the person to whom the appeal should be sent and that the warning will be put on their personal file and remain live for 18 months from the date that the warning is given. This means that any misconduct in the following 18 months is likely to lead to (at least) a final written warning.
- *Final written warning*—the police officer will be told the reason for the warning, that any future misconduct may result in dismissal, that they have a right to appeal, the name of the person to whom the appeal should be sent and that the final written warning will be put on their personal file. A misconduct hearing may impose a final written warning for between two and five years and it will remain live for this period from the date that the warning is given. This means that only in exceptional circumstances will further misconduct (that justifies more than management advice) not result in dismissal if proven.

Where a misconduct hearing finds that the conduct of an officer amounts to misconduct (but not gross misconduct), in addition to the two outcomes above, the persons conducting the hearing will also have available the outcomes of:

- *Reduction in rank*—this is available where there was a written warning in force at the date of the initial severity assessment and the misconduct hearing finds that the officer's misconduct arises from more than one incident and where those incidents are not closely factually connected.
- *Dismissal without notice*—dismissal without notice will mean that the police officer is dismissed from the police service with immediate effect.

Where a police officer appears before a misconduct hearing for an alleged act of gross misconduct, and the persons conducting the hearing find that the conduct amounts to misconduct rather than gross misconduct, then (unless the police officer already has a live final written warning) the disciplinary outcomes available to the panel are those that are available at a misconduct meeting only.

Where a misconduct hearing finds that the conduct of an officer amounts to gross misconduct, the persons conducting the hearing will have available the outcomes of:

- *Final written warning.*
- *Reduction in rank*, without the conditions stated above.
- *Dismissal without notice.*

So options A and C are incorrect as dismissal with or without notice is only available as a result of a misconduct hearing (not a misconduct meeting).

PC FOX could be given a final written warning (correct answer B).

General Police Duties, para. 3.17.6.10

Answer 17.2

Answer **D** — The Police (Conduct) Regulations 2020 are supported by a code of ethics—the Standards of Professional Behaviour. The Standards apply to police officers of *all* ranks from chief constable to constable (including special constables). Answers A and B are therefore incorrect. (If you answered A to this question, you may have been considering the Police (Performance) Regulations 2020, which only apply to police officers (including special constables) up to and including the rank of chief superintendent.)

The Standards of Professional Behaviour do apply to police officers who are subject to suspension; therefore, answer C is incorrect.

General Police Duties, para. 3.17.2

Answer 17.3

Answer **C** — The police friend can be a police officer, a police staff member or a person nominated by the police officer's staff association (making answers A and B incorrect). At a misconduct meeting, hearing or accelerated misconduct hearing under the Police (Conduct) Regulations 2020 or Police (Performance) Regulations 2020 where the police friend attends, he/she may ask questions of any witness, subject to the discretion of the person(s) conducting that hearing (correct answer C). Answer D is incorrect as a police friend who has agreed to accompany a police officer is entitled to take a reasonable amount of duty time to fulfil those responsibilities and is considered to be on duty when attending interviews, meetings or hearings.

General Police Duties, para. 3.17.4

Answer 17.4

Answer **A** — The decision to suspend a police officer may be taken only where there is an allegation of misconduct/gross misconduct (making answer D incorrect). The use of suspension must be reviewed at least every four weeks (making answer C incorrect). Answer B is incorrect as the Standards of Professional Behaviour continue to apply to police officers who are suspended from duty. Suspension must be authorised by a senior officer (which is an officer holding a rank above that of chief superintendent) although the decision can be communicated to the police officer by an appropriate manager (correct answer A).

General Police Duties, para. 3.17.5.1

Answer 17.5

Answer **A** — Where a police officer is on certificated sick leave, the investigator should seek to establish when the police officer will be fit for interview. It may be that the police officer is not fit for ordinary police duty but is perfectly capable of being interviewed. This is regardless of how serious the allegation is and answers B and C are incorrect.

Alternatively, the police officer concerned *may* be invited to provide a written response to the allegations within a specified period and *may* be sent the questions that the investigator wishes to be answered. Answer D is therefore incorrect.

General Police Duties, para. 3.17.5.9

Answer 17.6

Answer **D** — The written notification may be given to the officer in person, left with a person at or sent by recorded delivery to the officer's last known address, given to the officer in person by his/her police friend where the police friend has agreed (correct answer D) to this or given to the officer in any manner agreed with the officer. This means that answers A and C are incorrect as the written notification can be given to the officer in a number of ways. Answer B is incorrect as the notice can be sent by email as the notice can be given *in any manner* agreed with the officer (so if Inspector O'KANE agreed to the notice being given by email, it would be acceptable).

General Police Duties, para. 3.17.5.7

Answer 17.7

Answer **D** — A misconduct hearing for non-senior officers will consist of a three-person panel, chaired by a legally qualified person and assisted by an officer of at least the rank of superintendent and an independent member.

Answers A, B and C are therefore incorrect.

General Police Duties, para. 3.17.6.3

Answer 17.8

Answer **A** — The investigator is required to notify the police officer of the progress of the investigation at least every four weeks from the start of the investigation.

General Police Duties, para. 3.17.5.8

Answer 17.9

Answer **B** — A person chairing a misconduct hearing (but not a misconduct meeting) may decide to hold a misconduct pre-hearing under reg. 33 of the Police (Conduct) Regulations 2020. It is held in private (answer A is incorrect), can be held by telephone (answer C is incorrect) and does not have to be recorded (answer D is incorrect). Answer B is correct as the officer, the officer's police friend, the officer's counsel and counsel representing the appropriate authority (or the IOPC if they are the presenting authority) are entitled to attend.

General Police Duties, para. 3.17.5.15

Answer 17.10

Answer **C** — Answers A and B are incorrect as a police officer has a right of appeal against the finding and/or the outcome imposed at a misconduct meeting. Answer D is incorrect as the appeal will normally be heard within five (not ten) working days beginning with the working day after the determination that the officer concerned has arguable grounds of appeal. The person determining the appeal may confirm or reverse the decision appealed against. Where the person determining the appeal decides that the original disciplinary action imposed was too lenient, he/she may increase the outcome up to a maximum of a final written warning (correct answer C).

General Police Duties, paras 3.17.7 to 3.17.7.1

Answer 17.11

Answer **C** — A police officer has a right of appeal to a Police Appeals Tribunal against any disciplinary finding and/or disciplinary outcome imposed at a misconduct hearing or accelerated misconduct hearing held under the Police (Conduct) Regulations 2020 (making answer D incorrect). Senior police officers, in addition, have the right to appeal to a Police Appeals Tribunal against any disciplinary finding and/or outcome imposed at a misconduct meeting (making answer A incorrect). A police officer *may not* appeal to a tribunal against a finding of misconduct or gross misconduct where that finding was made following acceptance by the officer that his/her conduct amounted to that (making answer B incorrect).

General Police Duties, para. 3.17.9

Answer 17.12

Answer **C** — When a written warning is given, the warning will be put on the personal file of the officer concerned and will remain 'live' for a period of 18 months from the date that the warning was given.

General Police Duties, para. 3.17.6.10

Answer 17.13

Answer **C** — Answer A is incorrect as in the case of non-senior officers, the case will be heard by the police officer's chief constable (assistant commissioner in the Metropolitan Police). Answer B is incorrect as an accelerated misconduct hearing is held in public. The hearing may proceed in the absence of the police officer concerned, but the persons conducting the hearing should ensure that the police officer concerned has been informed of his/her right to be legally represented at the hearing or to be represented by a police friend where the police officer chooses not to be legally represented (so answer D is incorrect). There is no live witness evidence at an accelerated misconduct hearing, other than from the police officer concerned (correct answer C).

General Police Duties, para. 3.17.8

Answer 17.14

Answer **B** — Answer A is incorrect as the reviewer who conducts the process must be the line manager of or a police officer or staff member who is more senior to the officer. The Reflective Practice Review process is considered to be a performance rather than a disciplinary process, so that an officer participating in it may continue to apply for and obtain promotion (correct answer B). Similarly, an officer may not be represented during it—whether by a lawyer or a police friend and such persons may make no representations to the appropriate authority about any aspect of the process (making answers C and D incorrect).

General Police Duties, para. 3.17.9.10

18 Unsatisfactory Performance and Attendance

QUESTIONS

Question 18.1

Sergeant KHAN has been concerned about the attendance record of Constable HEALD and has asked the officer to attend a meeting to discuss the matter. It has been decided that the issue will be dealt with by informal intervention, rather than the unsatisfactory performance procedures. Constable HEALD admitted that her attendance could be better and has agreed to submit to an action plan to be set by Sergeant KHAN.

Which of the following statements is correct regarding the period of time Sergeant KHAN should set to allow an improvement in attendance by Constable HEALD?

A Because the matter is being dealt with by informal intervention, an automatic period of three months should be set.

B Because the matter relates to attendance, an automatic period of six months should be set.

C Because the matter is being dealt with by informal intervention, there is no limit to the period of time that may be set.

D There is no set period; however, Sergeant KHAN should allow sufficient time to provide a reasonable opportunity for Constable HEALD to improve attendance.

Question 18.2

PC FINNIGAN has been having problems with his performance over an extended period of time and informal intervention has not rectified the situation. Sergeant COLEMAN (PC FINNIGAN's line manager) decides that the issues need to be addressed using the Police (Performance) Regulations 2020 (UPPs). Sergeant COLEMAN notifies PC FINNIGAN in writing that he is required to attend a first stage meeting.

In relation to the date and time of the meeting, which of the comments below is correct?

A In the first instance, Sergeant COLEMAN must specify a date and time that the meeting should take place.

B Sergeant COLEMAN must ask PC FINNIGAN to specify a date and time that the meeting should take place.

C Sergeant COLEMAN must provide three prospective dates within five working days of each other; PC FINNIGAN must select one of those dates.

D Wherever possible, the meeting date and time should be agreed between the line manager and the police officer.

Question 18.3

Sergeant GANT has arranged a first stage unsatisfactory performance meeting with Constable RUSH to discuss the officer's poor attendance record. Sergeant GANT intends issuing the officer with an improvement notice, seeking an improvement in the officer's attendance at work. Sergeant GANT is newly promoted and wishes to seek advice on how to conduct the meeting and the possible outcomes.

Which of the following statements is correct in relation to the advice Sergeant GANT may seek?

A Sergeant GANT may ask a human resources professional to be present, or a police officer with relevant experience who is independent of the line management chain.

B Sergeant GANT may seek advice from a human resources professional, or a police officer with relevant experience, before the meeting, but they may not be present.

C Because the meeting is to do with attendance and not performance, Sergeant GANT must have a human resources professional present.

D Sergeant GANT may ask a human resources professional to be present, or a police officer who is part of the line management chain provided the officer is not the second line manager.

Question 18.4

Constable CROSS has been asked to attend a first stage unsatisfactory performance meeting to discuss the officer's poor performance. Before the meeting, Constable

CROSS met with Constable BECK, a Police Federation representative. They were discussing whether or not Constable BECK should make any representations on behalf of Constable CROSS in relation to the matter.

Which of the following statements is correct regarding any representations that either Constable CROSS or Constable BECK may make?

A Because this is a first stage unsatisfactory performance meeting, Constable BECK may not attend but may submit written representations beforehand; Constable CROSS may make verbal representations at the meeting.

B Constable BECK may attend but must submit written representations at the meeting; Constable CROSS may make verbal representations at the meeting.

C Because this is a first stage unsatisfactory performance meeting, Constable BECK may not attend and is not entitled to make representations; Constable CROSS may make written or verbal representations at the meeting.

D Constable BECK may attend and either she or Constable CROSS may make written or verbal representations at the meeting.

Question 18.5

Constable DALE attended a first stage unsatisfactory performance meeting with her line manager, Sergeant MALIK. The outcome of the meeting was that Constable DALE was given a written improvement notice relating to her paperwork submission, and was subject to an action plan to improve her paperwork (a 'specified period' which Sergeant MALIK set at three months). After three months, Sergeant MALIK considered that her performance had not improved. Constable DALE asked Sergeant MALIK if there was any way her specified period for improvement could be extended, rather than proceeding to the next stage.

Which of the following comments is correct in relation to the request to extend the improvement period?

A The improvement period can be extended for up to three months, unless there are exceptional reasons for extending the period beyond six months in total.

B The improvement period can be extended for up to six months, unless there are exceptional reasons for extending the period beyond nine months in total.

C The improvement period can be extended for up to nine months, but the period must not exceed 12 months in total.

D The improvement period can be extended for up to nine months, unless there are exceptional reasons for extending the period beyond 12 months in total.

Question 18.6

Constable POUNDS has been subject to a three-month action plan for poor attendance, following the issue of an improvement notice at a first stage unsatisfactory performance meeting. Constable POUNDS has not reported sick during this period and is now meeting Sergeant HALES to discuss the next steps. Sergeant HALES has informed the officer he needs to maintain attendance during the 'validity period' now that the current action plan has been achieved.

Which of the following statements is correct in relation to the 'validity period' during which Constable POUNDS has to maintain attendance?

A Constable POUNDS has to maintain attendance for another three months to avoid moving to the next stage.

B Constable POUNDS has to maintain attendance for another six months to avoid moving to the next stage.

C Constable POUNDS has to maintain attendance for another nine months to avoid moving to the next stage.

D Constable POUNDS has to maintain attendance for another 12 months to avoid moving to the next stage.

Question 18.7

PC FISK has had a number of problems with his performance at work and this has led to first and second stage meetings in relation to his performance. The last meeting resulted in a final written warning being issued to the officer. Despite all efforts to assist the officer, his performance is still poor and so at the end of the period in the final written improvement notice PC FISK's line manager, Inspector WINTERIDGE, sends a notification to PC FISK that he is required to attend a third stage meeting.

With regard to that third stage meeting, which of the following comments is correct?

A Any third stage meeting should take place no later than 15 working days after the date that the notification was sent to PC FISK.

B Any third stage meeting should take place no later than 25 working days after the date that the notification was sent to PC FISK.

C Any third stage meeting should take place no later than 30 working days after the date that the notification was sent to PC FISK.

D Any third stage meeting should take place no later than 40 working days after the date that the notification was sent to PC FISK.

Question 18.8

A meeting is being held between Inspector HAKES and JENNINGS, a human resources adviser, regarding the performance of Special Constable ANDERSON who works on the inspector's team. Special Constable ANDERSON is currently at the second stage of the unsatisfactory performance procedures and has recently failed an action plan. Inspector HAKES is seeking advice on what should happen next and whether it is appropriate for the officer to progress to the third stage of the procedures.

Which of the following statements is correct in relation to special constables and third stage meetings?

A Because special constables are unpaid volunteers, it is inappropriate for Special Constable ANDERSON to attend a third stage meeting.

B Special Constable ANDERSON may be required to attend a third stage meeting, but a senior special constable will be appointed to attend the meeting to advise her.

C Special Constable ANDERSON may be required to attend a third stage meeting, but a senior special constable will be appointed to attend the meeting to advise the panel.

D Special Constable ANDERSON may be required to attend a third stage meeting, but a senior special constable will be appointed to attend the meeting to form part of the panel.

Question 18.9

Constable PARKER was due to attend a third stage meeting in relation to his unsatisfactory performance, but three days before the meeting was due to take place the officer broke his leg in a football match. Constable PARKER is now unfit for duty and on sick leave (as a direct consequence of the broken leg) and has been for several weeks and is unable to attend the stage three meeting.

In relation to the attendance of the officer at the stage three meeting, which of the following comments is correct?

A As the officer is on sick leave, he cannot attend the stage three meeting.

B The force could conduct the stage three meeting using conferencing technology (video or telephone, for example).

C The meeting will be deferred indefinitely because Constable PARKER is unable to attend.

D The meeting cannot proceed until Constable PARKER is fit to attend it in person.

Question 18.10

Sergeant LORING was approached by Special Constable MALLET who was concerned about the behaviour of HEBDON who had recently resigned as a special constable. Special Constable MALLET told the sergeant that before he resigned HEBDON falsely claimed to have lost his warrant card and obtained a duplicate. HEBDON had recently been overheard in a pub boasting that he had a police warrant card that he could use to get favours.

If HEBDON is in possession of a warrant card in these circumstances, which of the following is correct in relation to offences under the Police Act 1996?

A HEBDON is guilty of impersonation because of his possession of the warrant card.

B HEBDON cannot be guilty of an offence under this Act because he is not in possession of a police uniform.

C HEBDON cannot be guilty of an offence under this Act unless evidence is available that he has used the warrant card to impersonate a police officer.

D HEBDON may be guilty of an offence under this Act because he does not have possession of the warrant card for a lawful purpose.

ANSWERS

Answer 18.1

Answer **D** — Management action should be used when a line manager identifies performance or attendance failures at an early stage. It provides an opportunity for the supervisor to discuss any improvement required, before progressing to the more formal unsatisfactory performance procedures. Ideally, performance or attendance will improve and continue to an acceptable level and where there is insufficient or unsustained improvement, it will then be appropriate to use the unsatisfactory performance procedures.

There is no set period of time for an action plan at this stage, whether the line manager is dealing with a performance or attendance failure (answers A and B are therefore incorrect). The length of the plan agreed or determined by the line manager must be *sufficient to provide a reasonable opportunity for the desired improvement or attendance to take place*. The period may not be unlimited; therefore, answer C is incorrect.

General Police Duties, para. 3.18.5

Answer 18.2

Answer **D** — Wherever possible, the meeting date and time should be agreed between the line manager and the police officer (correct answer D). However, where agreement cannot be reached the line manager must specify a time and date. If the police officer or his/her police friend is not available at the date or time specified by the line manager, the police officer may propose an alternative time. Provided that the alternative time is reasonable and falls within a period of five working days beginning with the first working day after that specified by the line manager, the meeting must be postponed to that time. Once the date for the meeting is fixed, the line manager should send to the police officer a notice in writing of the date, time and place of the first stage meeting.

General Police Duties, para. 3.18.9

Answer 18.3

Answer **A** — The formal procedures to deal with unsatisfactory performance and attendance are set out in the Police (Performance) Regulations 2020. There are potentially three stages to the process, each of which involves a different meeting composition and possible outcomes. However, the process is the same whether the officer is being asked to account for their poor performance or their attendance. Answer C is therefore incorrect.

A line manager may ask a human resources professional or police officer (who should have experience of unsatisfactory performance procedures) to attend a meeting to advise him/her on the proceedings at the first stage meeting. Answer B is therefore incorrect. The line manager may also seek such advice before the meeting and answer C is also incorrect in this respect because attendance at the meeting is optional and not mandatory.

If the experienced police officer is to attend the meeting, he/she must be independent of the line management chain (and not part of it at any level). Answer D is therefore incorrect.

General Police Duties, para. 3.18.9

Answer 18.4

Answer **D** — The purpose of the unsatisfactory performance procedures is to seek an improvement in performance and attendance; therefore, there is flexibility to achieve this aim.

A constable attending a first stage meeting is entitled to have a friend present. Answers A and C are therefore incorrect.

The line manager must provide the *police officer* or his/her *police friend* (if he/she has one) with an opportunity to make representations. The representations may be made verbally or in writing. Answers B and C are therefore incorrect for this reason.

General Police Duties, para. 3.18.9.1

Answer 18.5

Answer **D** — It is expected that the specified period for improvement would not normally exceed three months. On the application of the police officer or otherwise (e.g. on the application of his/her line manager), the appropriate authority may extend the 'specified period' if it considers it appropriate to do so.

In setting an extension to the specified period, consideration should be given to any known periods of extended absence from the police officer's normal role, e.g. if the police officer is going to be on long periods of pre-planned holiday leave, study leave or is due to undergo an operation. The extension should not lead to the improvement period exceeding 12 months; therefore, answers A and B are incorrect.

However, if the appropriate authority is satisfied that there are exceptional circumstances making it appropriate, the period may be extended beyond 12 months; therefore, answer C is incorrect.

General Police Duties, para. 3.18.9.2

Answer 18.6

Answer **C** — The 'validity period' of an improvement notice describes the period of 12 *months* from the date of the notice within which performance or attendance must be maintained (assuming improvement is made during the specified period). If the improvement is not maintained within this period, the next stage of the procedures may be used. Constable POUNDS has worked through a three-month action plan period and now has nine months of the 12-month 'validity period' left.

Answers A, B and D are therefore incorrect.

General Police Duties, para. 3.18.9.2

Answer 18.7

Answer **C** — Any third stage meeting should take place no later than 30 working days after the date that the notification was sent to the police officer, meaning that answers A, B and D are incorrect.

General Police Duties, para. 3.18.11.4

Answer 18.8

Answer **C** — First, special constables may be required to attend a third stage meeting to deal with unsatisfactory performance. In arranging a third stage meeting involving special constables, due consideration should be given to the fact that special constables are unpaid volunteers and may therefore have full-time employment or other personal commitments. Answer A is therefore incorrect.

In cases where a special constable is required to attend a third stage meeting, the force will appoint a member of the special constabulary to attend the meeting to advise the panel (as opposed to the officer—this is for the purpose of fairness). Answer B is incorrect.

The special constable advising the panel must have sufficient seniority and experience of the special constabulary to be able to advise the panel; however, he/

she will not form part of the panel and will not have a role in determining whether or not the police officer's performance or attendance is unsatisfactory. Answer D is therefore incorrect.

General Police Duties, para. 3.18.11.3

Answer 18.9

Answer **B** — Answer A is incorrect as attendance at any stage meeting is not subject to the same considerations as reporting for duty and the provisions of reg. 33 (sick leave) of the Police Regulations 2003 *do not apply*. An illness or disability may render a police officer unfit for duty without affecting his/her ability to attend a meeting. If the police officer is incapacitated, the meeting may be deferred until he/she is sufficiently improved to attend. A meeting will not be deferred indefinitely because the police officer is unable to attend, although every effort should be made to make it possible for the police officer to attend if he/she wishes to be present (making answer C incorrect). Where such circumstances apply at a stage three meeting, the force may wish to consider the use of video, telephone or other conferencing technology (correct answer B). Where, despite such efforts having been made and/or the meeting having been deferred, the police officer either persists in failing to attend the meeting or maintains his/her inability to attend, the person conducting the meeting will need to decide whether to continue to defer the meeting or whether to proceed with it, if necessary in the absence of the police officer (answer D is incorrect).

General Police Duties, para. 3.18.12

Answer 18.10

Answer **D** — There are several offences under the Police Act 1996 connected to such behaviour. First, there is impersonation under s. 90(1), but you would have to prove the person, with intent to deceive, impersonates a member of a police force or special constable or makes any statement or does any act calculated falsely to suggest that he/she is such a member or constable. There is no evidence that this has happened in this question; therefore, answer A is incorrect.

There are further offences under the 1996 Act: under s. 90(2) (wearing an article of police uniform of a member of a police force as to be calculated to deceive) and s. 90(3) (possessing an article of police uniform). An 'article of police uniform' for the purposes of s. 90(3) includes any article of uniform, any distinctive badge or mark or any document of identification usually issued to members of police forces or special constables (s. 90(4)). The document of identification would be a warrant card and this makes answer B incorrect.

Under subs. (3), a person can commit an offence by simply *possessing* the article of uniform unless he/she proves that he/she obtained possession of that article lawfully and has possession of it for a lawful purpose, making answer C incorrect. HEBDON is guilty of this offence and answer B is incorrect.

General Police Duties, para. 3.18.17.2

19 Road Policing Definitions and Principles

QUESTIONS

Question 19.1

JENKINS is sitting astride the seat of an old moped and riding it along a road. The moped was originally constructed as a motor vehicle and is fitted with pedals which JENKINS is using to propel the moped along the road although the engine is not working and there is no petrol in it.

Would the moped being ridden by JENKINS be a mechanically propelled vehicle?

A   No, as it is being used as a pedal cycle.
B   No, as the engine is not working.
C   Yes, provided it was constructed as one.
D   Yes, provided JENKINS intended to use it as one when he was riding it on the road.

Question 19.2

HARGREAVES was driving a diesel dumper truck on a road between two building sites. The dumper truck collided with a pedal cycle as HARGREAVES was negotiating a junction and the cyclist was injured. The police were called to deal with the accident. The dumper truck was intended for use solely on construction sites.

Considering the definition of a motor vehicle under s. 185(1) of the Road Traffic Act 1988, which of the following comments is correct in relation to the diesel dumper truck?

A   It would be considered a motor vehicle because HARGREAVES was driving it on a road.
B   It may be considered a motor vehicle if the prosecution is able to present evidence that it is suitable for use on a road.

C If it was intended for use solely on construction sites, it cannot be converted into a motor vehicle simply because it was being used on a road.
D It could not be considered as a motor vehicle as it was only being used temporarily on a road by HARGREAVES.

Question 19.3

BALL owns a Mini motor vehicle, which was manufactured for use on the road. BALL has decided to take up auto-cross racing which will take place off roads and he has completely rebuilt the Mini motor vehicle to use in those off-road races. BALL keeps the Mini in his garage off the road and has no intention of using the Mini on the road again.

Would the Mini be classed as a 'motor vehicle' at this time, under s. 185(1) of the Road Traffic Act 1988?
A No, because BALL does not intend to use it on the road.
B Yes, because it has retained its original character of a vehicle intended to be used on a road.
C No, because BALL keeps it off the road.
D Yes, because it was the manufacturer's intention that the vehicle would be used on the road.

Question 19.4

MERSON was thinking of buying a hoverboard to use as personal transportation to and from work. Most of MERSON's journey was through a large park (a public place), but parts of it were on public roads and pavements.

Which of the following statements is correct as to where MERSON could use this transportation device lawfully?
A The device could be used lawfully in the park but not on the road or the pavement.
B The device could not be used lawfully in any of these locations.
C The device could be used lawfully in the park or the pavement but not on the road.
D The device could be used lawfully in the park but not the pavement; it could be used lawfully on the road if it was registered as a road-legal vehicle.

Question 19.5

LOPEZ was giving his daughter driving lessons in his own private car. The first time he took her out on a road, LOPEZ allowed his daughter to sit in the driving seat of his car and to take control of the foot pedals while he leant over and took control of the steering wheel for the first 20 minutes or so. LOPEZ also kept his hand on the handbrake in case his daughter was unable to stop in enough time. He did this until his daughter gained enough confidence to drive on her own.

Would LOPEZ's actions be sufficient to satisfy a court that he was a 'driver' in these circumstances?

A No, only one person may be the driver of a vehicle at any one time.

B Yes, a court could decide LOPEZ was a 'driver' in these circumstances.

C Yes, a supervisor will always be a 'driver' while they are in a position to assume control of the vehicle if necessary.

D No, a supervisor will only be a 'driver' if they are supervising in a vehicle fitted with dual controls.

Question 19.6

MICHAELS was driving his car on a road when his mobile phone rang. He did not have a hands-free kit so he stopped at the side of the road. MICHAELS answered the phone while his car was stationary and with the engine still running. He remained in this position for ten minutes before completing the call and driving off.

In these circumstances, would MICHAELS have been the driver of the motor vehicle while it was stationary and he took the telephone call?

A No, as the vehicle was stationary, he was no longer a driver.

B Yes, he will be a driver until the end of his journey.

C No, the vehicle was stationary only for a short period of time.

D Yes, it's irrelevant how long the vehicle was stationary for.

Question 19.7

REID was sitting in the driver's seat of his car which was stationary and parked facing downhill on a road with a steep gradient. It had been snowing heavily and there was ice on the road. REID turned on the engine and released the handbrake and was about to set off slowly, but the vehicle started sliding down the hill. REID tried to apply the brakes and turn the vehicle into the skid but it continued sliding sideways down the hill and collided with a wall.

Could REID be held to have been 'driving' in these circumstances?

A No, at no time was REID in full control of the movement of the vehicle.

B Yes, even though REID did not have full control of the movement of the vehicle, the engine was running and this amounts to driving.

C No, a person may not be 'driving' when they are only attempting to control the movement of the vehicle.
D Yes, whether or not the engine is running is irrelevant when deciding if a person is driving; it is only whether they have some control of the movement of the vehicle that counts.

Question 19.8

KELLY was drunk and decided to drive home. He opened his car door and sat in the driver's seat. However, when KELLY tried to start the car he could not do so because he was using his house keys. Eventually, KELLY managed to find the correct ignition key, but the car would not start as the battery was flat.

At what point, if at all, would KELLY be considered as 'attempting to drive' his car?

A When he first sat in the driver's seat.
B When he tried to start the car with the house key.
C When he tried to start the car with the correct ignition key.
D He did not attempt to drive the car at any time.

Question 19.9

HEATH arranged a Scout fête and was given permission to use a field belonging to GILES, a local farmer. On the day of the fête, entry was restricted to a particular class of the public (in this case members of local Scout groups), and drivers of vehicles were charged £1 each for entry.

In relation to road traffic offences, would GILES's field qualify as a 'public' place in these circumstances?

A No, as entry to the field was restricted to a particular class of the public.
B Yes, as members of the public were allowed access.
C Yes, people were using the field with GILES's permission.
D No, as the people using the field were charged for entry.

Question 19.10

RICHLEY was stopped by police officers in the car park of the Red Lion public house at 9.30 pm and asked to provide a sample of breath for a screening test, which was positive. The car park had a sign up saying 'Red Lion Pub Customers Only'.

Is this car park a 'public place' at this time?

A Only if the prosecution can adduce clear evidence showing who uses the car park, when and for what purpose.

B No, as only a 'special class of public', i.e. only customers, are allowed to park there.

C Yes, even if the prosecution does not adduce evidence that the car park was a public place.

D No, as no invitation or permission was given to the public in general, only to persons wishing to use the public house.

Question 19.11

WINGFIELD is employed by POWE and as part of his job (and on behalf of POWE) he is driving a tractor on a road which is towing a trailer laden with hay. Constable SHAH stopped WINGFIELD for having an insecure load as some of the bales had fallen off the trailer onto the road. Constable SHAH reported WINGFIELD for the offence and later spoke to POWE who denied any responsibility as WINGFIELD had loaded the trailer himself. POWE stated that he would not have authorised the load to be carried in such a manner.

Which of the following comments is correct regarding POWE's liability for 'using' the vehicle in these circumstances?

A POWE would not be considered to be 'using' the vehicle as he did not authorise WINGFIELD to use the vehicle in such a way.

B Only the person who loaded the trailer (WINGFIELD) can 'use' so POWE cannot 'use' the vehicle.

C As WINGFIELD was drawing a trailer, only he could 'use' it.

D POWE would be 'using' the vehicle in these circumstances.

Question 19.12

WEST is the transport manager of a haulage company. He knows that most of his drivers make false entries on their tachograph sheets. WEST has not instructed them to do this, but as it means that the drivers work longer hours on behalf of the company, he does not stop them. FRAYLING, the owner of the company, is unaware of what is happening.

Who, if anyone, would be guilty of 'causing' offences in relation to drivers' hours in these circumstances?

A WEST only, as he has turned a blind eye to what is happening.

B Neither person is guilty of 'causing' offences in these circumstances.

C FRAYLING only as the owner of the company.

D Both people would be 'causing' offences in these circumstances.

Question 19.13

SILVER has recently re-applied for a driving licence following a period of disqualification but has been unable to afford to buy a new car because of the high cost of insuring it. SILVER has asked to borrow STAENBERG's car for the day. STAENBERG is aware of the recent disqualification but agrees to lend SILVER the car. STAENBERG has not discussed whether or not SILVER has insurance to drive the car on the road legally.

If SILVER does not have insurance and drives it on a road, which of the following would have to be proved if STAENBERG were to be guilty of 'permitting' the use of the vehicle without insurance?

A That STAENBERG knew SILVER did not have insurance and that the motor vehicle would be driven on a road.

B Only that STAENBERG knew SILVER would drive the motor vehicle on a road.

C That STAENBERG knew or believed SILVER did not have insurance and that the motor vehicle would be driven on a road.

D That STAENBERG knew SILVER did not have insurance or that the motor vehicle would be driven on a road.

Question 19.14

ALDERSON owed DIXON a considerable amount of money. DIXON threatened to set fire to ALDERSON's car if the money was not paid immediately. ALDERSON persuaded his brother to lend him the money and he drove to DIXON's house. On his way, ALDERSON was stopped by the police, who discovered he was a disqualified driver. ALDERSON claimed he was acting under duress and would not have driven had it not been for the threat made by DIXON.

Would ALDERSON be entitled to claim a defence of duress in these circumstances?

A Yes, if a reasonable person would have behaved in the same way as ALDERSON.

B No, the defence will apply only where death or serious injury are threatened.

C Yes, the defence will apply where serious damage has been threatened.

D No, the defence will not apply in a case of disqualified driving.

Question 19.15

Constable SAUNDERS is a Grade I advanced police driver. The officer was on duty in a marked police vehicle in the early hours of the morning and was following a vehicle which was being driven at speeds exceeding 100 mph on a road where the speed limit was 60 mph). The pursuit manager considered that Constable SAUNDERS was adequately trained and authorised the pursuit to continue. However, the officer lost control of the police vehicle on a bend and collided with a wall. Constable SAUNDERS's force submitted a file to the Crown Prosecution Service, seeking advice as to whether the officer should be prosecuted for dangerous driving.

Should the Crown Prosecution Service take Constable SAUNDERS's training into account when determining whether or not the officer's driving was dangerous?

A   No, Constable SAUNDERS is not entitled to have this training taken into account.
B   No, unless the police vehicle being driven by the officer is also displaying flashing lights.
C   Yes, Constable SAUNDERS was in an authorised pursuit situation and is entitled to have this training taken into account.
D   Yes, Constable SAUNDERS was on duty and is entitled to have this training taken into account.

Question 19.16

DC BELL is a trained advanced police driver and is part of a police surveillance unit tracking the activities of a gang who are suspected to be involved in a number of high-value robbery offences. DC BELL is driving a plain police surveillance vehicle and is following one of the chief suspects, TOMKINSON. All the information that DC BELL has at his disposal tells him that TOMKINSON is on his way to commit an offence of robbery at a bank. TOMKINSON is driving erratically and at speed and drives through a red traffic light. DC BELL believes that the seriousness of the situation requires him to do the same, and he follows TOMKINSON through the red traffic light at a considerable speed. DC BELL did this because he could see that there was nobody using the crossing or about to and believed the conditions were safe. Nobody is hurt in the incident but DC BELL's driving has been recorded by a camera at the traffic lights.

With regard to the offence of dangerous driving (contrary to s. 2 of the Road Traffic Act 1988) and case law in relation to police drivers and driving offences, which of the following comments is correct?

A The belief of DC BELL as to the conditions surrounding his driving will be taken into account by a court when considering whether he drove competently and carefully.

B Whilst the conditions that DC BELL found himself driving in may not provide a specific defence, they may provide significant mitigation for his actions.

C The fact that DC BELL is a highly skilled advanced police driver will be taken into account should he be charged with the offence of dangerous driving.

D DC BELL could rely on the defence of duress if he were prosecuted for dangerous driving.

Question 19.17

TABILO is a keen mechanic and likes to use his talents on all kinds of vehicles whether he is at work or at home. At his home address, he has several vehicles that he is working on for himself and some of his friends but he does not have the necessary space to work on all of them at the same time. As a result, he pushes a number of the vehicles onto the road outside his house. TABILO's neighbour, JOYCE, is annoyed by this behaviour and contacts the police to complain. PC TURNER visits TABILO's address and sees the vehicles in the road.

Considering only the issues in relation to the classification of vehicles, which of the following comments is correct?

A One of the vehicles in the road is an old Ford Escort constructed to be propelled by its mechanical engine. The Ford Escort has no engine in it as TABILO has re- moved it and is working on it in his garage 5 metres from the vehicle; the engine can easily be replaced in the Ford Escort. Just because there is no engine in the Ford Escort does not change the fact that it is a mechanically propelled vehicle.

B One of the vehicles in the road is a Nissan Terrano 4 × 4 originally intended for use on the road. TABILO has rebuilt the Terrano for one of his friends to use for 'off-road' racing; the Terrano is never going to be used on a road again and as such is no longer a motor vehicle.

C One of the vehicles in the road is an electrically assisted pedal cycle; this would be classed as a motor vehicle.

D One of the vehicles in the road is a Segway Personal Transporter (powered elec- trically); this would not be classed as a motor vehicle.

ANSWERS

Answer 19.1

Answer **C** — A mechanically propelled vehicle is, quite simply, a vehicle that is constructed so that it can be propelled mechanically. This is regardless of what the person driving/riding intends to use it for and for that reason answer D is incorrect.

Just because the engine in the moped is not working will not stop it being a mechanically propelled vehicle, making answer B incorrect. Answer A is incorrect as whilst it might be being used in the manner of a pedal cycle, it is still a mechanically propelled vehicle. In *McEachran* v *Hurst* [1978] RTR 462, the defendant was pedalling a moped to a friend's house for repair. It was not taxed and there was no current test certificate in force for the moped. The justices held that it was not a mechanically propelled vehicle on the grounds that it was being used as a pedal cycle, the engine did not work and there was no petrol in the tank. The Divisional Court, reversing the justices' decision, held that the test to be applied to determine whether the moped was mechanically propelled was the same as any other motor vehicle—on its construction. If it was constructed as a motor vehicle, it remained a mechanically propelled vehicle unless it could be said that there was no reasonable prospect of it again being mechanically propelled.

General Police Duties, para. 3.19.4

Answer 19.2

Answer **B** — A diesel dumper truck used solely for road construction work and not intended to be driven along the parts of the highway open to the public has been held not to be a motor vehicle for insurance purposes (*MacDonald* v *Carmichael* 1941 JC 27).

However, in a later case, while it was held that dumper trucks intended for use solely on construction sites will not generally be 'motor vehicles', the court did decide that if evidence can be adduced that they are suitable for use on a road, they *may* be held to be motor vehicles (*Daley* v *Hargreaves* [1961] 1 WLR 487). This does not mean that it will automatically be one, simply because it was being used on the road. Also, it has nothing to do with the owner's or manufacturer's intention (*Nichol* v *Leach* [1972] RTR 476), making answer C incorrect. Answer A is incorrect as just as HARGREAVES is driving the diesel dumper truck on the road would not automatically make it a motor vehicle.

It is the *use* of the vehicle that is important in this particular question, not the length of time it was driven on a road; therefore, answer D is incorrect.

General Police Duties, para. 3.19.5

Answer 19.3

Answer **B** — The test as to whether a vehicle is intended or adapted for use on roads is an objective one—would a reasonable person say that one of its uses would be general use on a road? (*Burns* v *Currell* [1963] 2 QB 433.) It has nothing to do with the owner's or manufacturer's intention. Answers A and D are therefore incorrect. Just because the vehicle is kept in a garage off the road would not have an impact on whether it is a motor vehicle or not, making answer C incorrect.

In *Nichol* v *Leach* [1972] RTR 476, the owner of a Mini car rebuilt it solely for 'autocross' racing, never intending it to be used on a road. Nevertheless, it was held to have retained its original intended road use character and remained a 'motor vehicle'.

General Police Duties, para. 3.19.5

Answer 19.4

Answer **A** — 'Self-balancing scooters' or 'personal transportation devices' (hoverboards) are illegal to ride on the road because they don't meet the requirements to be registered under the European or British schemes for road-legal vehicles. Since the device cannot be so registered, answer D is incorrect.

A person riding such a device on a pavement would commit an offence under s. 72 of the Highway Act 1835; therefore, answer C is incorrect.

On the other hand, riding the hoverboard in a park, a public place, would not contravene either piece of legislation and answer B is incorrect.

General Police Duties, para. 3.19.5

Answer 19.5

Answer **B** — Section 192(1) of the Road Traffic Act 1988 states that the 'driver' is a 'person engaged in the driving of the vehicle' and this section makes provision for the 'steersman' to be a 'driver'. This was confirmed in the case of *Tyler* v *Whatmore* [1976] RTR 83, when it was held that a girl in the front passenger seat of a car who leaned across the person in the driver's seat with both of her hands on the steering wheel, steering the car, with the ignition switch and handbrake within her reach, was 'actually driving'. Answer A is therefore incorrect.

Whether a person supervising a driver from the passenger's seat is a driver will be defined by the degree of control exercised throughout by the supervisor. In *Langman* v *Valentine* [1952] 2 All ER 803, it was held that an instructor who retains simultaneous control of the car by keeping their hands on the brake and steering wheel may be the driver. This case pre-dates dual-control learner vehicles and demonstrates that it would be possible for more than one person to be a 'driver', even if they are not in such a vehicle. Answer D is therefore incorrect.

However, a supervisor will not always be a 'driver'; in *Evans* v *Walkden* [1956] 1 WLR 1019, it was held that a person was not a 'driver' when the instructor was only in a position to assume control if necessary and therefore not in control at the material time. Answer C is therefore incorrect.

General Police Duties, para. 3.19.6

Answer 19.6

Answer **B** — For the purposes of road traffic offences, a person who takes out a vehicle remains the 'driver' of it, and he/she will be 'driving', until he/she has completed that journey. Therefore, even if the vehicle is stationary for some time, the person may still be the 'driver' if he/she has not completed the journey (*Jones* v *Prothero* [1952] 1 All ER 434) (answer C is therefore incorrect).

A person may still be 'driving' although the vehicle is stationary, when he is buying a newspaper or when he is changing a wheel (*Pinner* v *Everett* [1969] 1 WLR 1266); therefore, answer A is incorrect.

In *Edkins* v *Knowles* [1973] QB 748, it was emphasised that the reason for stopping is relevant as it might be part of the journey, e.g. stopping at a set of traffic lights or a junction, or may mark a break in the journey; however, the court did state that the length of the break and whether the driver leaves the vehicle *is* important and the court must consider the period of time and the circumstances before making its decision. Answer D is therefore incorrect.

General Police Duties, paras 3.19.6, 3.19.7

Answer 19.7

Answer **B** — There are many different cases ruling on whether or not a person is 'driving' a vehicle. In *DPP* v *Alderton* [2003] EWHC 2917 (Admin), it was held that operating the controls of a car (accelerator, clutch and steering) which was parked on a grass verge and wheel spinning was 'driving' even though there was no movement of the vehicle. Further, a person may be 'driving' even though they are only attempting to control the movement of the vehicle. In *Rowan* v *Merseyside Chief Constable* (1985), *The Times*, 10 December, the defendant knelt on the driving seat, released the hand-brake and thereafter attempted to re-apply it to stop the movement of the vehicle—he was held to be 'driving'. Answers A and C are therefore incorrect.

The Divisional Court has accepted a finding that a person sitting in the driver's seat of a car with the *engine running* had been 'driving' (*R (On the Application of Planton)* v *DPP* [2001] EWHC Admin 450). This has been extended in *Mason* v *DPP* [2010] RTR 120, where the Divisional Court suggested that 'driving' would occur when turning on the engine. This can be compared to the situation where the person sitting in the driving seat of a stationary motor vehicle with their hands on the steering wheel and the *engine off* was held *not* to be 'driving' (*Leach* v *DPP* [1993] RTR 161). Therefore, whether or not the engine is running *is* relevant when deciding if a person is driving and answer D is incorrect.

General Police Duties, paras 3.19.7, 3.19.8

Answer 19.8

Answer **B** — Acts which are merely preparatory will not amount to attempting to drive. Merely sitting in a car would not be sufficient as this is still a preparatory act. Answer A is therefore incorrect.

It has been held that where a defendant sits in the driver's seat of a car and tries to put his/her house keys in the ignition, that behaviour may be enough to prove a charge of 'attempting to drive' (*Kelly* v *Hogan* [1982] RTR 352). Answer D is therefore incorrect.

The fact that the vehicle is incapable of being driven will not prevent a charge involving an 'attempt' to drive (*R* v *Farrance* [1978] RTR 225). Answer C is incorrect because the question asks for the first point at which the defendant could be guilty of 'attempting' to drive.

General Police Duties, para. 3.19.8

Answer 19.9

Answer **A** — In order for a place to be a 'public place', it must be shown by the prosecution that:

• the people admitted to the place are members of the public and are admitted for that reason, and not because they belong to a certain or special class of the public; *and*

• those people are so admitted with the permission, express or implied, of the owner of the land.

(*DPP* v *Vivier* [1991] RTR 205.)

This case shows that the place in question must be open to *all* members of the public, without restriction (answer B is therefore incorrect). It is irrelevant whether the people are there with permission if only restricted members of the public are present. The two requirements from the *Vivier* case go hand in hand and answer C is therefore incorrect.

The fact that people had to pay to enter the land is completely irrelevant as to whether it is a public place. It is the *class of people* that are allowed entry (or not) that is important. If the fête had been open to *all* members of the public and they had all been made to pay, it would have been a public place. Answer D is therefore incorrect.

General Police Duties, para. 3.19.11

Answer 19.10

Answer **C** — In order to prove that a place is in fact a 'public place' for the purposes of road traffic offences, it must be shown by the prosecution that:

• those people who are admitted to the place in question are members of the public and are admitted as such, not as members of some special or particular class of the public (e.g. people belonging to an exclusive club) or as a result of some special characteristic that is not shared by the public at large; *and*
• those people are so admitted with the permission, express or implied, of the owner of the land in question.

(*DPP* v *Vivier* [1991] RTR 205.)

Customers of this pub are members of the general public who are invited to use it by the licensee, therefore making it public and not a 'special class' of persons, e.g. members of a club, and therefore answers B and D are incorrect.

The importance of police officers providing enough evidence to show that a particular location amounted to a public place was highlighted in *R* v *DPP, ex parte Taussik* [2001] ACD 10. In that case, the defendant was stopped as she drove out of an access road leading from a block of flats. The road was a cul-de-sac leading off a highway and was maintained by the local housing department. At the entrance to it, there was a large sign saying 'Private Residents Only'. As there was no evidence from the officers themselves that they had seen motorists (other than residents) using the road, the court was unable to conclude that the road was anything other than a private one. Contrast this with *R (On the Application of Lewis)* v *DPP* [2004] EWHC 3081 (Admin), where the court held that it was not necessary for the prosecution to adduce evidence that a pub car park was a public place, given that it was attached to the public house and given a general invitation to use it by the licensee. Therefore, answer A is incorrect.

General Police Duties, para. 3.19.11

Answer 19.11

Answer **D** — Offences relating to 'using' a vehicle are generally committed by the driver and the driver's employer. For the employer to commit the offence of 'using', the person driving the vehicle must be doing so in the ordinary course of his/her employer's business (*West Yorkshire Trading Standards Service* v *Lex Vehicle Leasing Ltd* [1996] RTR 70). It must be proved that:

- the employer owned the vehicle;
- the driver was employed by the employer; *and*
- the driver was driving in the ordinary course of his/her employment.

(*Jones* v *DPP* [1999] RTR 1.)

It is immaterial that the employer has not specifically authorised the employee to use the vehicle in such a way (*Richardson* v *Baker* [1976] RTR 56). Answers A and B are therefore incorrect.

The owner of a trailer who is responsible for putting it on a road will not escape liability by arguing that it was being drawn and therefore 'used' by someone else (*NFC Forwarding Ltd* v *DPP* [1989] RTR 239). Answer C is therefore incorrect.

General Police Duties, para. 3.19.12.1

Answer 19.12

Answer **B** — 'Causing' will involve some degree of dominance or control, or express mandate from the 'causer'.

Causing requires both positive action and knowledge by the defendant (*Price* v *Cromack* [1975] 1 WLR 988). Therefore, it is not enough that the person in charge is aware that an offence is being committed; he/she must have done something to contribute to it. Neither person in the scenario could meet these criteria, as neither 'ordered' the offences to be committed (one person was unaware of what was going on).

Further, wilful blindness by employers to their employees' unlawful actions is not enough to amount to 'causing' the offence (*Redhead Freight Ltd* v *Shulman* [1989] RTR 1). Answers A, C and D are incorrect for these reasons.

General Police Duties, para. 3.19.12.2

Answer 19.13

Answer **A** — Generally, in order to prove a case of 'permitting' there must be proof of knowledge by the defendant of the vehicle's use *and* of the unlawful nature of that use. In other words, there must be proof that the defendant knew the vehicle was being used and that the driver was committing an offence by using it (i.e. by driving it on a road without insurance). Answers B, C and D are incorrect for this reason.

General Police Duties, para. 3.19.12.3

Answer 19.14

Answer **B** — The defence(s) of duress and *necessity* will apply to cases of dangerous driving, careless and inconsiderate driving *and* driving while disqualified (*R* v *Martin* [1989] RTR 63 and *R* v *Backshall* [1998] 1 WLR 1506). Answer D is therefore incorrect. The defence of duress will only apply where the defendant was forced to commit an offence to avoid death or serious injury (*R* v *Conway* [1989] RTR 35), meaning that answers A and C are therefore incorrect.

General Police Duties, para. 3.19.13.1

Answer 19.15

Answer **A** — In *R* v *Bannister* [2009] EWCA Crim 1571, the Court of Appeal overruled a previous authority (*Milton* v *CPS* [2007] EWHC 532 (Admin)) finding that an advanced police driver with highly developed driving skills was *not* entitled to have that ability taken into account when deciding whether or not the driving in question was dangerous (correct answer A) and whether the flashing lights were displayed on the vehicle is irrelevant (answer B is incorrect).

The statutory test is based simply on the standard of the competent and careful driver, who is not to be vested with any particular level of skill or ability not found in the ordinary motorist, so answers C and D are therefore incorrect.

General Police Duties, para. 3.19.13.3

Answer 19.16

Answer **B** — The beliefs of DC BELL as to the conditions surrounding his driving at the time of the incident are not relevant to the issue of whether he drove competently and carefully (*R v Collins* [1997] EWCA Crim 657), making answer A incorrect. In *R v Bannister* [2009] EWCA Crim 1571, the Court of Appeal held that the fact that the defendant was a highly skilled advanced police driver was not a relevant circumstance that could be taken into account, making answer C incorrect. Answer D is incorrect as duress is a defence where the defendant is compelled to commit an offence having been threatened with death or serious injury. However, in *Agnew v DPP* [1991] RTR 144, the court stated that whilst the particular circumstances under which the police driver found him/herself driving may not provide a specific defence, they may provide significant mitigation for their actions and, where appropriate, special reasons for not disqualifying the driver.

General Police Duties, paras 3.19.13.3, 3.21.2.2, 3.21.4

Answer 19.17

Answer **A** — A 'mechanically propelled vehicle' is, quite simply, a vehicle that is constructed to be propelled mechanically. Removing the engine from the vehicle does not stop it being mechanically propelled if you can show the engine can easily be replaced (*Newbury v Simmons* [1961] 2 All ER 318), making answer A correct. Answer B is incorrect as a motor vehicle which is rebuilt for off-road racing continues to be 'intended' for use on a road even though those rebuilding it never intended to use it so again (*Nichol v Leach* [1972] RTR 476). Answer C is incorrect as an electrically assisted pedal cycle is not classed as a motor vehicle. A Segway Personal Transporter was held to be a motor vehicle within the definition of the Road Traffic Act 1988 (*Coates v CPS* [2011] EWHC 2031 (Admin)), making answer D incorrect.

General Police Duties, paras 3.19.4, 3.19.5

20 | Key Police Powers Relating to Road Policing

QUESTIONS

Question 20.1

DC MORENO was on mobile patrol late at night in plain clothes in an unmarked vehicle. There had been a number of burglaries in the area and the officer was on the lookout for suspicious people. The officer saw a vehicle being driven by KNIGHT stop at a set of traffic lights and pulled up alongside. DC MORENO did not suspect the driver had committed any offences relating to the vehicle, but wanted to ask why the driver was out late at night. The officer produced a warrant card and asked KNIGHT, 'Can you pull over, I just want to have a chat?' KNIGHT immediately got out of the car, ran across the road and entered a dwelling house.

In relation to s. 163 of the Road Traffic Act 1988 and the power of entry associated with it under s. 17(1)(c)(iiia) of the Police and Criminal Evidence Act 1984, which of the following comments is correct?

A This power may only be used when a person has failed to stop after committing an offence relating to the use of a vehicle on a road.

B DC MORENO could not use the power as a police officer must be in uniform to exercise a power of entry under this section.

C DC MORENO could only use this power of entry if KNIGHT had failed to stop for a constable in uniform.

D DC MORENO has the power to enter the premises because KNIGHT has failed to stop for a constable.

Question 20.2

Constable GREEN had been tutoring Constable COSGROVE for four weeks and had identified that the officer needed more experience in dealing with breathalysers.

On a night shift, Constable GREEN decided to set up a checkpoint on a housing estate with the intention of stopping all vehicles that came along. The plan was for Constable COSGROVE to speak to the drivers to identify if grounds existed to conduct breath test procedures.

Would the officers' actions be lawful in these circumstances?
A Yes, it is perfectly acceptable to randomly stop vehicles to train newly appointed officers in traffic procedures.
B No, they must at least anticipate detecting an offence or a crime before stopping the vehicle.
C No, this represents random breath testing, which is unlawful.
D Yes, it is perfectly acceptable to stop vehicles to conduct random breath tests.

Question 20.3

Constable ROBERTS attended a large retail store where the occupants of a green 4 × 4 vehicle had been captured on closed circuit television as they entered the store and stole several laptop computers (worth approximately £3,000) from within. The vehicle was seen to make off immediately prior to Constable ROBERTS's arrival. Constable ROBERTS contacted the control room and asked the duty sergeant to authorise an urgent road check, under s. 4 of the Police and Criminal Evidence Act 1984, for the vehicle and its occupants.

Can the officer's request be granted in these circumstances?
A Yes, but Constable ROBERTS could have authorised the road check himself.
B Yes, provided the sergeant authorises it.
C No, only an inspector may authorise a road check in urgent circumstances.
D No, only a superintendent may authorise a road check in any circumstances.

Question 20.4

Superintendent HAYES has provided written authorisation for a road check (under s. 4 of the Police and Criminal Evidence Act 1984) to take place in relation to an offence of rape. The purpose of the road check is to locate witnesses to the offence who may have seen the offence take place. Superintendent HAYES has authorised that all vehicles are to be stopped at the location of the incident, at the approximate time of day it occurred, for the next seven days. No useful information was gleaned during the initial period of seven days and the officer in the case has asked Superintendent HAYES to extend the duration of the road check.

If Superintendent HAYES agrees to extend this period, what would be the maximum period that may be granted beyond the initial seven days?

A It would be limited to one further period of seven days.

B It would be limited to two further periods, each lasting seven days.

C It would be limited to three further periods of seven days, subject to an overall maximum period of 28 days.

D There is no maximum period, provided the authorisations are for no more than seven days at a time.

Question 20.5

BRIARS was involved in a non-injury road traffic collision which the police attended. BRIARS was issued with an HORT/1 form to produce a driving licence and certificate of insurance. BRIARS was due to go on holiday the next day for a week and asked a friend, HAGGER, to take the documents to the station with the HORT/1 form.

In relation to the production of both documents, which of the following statements is correct?

A HAGGER may not produce these documents; they must both be produced by BRIARS.

B HAGGER may produce the driving licence, but BRIARS must produce the certificate of insurance.

C HAGGER may produce both the driving licence and the certificate of insurance.

D HAGGER may produce the certificate of insurance, but BRIARS must produce the driving licence.

Question 20.6

Constable HOLDSWORTH attended a road traffic collision that had taken place on a road. One of the vehicles was being driven by SAUNDERS, a provisional licence holder. The officer was told that another vehicle had driven into the rear of SAUNDERS's car while it was stationary at a set of traffic lights. At the time, SAUNDERS was being supervised by AMIN, a full licence holder. Both SAUNDERS and AMIN produced driving licences at the scene, but neither could produce a certificate of insurance. Constable HOLDSWORTH issued SAUNDERS with an HORT/1 form for the production of this document.

What is Constable HOLDSWORTH entitled to ask of AMIN, according to s. 165(5) of the Road Traffic Act 1988 (requirement to produce insurance)?

A Constable HOLDSWORTH is entitled to ask for AMIN's name and address and the name and address of the owner of the vehicle.

B Constable HOLDSWORTH is entitled to ask for AMIN's name, address and date of birth, but only if it is suspected that SAUNDERS has committed an offence.

C Constable HOLDSWORTH is entitled to ask AMIN whether or not SAUNDERS was insured to drive the motor vehicle on a road.

D Nothing, the duties under s. 165 only apply to the driver of a motor vehicle on a road.

Question 20.7

JORDAN is a designated police community support officer working on a housing estate. Numerous complaints have been received about a motor cycle being ridden around the estate by NEAL. JORDAN saw NEAL sitting astride the motor cycle outside a shopping centre and conducted a Police National Computer check on the vehicle, which showed that the vehicle was uninsured.

In relation to s. 165A of the Road Traffic Act 1988 (the power to seize a vehicle), which of the following comments is correct?

A JORDAN could not seize the motor cycle unless he was authorised to do so by an officer of or above the rank of inspector.

B JORDAN has the power to seize and remove the vehicle in these circumstances.

C The only people who could seize the motor cycle would be a constable in uniform or an authorised vehicle examiner.

D The vehicle can be seized but only by a constable in uniform.

Question 20.8

Constable GREEN was on uniform mobile patrol in a marked police vehicle and was following a vehicle being driven by STONE, who was unaccompanied at the time. The officer conducted a Police National Computer (PNC) check on the vehicle, which showed that it was uninsured. STONE began to make off and, not being pursuit trained, Constable GREEN stood down from following the vehicle. The officer traced the vehicle about two hours later, outside STONE's house. STONE produced a certificate of insurance, which was dated the day before and the officer concluded that PNC had not yet been updated; however, STONE did admit to only being a provisional driving licence holder.

Does Constable GREEN have the power to seize STONE's vehicle under s. 165A of the Road Traffic Act 1988 in these circumstances?

A Yes, the vehicle can be seized because the driver failed to stop, and Constable GREEN has reasonable grounds for believing the vehicle was being driven otherwise than in accordance with a licence.

B No, STONE has produced a valid certificate of insurance which was the original reason for stopping the vehicle.

C No, STONE is no longer 'driving' the vehicle.

D Yes, the vehicle can be seized simply because the driver failed to stop, without any of the other conditions being met.

Question 20.9

Constable BRIGHT was on uniform mobile patrol in a marked vehicle and was attempting to stop a vehicle, which made off without stopping. The officer conducted a Police National Computer check which showed that the vehicle did not have insurance. Constable BRIGHT attended the address of the registered owner, HANSON, a short while later and spoke to HANSON who admitted that the vehicle was uninsured. HANSON stated that the vehicle was parked in the detached garage in the grounds of the house.

Would Constable BRIGHT be entitled to seize the vehicle under s. 165A(1) of the Road Traffic Act 1988 in these circumstances?

A No, because the vehicle was in a private dwelling house.

B Yes, because the vehicle was not in a private dwelling house.

C Yes, a constable may enter any premises in order to exercise this power.

D No, because the vehicle was on private property.

Question 20.10

Constable PIERCE was dealing with a road traffic collision which involved serious injuries to one driver. The driver of the other vehicle left the scene without stopping. A Police National Computer check revealed that the registered keeper of the vehicle, TAYLOR, lived nearby. Constable PIERCE attended TAYLOR's address immediately to ascertain who was driving the vehicle.

What does s. 172 of the Road Traffic Act 1988 say in relation to Constable PIERCE's ability to ascertain these details?

A A request may be made verbally by Constable PIERCE, and TAYLOR has 28 days in which to reply.

B A request may only be made by post, and TAYLOR would have 28 days in which to reply.

C A request may be made verbally by Constable PIERCE, and TAYLOR must reply within a reasonable time.

D Constable PIERCE may not make the request: this power is restricted to people authorised by the chief officer of police.

Question 20.11

SHARMA was served with a notice under s. 172(2) of the Road Traffic Act 1988 after a vehicle registered to him had driven through a red light and been caught on camera. SHARMA returned the notice with a letter stating that he had lent his car to HOLLAND on the day of the offence; however, HOLLAND had told SHARMA that he in turn had lent the car to another person, but refused to say who that person was. SHARMA stated that he was unable to identify the driver and provided HOLLAND's details in the form.

What options are now open to the police, under s. 172, in these circumstances?

A A notice may only be served on the registered keeper under this section; therefore, the police will have to prosecute SHARMA for failing to comply with s. 172 and he has no defence.

B The police should serve a notice on HOLLAND; s. 172 only requires SHARMA to provide details of the actual driver, not a potential driver; since he could not, he has no other liability under this section.

C The police should serve a notice on HOLLAND; however, SHARMA may still be liable under s. 172.

D The police should serve a notice on HOLLAND but they should also prosecute SHARMA for failing to comply with s. 172 and he has no defence.

Question 20.12

A road traffic collision occurs in which HAVERY and BARROW, who were pedestrians walking along a pavement, are seriously injured. A witness to the collision has described the driving of the person responsible; this description causes the officer attending the scene, PC ROGERSON, to believe that an offence of causing serious injury by dangerous driving (contrary to s. 1A of the Road Traffic Act 1988) has occurred. PC ROGERSON has a description of the vehicle concerned and wishes to authorise a road check to locate the person responsible for the offence.

Considering the law relating to road checks, which of the following comments is correct?

A   A road check cannot be authorised to ascertain whether a vehicle is carrying a person who is responsible for a road traffic offence.

B   PC ROGERSON can authorise a road check in these circumstances.

C   A road check cannot be authorised unless it is for the purpose of ascertaining whether a vehicle carries a person who is unlawfully at large.

D   A road check can be authorised but this authorisation must come from an officer of the rank of superintendent or above.

Question 20.13

BRATLEN is driving her Ford Fiesta along a road when she is stopped by PC KHAN (on uniform foot patrol). The officer speaks to BRATLEN and asks her if she has insurance for the vehicle. BRATLEN replies, 'I might have and I might not, but either way what are you going to do about it?' and drives off. PC KHAN took the registration number of the vehicle and finds out BRATLEN's home address. PC KHAN visits the address and when he arrives he can see the Ford Fiesta parked in a garage adjoining BRATLEN's home address. PC KHAN suspects that BRATLEN has no insurance for the Ford Fiesta and is considering seizing the vehicle under the powers of the Road Traffic Act 1988.

Which of the following comments is correct?

A   The power cannot be used as the garage that the Ford Fiesta is in is connected to a dwelling house.

B   The power can be used but PC KHAN will require another officer (of any rank) to be present to witness the seizure.

C   The power cannot be used as PC KHAN only suspects that BRATLEN has no insurance for the Ford Fiesta.

D   The Ford Fiesta can be seized by the officer as he has reasonable grounds to suspect that BRATLEN has no insurance certificate to drive it.

ANSWERS

Answer 20.1

Answer **C** — Under s. 163(1) of the Road Traffic Act 1988, a person driving a mechanically propelled vehicle on a road must stop the vehicle on being required to do so by a constable in uniform or a traffic officer. If a person fails to comply with this section, he/she is guilty of an offence (s. 163(3)).

Section 163 carries with it a power of entry under s. 17(1)(c)(iiia) of the Police and Criminal Evidence Act 1984, which states:

> Subject to the following provisions of this section, and without prejudice to any other enactment, a constable may enter and search any premises for the purpose of arresting a person for an offence under
>
> ...
>
> (iiia) section 4 (driving etc. when under the influence of drink or drugs) or section 163 (failure to stop when required to do so by a constable in uniform) of the Road Traffic Act 1988.

The use of the *power of entry* under this section is not restricted to police officers in uniform; therefore, a plain-clothed police officer may exercise this power (answer B is incorrect). However, the suspect must have initially *failed to stop* for a constable in uniform before the power may be used; therefore, answer D is incorrect.

There is no requirement for the person to have committed an offence relating to use of a vehicle on a road *and* failed to stop; simply failing to stop when required to do so by a constable in uniform would trigger the use of the power under s. 17. Answer A is therefore incorrect.

General Police Duties, para. 3.20.2

Answer 20.2

Answer **A** — Section 163(1) of the Road Traffic Act 1988 states that a person driving a mechanically propelled vehicle on a road must stop the vehicle on being required to do so by a constable in uniform or a traffic officer. This is a power for an officer in uniform randomly to stop vehicles. That said, like any power available to the police, its use must be able to be justified. In *Stewart* v *Crowe* 1999 SLT 899, it was said that the power under s. 163 represented a necessary and proportionate response to the prevention of crime and that the only limit on the power is that it should not be used whimsically or oppressively.

In *Chief Constable of Gwent* v *Dash* [1986] RTR 41, vehicles were being randomly stopped in order to give a police officer further experience of the breath test procedure under the supervision of her senior. The court held that the actions of the police were not an abuse of power and did not amount to malpractice; therefore, the requirement of a breath specimen and the subsequent procedure were lawful. Random stopping of cars for the purpose of ascertaining whether their drivers have alcohol in their bodies is perfectly permissible; random breath testing, however, is not. This case adds yet another reason for a police officer to stop a vehicle—to train newly appointed officers in traffic procedure. Answers B and D are therefore incorrect.

In *Miller* v *Bell* 2004 GWD 26-564, it was held that the requirement to stop the vehicle is a legal one and, as a result of a response given by the driver and/or the officer's observations, a suspicion may form in the officer's mind that the driver has alcohol in their body and they may require the driver to take a preliminary test. This is a random stop but *not* a random preliminary test. Answer C is therefore incorrect.

General Police Duties, para. 3.20.2

Answer 20.3

Answer **A** — Section 4 of the Police and Criminal Evidence Act 1984 states that a road check may be authorised only where the officer has reasonable grounds for believing that the offence committed is an indictable offence—this is an indictable offence so a road check can be authorised. Generally speaking, an officer of at least the rank of superintendent must authorise a road check.

In urgent cases, the authorising officer may be any rank below the rank of superintendent, and in this case Constable ROBERTS could have authorised the check provided a written record is made and a superintendent informed as soon as possible; answers B, C and D are therefore incorrect as the officer could have authorised the road check himself.

General Police Duties, para. 3.20.3

Answer 20.4

Answer **D** — Section 4 of the Police and Criminal Evidence Act 1984 states that a road check may be authorised only where the officer has reasonable grounds for believing that the offence committed is an indictable offence. Generally, the authorisation will be given by a superintendent; however, an officer of any rank may authorise the road check in urgent circumstances.

Section 4(11)(a) states that the authorising officer must specify a period, not exceeding seven days, during which the road check may continue. This period may be either continuous or conducted at specified times during that period. If it appears to a superintendent that the road check ought to continue beyond the initial seven days, he/she may authorise a further period of seven days during which it may continue. There is no limit as to how many road checks may be authorised, provided each period does not exceed seven days. Answers A, B and C are therefore incorrect.

General Police Duties, para. 3.20.3.1

Answer 20.5

Answer **D** — Under s. 164(8)(a) of the Road Traffic Act 1988, the person must show that within seven days after the production of his/her licence was required, he/she produced it *in person* at a police station that was specified by him/her at the time their production was required.

On the other hand, under s. 165 (4)(a), the person must show that within seven days, the certificate of insurance *was produced* at a police station, removing the requirement for it to be produced in person.

Since answer D is the only one containing the correct combination, answers A, B and C are incorrect.

General Police Duties, paras 3.20.4.4, 3.20.5

Answer 20.6

Answer **A** — Section 165(5) of the Road Traffic Act 1988 states that a person:

(a) who supervises the holder of a provisional licence granted under Part III of this Act while the holder is driving on a road a motor vehicle, or

(b) whom a constable or vehicle examiner has reasonable cause to believe was supervising the holder of such a licence while driving, at a time when an accident occurred owing to the presence of the vehicle on a road or at a time when an offence is suspected of having been committed by the holder of the provisional licence in relation to the use of the vehicle on a road,

must, on being so required by a constable or vehicle examiner, give his name and address and the name and address of the owner of the vehicle.

Since the officer may ask the supervisor for these details, answer D is incorrect.

Constable HOLDSWORTH may ask for these details if the vehicle was involved in a collision on the road or if it is suspected that SAUNDERS has committed an offence. Answer B is therefore incorrect.

There is no power under this section to deal with the supervisor in respect of insurance issues. These duties belong to the driver and therefore answer C is incorrect.

General Police Duties, para. 3.20.5

Answer 20.7

Answer **D** — Vehicles may be seized under s. 165A of the Road Traffic Act 1988, subject to certain conditions being satisfied. The first condition is where a constable in *uniform* requests that a person produces evidence that a motor vehicle is or was not being driven in contravention of s. 87(1) of the Act (driving otherwise than in accordance with a licence); the second condition is that a similar request is made for evidence that the vehicle was not being driven in contravention of s. 143 (driving without insurance). Where the person fails to produce such evidence, provided the constable has reasonable grounds for believing that the vehicle was being so driven, he/she may seize the vehicle.

The power is restricted to police officers, in uniform, and is not given to authorised vehicle examiners or PCSOs.

Answers A, B and C are therefore incorrect.

Note that PCSOs do have a power to seize a motor vehicle under s. 59 of the Police Reform Act 2002 (using a motor vehicle in an anti-social manner).

General Police Duties, para. 3.20.6

Answer 20.8

Answer **A** — Vehicles may be seized under s. 165A of the Road Traffic Act 1988, subject to certain conditions being satisfied. Under s. 165A, the first condition is where a constable in uniform requests that a person produces evidence that a motor vehicle is or was not being driven in contravention of s. 87(1) of the Act (driving otherwise than in accordance with a licence); the second condition is that a similar request is made for evidence that the vehicle was not being driven in contravention of s. 143 (driving without insurance).

There is a third condition attached to s. 165A, which is when a constable in uniform requires a person driving a motor vehicle to stop (under s. 163), the person fails to stop the vehicle, or to stop it for long enough, for the constable to make such lawful inquiries as he/she considers appropriate, and the constable has reasonable grounds for believing that that vehicle is or was being driven in contravention of s. 87(1) or s. 143.

If any of these conditions apply, and the person fails to produce evidence that the vehicle was not being driven in contravention of these two sections, provided the constable has reasonable grounds for believing that the vehicle was being so driven, he/she may seize the vehicle, notwithstanding that the person is no longer driving it. Answer C is therefore incorrect.

The vehicle may be seized if one condition is not met (i.e. the driver has insurance) and the other condition is (i.e. he/she has no driving licence). Answer B is therefore incorrect.

Finally, a vehicle cannot be seized simply because the driver failed to stop. The constable must have reasonable grounds for believing that at least one of the other conditions is met. Answer D is therefore incorrect.

General Police Duties, para. 3.20.6

Answer 20.9

Answer **B** — Vehicles may be seized under s. 165A of the Road Traffic Act 1988, subject to certain conditions being satisfied. Under s. 165A(4), where a constable in uniform has required a person to stop a motor vehicle and the person fails to do so, the constable may seize the vehicle where the constable has reasonable grounds for believing the vehicle is or was being driven contrary to s. 143 of the Act.

For the purposes of exercising the power under s. 165A, a constable may enter any premises other than a private dwelling house on which he/she has reasonable grounds for believing the vehicle to be. Answer C is therefore incorrect.

Under s. 165A(9)(d), the definition of a 'private dwelling house' does *not* include any garage or other structure occupied with the dwelling house or land belonging to it. Since a garage is not a private dwelling house, answer A is incorrect.

This exception refers to private dwelling houses and not private property; therefore, if the vehicle had been parked on property which was private but not a dwelling, it could have been seized and therefore answer D is incorrect.

Note that the powers referred to in s. 165A also apply to circumstances where a person is believed to be driving a vehicle contrary to s. 87(1) of the Act (driving otherwise than in accordance with a licence).

General Police Duties, para. 3.20.6

Answer 20.10

Answer **C** — Under s. 172(2) of the Road Traffic Act 1988, where the driver of a vehicle has committed an offence to which the section applies (this includes ss. 3 and

170), the keeper of the vehicle shall give information as to the identity of the driver as required by or on behalf of a chief officer of police.

There is no mention of a person having to be authorised to make such a request on behalf of the chief officer so answer D is therefore incorrect.

When a request is made by post, the keeper has 28 days in which to reply. The 1988 Act does not state that *all* requests must be made by post and answer B is therefore incorrect. On the contrary, the case of *Lowe* v *Lester* [1987] RTR 30 indicates that requests may be made verbally, and the information must be provided within a reasonable time. Therefore, answer A is incorrect.

General Police Duties, para. 3.20.7

Answer 20.11

Answer **C** — A person is guilty of an offence if they fail to comply with a requirement under s. 172(2) of the Road Traffic Act 1988 to supply the details of the person who was driving a vehicle at the time an offence was committed. A s. 172 notice will be sent by the police to the registered keeper and compliance will be achieved by returning it with details of who was driving. A section of the form allows the registered keeper to enter another person's details if he/she was not the driver at the time of the offence. If the keeper is unable to provide details of the driver, the form asks for reasons for that inability.

Where a registered keeper returned the form with a covering letter stating that he had not completed the form because on the day of the alleged offence more than one person had used the vehicle, he was convicted of failing to comply with the requirement under s. 172. The defendant argued that he had complied with s. 172 because the form only required him to provide details of the actual driver, not a potential driver (which he could not do).

The Divisional Court disagreed, holding that a notice issued pursuant to s. 172 requires an accurate response and not an inaccurate or misleading statement. The defendant's claim was clearly contrary to the legislative intention, as it would frequently be the case that the registered owner of a vehicle would at least suspect who the driver was, even if he/she did not know for certain, e.g. where the owner lent the vehicle to a friend but was not in the vehicle at the time of the alleged offence (*R (On the Application of Flegg)* v *Southampton and New Forest Justices* [2006] EWHC 396 (Admin)). Answer B is therefore incorrect.

Answer A is incorrect because s. 172(2) allows for a notice to be sent to the keeper, or any other person who will be required to give 'any information which it is in his power to give and may lead to identification of the driver'. This means that a notice should be sent to HOLLAND regardless of any decision to prosecute SHARMA.

Section 172(4) provides that a person shall not be convicted of this offence if that person can show that he/she did not know and could not have ascertained with reasonable diligence who the driver of the vehicle was. This does not negate the keeper's liability, as seen in *R (On the Application of Flegg)*; it will depend whether the prosecution decides to pursue a case against HOLLAND, who would commit the offence if he failed to disclose details of the driver, or both persons. Answer D is therefore incorrect.

General Police Duties, paras 3.20.7, 3.20.7.1

Answer 20.12

Answer **A** — A road check can take place to ascertain whether a vehicle is carrying:

- a person who has committed an offence other than a road traffic offence or a vehicle excise offence;
- a person who is a witness to such an offence;
- a person intending to commit such an offence; or
- a person who is unlawfully at large.

So answer C is incorrect as there are a variety of reasons why a road check can be authorised. In an 'urgent' situation ('urgent' is not defined), any officer can authorise a road check. Ordinarily they are authorised by an officer of the rank of superintendent or above. However, a road check cannot be authorised in relation to a road traffic offence or a vehicle excise offence. As the offence described is most definitely a road traffic offence (regardless of its seriousness), a road check could not be authorised, making answers B and D incorrect.

General Police Duties, para. 3.20.3

Answer 20.13

Answer **C** — Where a constable in uniform requires a person driving a motor vehicle to stop the vehicle (as per s. 163 of the Road Traffic Act 1988) and that person fails to stop the vehicle, or to stop the vehicle for long enough, for the constable to make such lawful inquiries as he/she considers appropriate and the constable has reasonable grounds for *believing* that the vehicle is or was being driven without insurance, then he/she may seize the vehicle. PC KHAN only *suspects* so the power is not available (answer D is incorrect). The fact that the car is in a garage next to a house would not stop the use of the power in the right circumstances (answer A). There is no requirement for a witness to the seizure should the powers be used (answer B).

General Police Duties, para. 3.20.6

21 | Offences Involving Standards of Driving

QUESTIONS

Question 21.1

Fifty cars were gathered in a supermarket car park one evening, racing in an un-authorised rally. GLEESON was driving one of the cars at high speed and KRAMER was in the front passenger seat. GLEESON lost control of the car and crashed into a shelter. GLEESON survived the crash, but KRAMER did not. The car park was only open to the public when the supermarket was open. A barrier prevented vehicular access outside these hours, but the people attending the rally damaged it to gain access.

Could GLEESON be found guilty of causing death by dangerous driving under s. 1 of the Road Traffic Act 1988 in these circumstances?

A No, GLEESON was not driving on a road.

B Yes, because GLEESON was trespassing, the offence could be complete.

C No, GLEESON was not driving on a road or public place.

D Yes, there are no restrictions on where the offence may take place.

Question 21.2

INGHAM was a delivery driver and was working in the early hours of the morning while it was still dark and visibility was poor. INGHAM stopped the delivery van on a country road, which had no on-street lighting, to deliver goods to a premises which was situated on a sharp bend. While INGHAM was out of the van delivering goods, another vehicle driving on the road collided with the van, causing the death of the only occupant. When the police accident investigation team arrived, they noted that the van could not be seen by a person driving towards the bend and that INGHAM had left no warning lights on the vehicle.

In relation to the offence of causing death by dangerous driving under s. 1 of the Road Traffic Act 1988, could INGHAM be said to have 'caused' the death of the other driver in these circumstances?

A No, INGHAM was not driving at the time of the accident.

B Yes, there was a causal link between INGHAM parking the van at the location and the fatal accident.

C Yes, in the circumstances the prosecution will be able to show that INGHAM's actions were a substantial cause of the death, which is required in such cases.

D No, the prosecution would have to show that INGHAM's driving fell far below what would be expected of a competent and careful driver which, in the circumstances, would not be possible.

Question 21.3

DALEY was driving her car on the approach to a zebra crossing when some children were crossing the road. When DALEY applied her brakes, they failed and she knocked over a child, injuring the child. DALEY's car was examined and it was found that her brake discs were so worn that they did not work. DALEY stated that she had heard the brakes squealing earlier in her journey but had not realised how bad they were.

Considering only the 'dangerous condition' of the vehicle, what further evidence, if any, would be required in order to convict DALEY of driving dangerously?

A That it would have been obvious to a competent and careful driver that driving the vehicle in that condition would be dangerous.

B No further evidence is required; DALEY may be convicted on these facts alone.

C DALEY could not be convicted of dangerous driving as she was unaware of the dangerous condition of her car.

D That it should have been obvious to DALEY that driving the vehicle in that condition would be dangerous.

Question 21.4

SHARPE was driving a bus towards a zebra crossing while two people were crossing the road. Witnesses have stated that SHARPE drove into the two people while they were still on the crossing; both persons were taken to hospital but later died of their injuries. SHARPE has been charged with an offence under s. 1 of the Road Traffic Act 1988 (causing death by dangerous driving) but intends pleading not guilty because, on the approach to the crossing, he inadvertently pressed the accelerator pedal instead of the brake which meant that he had no intention to commit the offence.

Which of the following statements is correct in relation to SHARPE's proposed defence to a charge for this offence?

A The fact that SHARPE had no intention to commit the offence is irrelevant; he could be convicted on these facts alone.

B For SHARPE to be convicted of this offence, the prosecution would have to show that he intended his driving to be dangerous.

C The court might not convict SHARPE of this offence because of his lack of intent; however, it may convict him of the alternative charge of causing death by careless driving.

D The court might not convict SHARPE of this offence because of his lack of intent, unless the prosecution can show that he knew his driving was dangerous.

Question 21.5

LLOYD is appearing in Crown Court for an offence of dangerous driving. Witnesses saw LLOYD speeding towards a junction on a housing estate and failing to brake in time. The defendant's vehicle shot through the junction and collided with another vehicle. A nearby resident, REID, has also provided a written statement stating that she saw LLOYD doing handbrake turns in the road shortly before the collision, before the vehicle sped off out of her sight towards the junction where the collision occurred. In her statement, REID has stated that LLOYD was well known on the estate for the dangerous way he drove and she had heard from other residents that there had been several other near misses such as the current case.

Would the prosecution be able to admit REID's evidence in asking the court to decide whether LLOYD is guilty of dangerous driving?

A Yes, the court may hear the evidence of LLOYD's driving immediately before the incident, but the information regarding previous bad driving would be considered inadmissible.

B Yes, the court may hear all of REID's testimony—evidence such as this is admissible in cases of dangerous driving.

C No, only an expert witness could give this evidence and REID will not be regarded as such.

D No, REID's entire evidence would not be admissible in this case.

Question 21.6

HIGGINSON has been charged with causing death by dangerous driving in relation to a road traffic accident.

In relation to the actual causes of the accident, which of the following is true?
A Any police officer may give an opinion, but it must be supported with factual evidence.
B A court may allow a police officer who is an expert in the investigation of collisions to give evidence of opinion as to the cause of that collision.
C A police officer who has experience in collision investigation may give such opinion, but it must be supported with factual evidence.
D Only factual evidence in relation to the dangerous driving is allowed; opinion as to the cause of the accident is not.

Question 21.7

Constable CHAPMAN was dealing with a fatal road traffic accident where LYNCH (the suspected driver of the vehicle involved) had made off. According to witness accounts, LYNCH had caused the accident by driving carelessly beforehand. Constable CHAPMAN eventually traced LYNCH some five hours after the accident occurred. LYNCH admitted to having taken drugs since the accident and was exhibiting signs of being unfit. Constable CHAPMAN asked LYNCH to provide a preliminary drug test under s. 6C of the Road Traffic Act 1988, using an approved device; however, LYNCH refused to provide a sample because he had taken drugs after the accident.

Would LYNCH be guilty of an offence under s. 3A(1)(d) of the Road Traffic Act 1988 (causing death by careless driving when under the influence of drink or drugs) in these circumstances?
A Yes, the request was made within the timescale required under s. 3A.
B Yes, the timescale required under s. 3A is not relevant because LYNCH has deliberately attempted to evade arrest.
C No, at this stage an offence is not committed under this section; however, LYNCH could be guilty if he subsequently refuses to provide a sample under s. 7 of the Act.
D Yes, Constable CHAPMAN reasonably suspects that LYNCH is unfit to drive now; therefore, the offence is complete.

Question 21.8

CAGE works for a building company and has a drug habit. CAGE turned up for work while under the influence of drugs and was fired. To get revenge, CAGE stole a dumper truck from the site, intending to take it to the head office and cause damage. On the way, CAGE was involved in a road traffic accident where a pedestrian walked into the road in front of the dumper truck, and was killed. CAGE was still under the influence of drugs at this time and was unfit to drive.

Has CAGE committed an offence under s. 3A of the Road Traffic Act 1988 in these circumstances?

A No, CAGE was not under the influence of drink at the time of the accident.

B No, it must be shown that CAGE drove without due care and attention or without due consideration to other road users.

C Yes, he was driving a motor vehicle whilst unfit to drive and caused the death of the pedestrian (the location of the accident is irrelevant).

D Yes, he was driving a mechanically propelled vehicle on a road while under the influence of drugs.

Question 21.9

FRANCIS was driving a van on a road and was approaching a junction with a side road. FRANCIS indicated to turn left and was in the middle of doing so when, without warning, HASTINGS stepped off the pavement into the path of the vehicle driven by FRANCIS and was knocked over. HASTINGS turned out to be an elderly man who suffered minor injuries, but he had to be taken to hospital with breathing difficulties and later died of a heart attack. It transpired that FRANCIS had been driving the vehicle without insurance.

Would the fact that FRANCIS did not cause the accident be relevant in relation to an offence under s. 3ZB of the Road Traffic Act 1988 (causing the death of another person)?

A No, the fact that FRANCIS was driving without insurance would be sufficient to prove this offence.

B Yes, there must be evidence that FRANCIS's driving in some way contributed to HASTINGS's death beyond the mere presence of the vehicle on the road.

C No, the mere presence of the vehicle on the road would make FRANCIS guilty of this offence.

D Yes, because HASTINGS's injuries as a result of the collision were not serious, FRANCIS has not 'caused' his death.

Question 21.10

LUTHER is a disqualified driver and was driving his friend's car on a road. Whilst approaching a junction, LUTHER was guilty of a minor lapse in concentration, which resulted in him not seeing a cyclist on his nearside. The wing mirror of the car LUTHER was driving clipped the cyclist, who then fell off the cycle. The cyclist was later taken to hospital suffering from a broken leg.

Could LUTHER be guilty of an offence under s. 3ZD of the Road Traffic Act 1988 in these circumstances?

A Yes, as a disqualified driver, he meets both requirements under the section (having no driving licence and having no insurance).

B Yes, LUTHER has committed this offence simply by being a disqualified driver.

C No, LUTHER has not caused the death of another person.

D Yes, as a disqualified driver, he meets one of the requirements under the section (having no driving licence or having no insurance).

Question 21.11

PC FACEY is investigating an allegation of careless and inconsiderate driving (contrary to s. 3 of the Road Traffic Act 1988). He has interviewed HASSAN (the driver of the vehicle) who has stated that he only passed his driving test two months ago and consequently was very nervous when he was driving his vehicle along the road where the offence is alleged to have taken place. HASSAN states that there were several children playing in the road and that he was distracted by them, causing him to involuntarily veer slightly to the left of the road and drive through a puddle which sprayed water on several pedestrians walking along the pavement (the source of the allegation of careless and inconsiderate driving).

Considering the law surrounding careless and inconsiderate driving and the offence under s. 3 of the Act, which of the following comments is correct?

A The offence has not been committed as HASSAN's driving has not caused inconvenience to other road users who are driving or riding mechanically propelled vehicles.

B For the offence to be committed, it must be proved that HASSAN departed from the standard of driving that would be expected from a competent and careful driver and that his actions were voluntary.

C A court would be able to consider the fact that HASSAN was a 'new' driver and that he could not be expected to drive in the same way as an experienced driver would in the same circumstances.

D The fact that there were children playing in the road is entirely immaterial, so if HASSAN were charged with the offence this element of the circumstances could not amount to a defence.

Question 21.12

EVATT is driving a dumper truck on a building site. He leaves the building site and drives into a public car park next to the building site to visit a newsagent and purchase some cigarettes. There is a car parking space directly outside the newsagent and EVATT drives towards it. As he does so, LINDLEY, driving her Nissan Micra, begins to reverse into the parking space. EVATT is outraged that someone is going to beat him to the parking spot and presses down on the accelerator of the dumper truck, taking it to its maximum speed in an attempt to beat LINDLEY to the parking space. Unfortunately, EVATT loses control of the dumper truck, which collides with LINDLEY's Nissan Micra. The collision has serious consequences as LINDLEY is six months pregnant and, due to the shock of the accident, she suffers a miscarriage, losing her unborn child.

Which comment is true with regard to the offence of causing death by dangerous driving (contrary to s. 1 of the Road Traffic Act 1988)?

A EVATT is not liable for the offence as he was driving a dumper truck which is classed as a mechanically propelled vehicle and this offence only applies to motor vehicles.

B EVATT is not liable for the offence as the incident occurred in a public place rather than on a road.

C EVATT is not liable for the offence as he has not caused the death of another person.

D EVATT has committed the offence in these circumstances.

Question 21.13

At 5.30 pm, a car driven carelessly by TRICKETT is involved in an accident during which YORK (a pedestrian) is seriously injured. TRICKETT does not stop at the scene of the accident. YORK is taken to hospital but at 10 pm the same evening he dies from injuries sustained in the accident. The police are making inquiries to locate TRICKETT and require a specimen from him under s. 7 of the Road Traffic Act 1988.

What is the latest time that TRICKETT can be asked to provide the specimen where a refusal would constitute an offence under s. 3A of the Act (causing death by careless driving when unfit through drink or drugs)?

A Within 18 hours of 5.30 pm (the time of the accident).

B Within 18 hours of 10 pm (the time of death).

C Within 24 hours of 5.30 pm (the time of the accident).

D Within 24 hours of 10 pm (the time of death).

ANSWERS

Answer 21.1

Answer **C** — The offence of causing death by dangerous driving under s. 1 of the Road Traffic Act 1988 may be committed by a person driving a mechanically pro-pelled vehicle *on a road or public place*. The Act gives a wide meaning to the types of vehicle that may commit the offence (including dumper trucks, cranes and quad-bikes), and the location. Answers A and D are therefore incorrect.

A place will only be public if people are admitted with the permission, express or implied, of the owner of the land in question (*DPP* v *Vivier* [1991] RTR 205). Because drivers of the vehicles were trespassing, the offence will *not* be complete as it may only take place on a road or public place and therefore answer B is incorrect.

General Police Duties, paras 3.19.11, 3.21.2

Answer 21.2

Answer **B** — Section 1 of the Road Traffic Act 1988 states that a person who causes the death of another person by driving a mechanically propelled vehicle danger-ously on a road or other public place is guilty of an offence.

In this particular scenario, because INGHAM was not actually sitting in the van and 'driving' it in the ordinary sense, the court would have to decide whether or not this impacts on the ability of the defendant to commit the offence. The Court of Appeal have clarified that this offence relates to causing death *by* driving and not causing death *while* driving and therefore the 'driving' does not have to be coextensive (or coterminous) with the accident that resulted in the death. In other words, INGHAM's *earlier* driving was a contributing factor to the victim's death.

In *R* v *Jenkins* [2012] EWCA Crim 2909, the court held that parking a vehicle to make a delivery and leaving it in conditions of poor visibility where another ve-hicle collided with it was certainly a causal link to the fatality that occurred.

Answers A and D are incorrect, because the defendant *has* driven in a way which would fall far below what would be expected of a competent and careful driver.

It is not necessary to show that the driving by the defendant was the sole or even a substantial cause of death; it must only be shown to have been *a* cause of the death (*R* v *Hennigan* [1971] 3 All ER 133). Answer C is therefore incorrect.

General Police Duties, paras 3.21.2.1, 3.21.2.2

Answer 21.3

Answer **A** — Section 2A(2) of the Road Traffic Act 1988 states:

(2) A person is also to be regarded as driving dangerously for the purposes of sections 1 and 2 above if it would be obvious to a competent and careful driver that driving the vehicle in its current state would be dangerous.

The test is an objective one which looks at the manner of driving and *not* at the defendant's state of mind. It must be proved that:

- the dangerous condition would itself have been obvious to a competent and careful driver; *or*
- the defendant actually *knew* of its condition.

(*R* v *Strong* [1995] Crim LR 428.)

Answer B is incorrect as the prosecution has to prove one of these requirements. Answer C is incorrect for the same reason.

Answer D is incorrect as the dangerous driving must have been obvious to a competent and careful driver—not simply to DALEY herself.

However, see the case of *R* v *Marchant and Muntz* [2003] Crim LR 806, where the prosecution failed to convince the Court of Appeal that a vehicle was dangerous as a result of its being 'manufactured' in that way.

General Police Duties, paras 3.21.2.2, 3.21.2.3

Answer 21.4

Answer **A** — Section 1 of the Road Traffic Act 1988 states that a person who causes the death of another person by driving a mechanically propelled vehicle dangerously on a road or other public place is guilty of an offence.

Under s. 2A(1) of the Act, a person is to be regarded as driving dangerously if the way he/she drives falls far below what would be expected of a competent and careful driver, and it would be obvious to a competent and careful driver that driving in that way would be dangerous.

This is an objective test, which focuses on the manner of driving rather than the defendant's state of mind and on what would have been obvious to a hypothetical 'competent and careful driver'. Answer D is incorrect as the prosecution is not required to prove any knowledge on the defendant's part.

The Court of Appeal reviewed the requirements of s. 2A in *Attorney-General's Reference (No. 4 of 2000)* [2001] EWCA Crim 780, where a bus driver inadvertently pressed the accelerator pedal instead of the brake, killing two pedestrians. The court held that it was no defence to claim that he had not intended to press the accelerator; under s. 2A, the test is an objective one and there is no requirement to show any specific intent to drive dangerously. Answer B is therefore incorrect.

As with dangerous driving, the test for careless driving is entirely objective in nature and focuses on the manner of driving rather than the defendant's state of mind. Answer C is incorrect for this reason.

General Police Duties, paras 3.21.2.2, 3.21.6.1

Answer 21.5

Answer **A** — Evidence showing how the particular vehicle was being driven before the incident *may* be given in support of the charge of dangerous driving.

However, care needs to be taken by the prosecution not to seek to adduce inadmissible evidence about the defendant's past bad driving (*R v McKenzie* [2008] EWCA Crim 758). Answer B is therefore incorrect.

The evidence REID is able to give of LLOYD's driving immediately before the incident is direct evidence and could be admitted in this case—even though REID is not an expert witness. On the other hand, the information regarding previous bad driving is hearsay and inadmissible. Answers C and D are therefore incorrect.

General Police Duties, para. 3.21.4

Answer 21.6

Answer **B** — Whether a witness is properly qualified in the subject calling for expertise is a question for the court. Such competence or skill may stem from formal study or training, experience or both.

In *R v Oakley* [1979] Crim LR 657, a police officer who had attended a course, passed an exam as a collision investigator and attended more than 400 accidents was entitled to give expert evidence as to the cause of an accident. Answers A and D are therefore incorrect.

The investigation of road traffic accidents is a science that has professional qualifications attached to it, and mathematical calculations that would not look out of place on a rocket scientist's desk! Although it is likely that factual evidence will be available, a police officer meeting the *Oakley* criteria may give purely an opinion of how the accident occurred. Answer C is therefore incorrect.

General Police Duties, para. 3.21.4

Answer 21.7

Answer **C** — Under s. 3A(1) of the Road Traffic Act 1988, if a person causes the death of another person by driving a mechanically propelled vehicle on a road or other public place without due care and attention, or without reasonable consideration for other persons using the road or place, and:

(a) he is, at the time when he is driving, unfit to drive through drink or drugs, or

(b) he has consumed so much alcohol that the proportion of it in his breath, blood or urine at that time exceeds the prescribed limit, or

(ba) he has in his body a specified controlled drug and the proportion of it in his blood or urine at that time exceeds the specified limit for that drug, or

(c) he is, within 18 hours after that time, required to provide a specimen in pursuance of section 7 of this Act, but without reasonable excuse fails to provide it, or

(d) he is required by a constable to give his permission for a laboratory test of a specimen of blood taken from him under section 7A of this Act, but without reasonable excuse fails to do so,

he is guilty of an offence.

In the first instance, a person must have driven a mechanically propelled vehicle on a road or other public place without due care and attention, or without reasonable consideration for other persons using the road or place. Once this has been proved, the prosecution would seek to show that one of the circumstances in paras (a) to (d) applies. These require the driver to have been unfit to drive, or over the prescribed limit for drink or drugs, *at the time of the accident* and answer D is incorrect.

There are timescales which are relevant under s. 3A(1)(c); however, these relate to a failure to provide a relevant specimen requested in pursuance of s. 7 of the Act (requests made at the station or hospital) within 18 hours of the accident. Answer C is correct (and answers A and B are incorrect) because LYNCH could only be guilty if he subsequently refuses to provide a sample under s. 7.

Note that LYNCH could have committed offences under s. 6 (failure to provide) and/or s. 2B (causing death by careless or inconsiderate driving); however, the prosecution would seek to prove the offence under s. 3A(1) in the first instance because it carries a maximum term of imprisonment of 14 years (as opposed to five years under s. 2B).

General Police Duties, para. 3.21.5

Answer 21.8

Answer **B** — Under s. 3A(1) of the Road Traffic Act 1988, if a person causes the death of another person by driving a mechanically propelled vehicle on a road or other public place without due care and attention, or without reasonable consideration for other persons using the road or place, and:

(a)   he is, at the time when he is driving, unfit to drive through drink or drugs, or

(b)   he has consumed so much alcohol that the proportion of it in his breath, blood or urine at that time exceeds the prescribed limit, or

(ba) he has in his body a specified controlled drug and the proportion of it in his blood or urine at that time exceeds the specified limit for that drug, or

(c)   he is, within 18 hours after that time, required to provide a specimen in pursuance of section 7 of this Act, but without reasonable excuse fails to provide it, ...

he is guilty of an offence.

In the first instance, a person must have driven without due care and attention, or without reasonable consideration for other persons using the road or place, which is why answer B is correct, and answer D is incorrect.

A dumper truck is a mechanically propelled vehicle not a motor vehicle and the offence can only be committed on a road or public place so answer C is incorrect.

Finally, the defendant may commit this offence if, at the time, he/she is unfit to drive through drink or drugs or over the limit due to drink. Answer A is therefore incorrect.

General Police Duties, para. 3.21.5

Answer 21.9

Answer **B** — Under s. 3ZB of the Road Traffic Act 1988, a person is guilty of an offence if he/she causes the death of another person by driving a motor vehicle on a road, and at the time the circumstances are such that he/she is committing an offence under:

(a)   section 87(1) of this Act (driving otherwise than in accordance with a licence);

(b)   ... or

(c)   section 143 of this Act (using a motor vehicle while uninsured or unsecured against third party risks).

This offence was initially construed as a 'but for' offence, i.e. 'but for' the presence of the person on a road at the time, who was disqualified, had no insurance or no driving licence, a fatality may not have occurred. This was confirmed by the Court of Appeal in *R* v *Williams* [2010] EWCA Crim 2552, where the deceased walked directly into the path of the uninsured defendant's car. The conviction was upheld despite the lack of any fault in the quality of the defendant's driving.

However, in *R* v *Hughes* [2013] UKSC 56, their lordships made clear that the 'but for' interpretation 'confuses criminal responsibility for the serious offence of being uninsured with criminal responsibility for the infinitely more serious offence of killing another person'. The following directions should be made to the jury where such an offence is charged:

> ... it is not necessary for the Crown to prove careless or inconsiderate driving, but there must be something open to proper criticism in the driving of the defendant, beyond the mere presence of the vehicle on the road, and which contributed in some more than minimal way to the death.

Answers A and C are therefore incorrect.

The elements in relation to 'causing the death of' and 'another person' are, generally, the same as those under s. 1. In *R* v *Hennigan* [1971] 3 All ER 133, it was held that the driving by the defendant must be shown to have been a cause of the death; it is not necessary to show that it was the sole or even a substantial cause of death. It is irrelevant whether or not the person killed contributed to the incident which resulted in his/her death (*R* v *Girdler* [2009] EWCA Crim 2666). The heart attack, which arguably occurred as a result of the collision, *could* result in a person being charged in these circumstances (provided all the other elements of the offence are present); therefore, answer D is incorrect.

General Polices Duties, paras 3.21.2.1, 3.21.8

Answer 21.10

Answer **B** — Under s. 3ZD of the Road Traffic Act 1988, a person is guilty of an offence if he/she:

(a) causes serious injury to another person by driving a motor vehicle on a road, and
(b) at that time, is committing an offence under section 103(1)(b) of this Act (driving while disqualified) ...

Causing the *death* of another person, whilst committing an offence under s. 103(1)(b), is a separate offence under s. 3ZC; since the offence under s. 3ZD may be committed by causing a serious injury to another person, answer C is incorrect.

There is no offence of causing serious injury to another person whilst committing an offence under s. 143 of the Act (driving without insurance); this behaviour is covered in s. 3ZB, where a driver must cause the death of a person. Answers A and D are therefore incorrect.

General Police Duties, para. 3.21.8

Answer 21.11

Answer **B** — The offence under s. 3 of the Road Traffic Act 1988 is committed if a person drives a mechanically propelled vehicle on a road or other public place without due care and attention, or without reasonable consideration for other persons using the road or place. Other persons using the road/public place can include pedestrians who are deliberately sprayed with water from a puddle or passengers in a vehicle (*Pawley* v *Wharldall* [1966] 1 QB 373), so answer A is incorrect. Answer C is incorrect as a person is to be regarded as driving without due care and attention if (and only if) the way he/she drives falls below what would be expected of a competent and careful driver (s. 3ZA(2)). There is one *objective* standard of driving which is expected of all drivers, including learner drivers (*McCrone* v *Riding* [1938] 1 All ER 157). Answer D is incorrect as the Administrative Court has accepted that a distraction (such as children on the carriageway) can amount to a defence to a charge of careless driving (*Plunkett* v *DPP* [2004] EWHC 1937 (Admin)). Answer B is correct as once you have proved that a defendant departed from that standard of driving, and that the defendant's actions were 'voluntary', the offence is complete. There is no need to prove any *knowledge* or *awareness* by the defendant that his/her driving fell below that standard (*R* v *Lawrence* [1982] AC 510).

General Police Duties, paras 3.21.6.1, 3.21.9

Answer 21.12

Answer **C** — Section 1 of the Road Traffic Act 1988 states:

> A person who causes the death of another person by driving a mechanically propelled vehicle dangerously on a road or other public place is guilty of an offence.

Answer A is incorrect as this offence applies to a 'mechanically propelled vehicle' and would therefore include a dumper truck. Answer B is incorrect as the offence can be committed on a road or public place and a public car park is certainly a public place. Answer D is incorrect as the death must be that of 'another person'. Whilst this would cover the situation where a foetus is, after an incident of dangerous driving, later born alive but which subsequently dies (this would be the death of another person), it would not cover the situation where the foetus is never born alive.

General Police Duties, paras 3.21.2 to 3.21.2.2

Answer 21.13

Answer **A** — The offence under s. 3A of the Road Traffic Act 1988 is committed if a person causes the death of another by driving a mechanically propelled vehicle on a road or other public place without due care and attention, or without reasonable consideration for other persons using the road or place, and (under s. 3A(c)) he is, within 18 hours after that time, required to provide a specimen in pursuance of s. 7 of this Act, but without reasonable excuse fails to provide it. This makes answers C and D incorrect. The request must be made within 18 hours *after the driving which caused the death* and not after the death itself making answer B incorrect.

General Police Duties, para. 3.21.5

22 | Drink, Drugs and Driving

QUESTIONS

Question 22.1

Constable BROWN was walking past a public car park when PALMER called him over. PALMER pointed out HODGES, who was driving around the car park on a quad-bike and being cheered on by a group of teenagers. PALMER had seen HODGES drinking cans of lager earlier and was concerned for the safety of people using the car park. Constable BROWN managed to stop the vehicle and, on speaking to HODGES, formed the opinion that he was drunk.

Given that the quad-bike was a mechanically propelled vehicle (and not a motor vehicle), could HODGES commit an offence under either s. 4(1) (unfit to drive through drink or drugs) or s. 5(1) (driving while over the prescribed limit) of the Road Traffic Act 1988 in these circumstances?

- **A** Yes, under s. 4(1), as HODGES was driving a mechanically propelled vehicle in a public place.
- **B** Yes, under either section, as HODGES was driving a mechanically propelled vehicle in a public place.
- **C** No, HODGES was not driving a motor vehicle on a road.
- **D** No, HODGES was not driving a motor vehicle or a mechanically propelled vehicle on a road.

Question 22.2

Constable LANGLEY was following a vehicle being driven by FORSYTHE. The officer observed the vehicle being driven erratically, swerving across the road. Constable LANGLEY forms the opinion that the driver is drunk but loses sight of the vehicle. Following a computer check, the officer attended FORSYTHE's home address. On arrival, Constable LANGLEY saw FORSYTHE asleep inside the vehicle which was inside a detached garage, a building adjacent to FORSYTHE's house. The garage door was open. Constable LANGLEY was considering arresting FORSYTHE for an offence under s. 4 of the Road Traffic Act 1988 (unfit through drink or drugs).

Does Constable LANGLEY have the power to enter the garage and/or the vehicle under s. 17 of the Police and Criminal Evidence Act 1984 in these circumstances?

A No, because s. 17 does not provide a power of entry to arrest a person for the offence under s. 4 of the Road Traffic Act 1988.

B No, because the vehicle has not been involved in an accident where injury was caused to any person.

C Yes, but only the garage as a vehicle is not a 'premises' for the purposes of s. 17.

D Yes, both the garage and the vehicle are 'premises' for the purposes of s. 17.

Question 22.3

Constable DERECK attended the Fox and Hounds public house as a result of a call from the licensee, BELL. BELL had seen MEARS enter the premises from the car park in a drunken condition with some friends. They had bought two rounds of drinks when it had been brought to BELL's attention that MEARS had driven to the premises. Constable DERECK spoke to MEARS who admitted he had driven to the premises, but stated that he had only drunk two pints, which had been bought since he'd arrived. BELL was adamant that MEARS had been drunk when he'd arrived and that he was too intoxicated for someone who had only drunk two pints.

Considering the offence under s. 4 of the Road Traffic Act 1988, which of the following statements is correct in relation to the information BELL has provided so far?

A BELL could give an opinion of MEARS's impairment and his ability to drive a vehicle on a road, which would provide reasonable suspicion for Constable DERECK to arrest him for this offence.

B BELL's suspicion that MEARS had been drunk when he had arrived would provide reasonable suspicion for Constable DERECK to arrest him for this offence.

C BELL's opinion of MEARS's impairment would not be sufficient for the officer to arrest MEARS; Constable DERECK must formulate a separate reasonable suspicion of the defendant's condition before arresting him.

D BELL's opinion of MEARS's impairment would only provide reasonable suspicion for Constable DERECK to arrest him for this offence if BELL was an expert on such matters.

Question 22.4

Constable SQUIRE stopped HENSON who was driving a motor vehicle on a road at night. Constable SQUIRE noticed that HENSON smelled of intoxicants and requested a sample of breath. The screening test proved negative; however, as HENSON was returning to her car, Constable SQUIRE noticed that she was staggering which gave the officer reason to believe that she was unfit to drive through drink, despite the negative screening test. Constable SQUIRE then arrested HENSON under s. 4 of the Road Traffic Act 1988 (unfit to drive through drink or drugs).

Did Constable SQUIRE act correctly in these circumstances?

A Yes, the officer was entitled to arrest HENSON in these circumstances alone.

B No, Constable SQUIRE should have required HENSON to provide a further sample of breath before making this decision.

C No, Constable SQUIRE could not have formed a reasonable suspicion that HENSON was unfit to drive through drink as the screening test was negative.

D No, the arrest would only have been lawful if Constable SQUIRE had initially suspected HENSON was unfit to drive through drugs.

Question 22.5

BEDFORD is appealing against a conviction for driving a motor vehicle on a road while over the prescribed limit. The circumstances were that BEDFORD was on a night out and was bought several alcoholic drinks by friends. BEDFORD claims that she had told her friends to buy her soft drinks and she was unaware that the drinks she had consumed contained alcohol.

Which of the following statements is correct, regarding the responsibility BEDFORD had in relation to the proportion of alcohol in her body?

A BEDFORD had some positive duty to inquire whether the drinks contained alcohol before consuming them.

B BEDFORD had an absolute duty to inquire whether the drinks contained alcohol before consuming them.

C BEDFORD had no particular duty to inquire whether the drinks contained alcohol before consuming them.

D If BEDFORD's claim is correct, her friends had an absolute duty to inform her that the drinks contained alcohol before she consumed them.

Question 22.6

RICHMOND is appearing in court having been charged with driving a motor vehicle on a road when there was a specified controlled drug in her body and the proportion of the drug in her blood exceeded the specified limit. The drug in question is diazepam and RICHMOND is claiming a defence because the drug was prescribed by her GP.

In relation to the 'medical defence' that s. 5A of the Road Traffic Act 1988 provides, which of the following comments is correct?

A Diazepam is a controlled drug under the Misuse of Drugs Act 1971; this defence is not available for such a drug.

B Provided the drug was lawfully prescribed to RICHMOND, this defence may be available on that basis alone.

C Provided the drug was lawfully prescribed and it was taken in accordance with any directions given by the person who prescribed it, RICHMOND could use the defence.

D RICHMOND must demonstrate that the drug was prescribed to her in error and that she was unaware that she had taken that particular drug for the defence to be available.

Question 22.7

CHANEY works for a building company which was contracted to conduct work in a supermarket car park. In his lunch break, CHANEY took cocaine and, when he returned to work, he drove a dumper truck erratically around the car park, clipping the wing mirror of a car parked on the car park and damaging the wing mirror in the process. Several customers complained and Constable OLNEY was called to deal with the incident; the officer immediately suspected CHANEY had been taking drugs because of his behaviour.

Given that the dumper truck was not intended or adapted for use on the road, would Constable OLNEY be able to request a preliminary drugs test from CHANEY under s. 6 of the Road Traffic Act 1988 in these circumstances?

A Yes, CHANEY was driving a mechanically propelled vehicle in a public place at the time of the incident.

B No, CHANEY was not driving a motor vehicle on a road or other public place at the time of the incident.

C Yes, CHANEY was driving a motor vehicle that had been involved in an accident.

D No, CHANEY was not driving a mechanically propelled vehicle on a road at the time of the incident.

Question 22.8

DC PARR was in plain clothes on inquiries in the Swan public house. The officer saw BAKER stumble through the bar to the exit door, leave the pub and get into a car outside. DC PARR left the premises and got into a police vehicle as BAKER was driving away. At the end of the street, BAKER failed to observe a stop sign, turned into a main road and then collided with the rear of another car which was stationary at a red traffic light.

What is the earliest point when DC PARR would have been entitled to require BAKER to cooperate with one of the preliminary tests under s. 6 of the Road Traffic Act 1988?

A When BAKER first got into the car.

B When BAKER drove through the stop sign.

C When BAKER collided with the rear of the other car.

D At no point, as DC PARR was in plain clothes and had no power to require BAKER to submit to one of the preliminary tests.

Question 22.9

WHEELAN attended a police station to report a crime and spoke to Constable BLOOM. As they were speaking, the officer suspected that WHEELAN may have been drinking and asked whether she had been. WHEELAN stated that she had and the officer asked whether or not she had driven to the station. Again, WHEELAN stated that she had. Constable BLOOM requested a sample of breath from WHEELAN, which proved to be positive. WHEELAN was charged with the offence of driving whilst over the prescribed limit but pleaded not guilty in court, stating that Constable BLOOM should have cautioned her prior to administering the breath test as their conversation constituted an interview.

In relation to the need to caution WHEELAN, which of the following comments is correct?

A As the conversation occurred prior to the breath test, Constable BLOOM had formed the suspicion that WHEELAN had committed an offence and a caution was required.

B Constable BLOOM only formed the suspicion that an offence had been committed after the breath test was administered; therefore, a caution was not required.

C The questions asked by Constable BLOOM were preliminary to a breath test and designed to establish whether an offence had taken place; therefore, a caution was required.

D Constable BLOOM knew that WHEELAN had been drinking; therefore, the question as to whether she had driven there constituted an interview and a caution was required.

Question 22.10

Constable COURT was conducting her first breath test procedure, having stopped KAY who was driving with a defective light. During the test, Constable COURT failed to hold down a button on the breath test device for the recommended amount of time. However, the reading still showed a positive breath result and Constable COURT arrested KAY.

Which of the comments below is correct in respect of the arrest made by Constable COURT?

A Constable COURT has acted correctly in the circumstances and the arrest is lawful.

B As Constable COURT made a mistake with the procedure, the arrest is unlawful.

C The arrest is unlawful but this would not affect the result of the case if KAY provided a positive sample at the station.

D KAY should have been made to take the test again and, as this was not done, it means that the arrest was unlawful.

Question 22.11

Constable CLEMENT attended a road traffic accident involving two vehicles. One of the drivers, MARINER, smelled of intoxicants but the other driver, McCLAREN, did not. Constable CLEMENT requested both drivers to cooperate with a preliminary breath test (under s. 6(5) of the Road Traffic Act 1988). However, the officer's breath test machine was defective; after several attempts to get another officer to attend the scene with a machine that worked, Constable CLEMENT realised that the rest of the team were too busy to assist. The officer considered whether or not to take MARINER and McCLAREN to the nearest police station to conduct the test.

Who, if anyone, is Constable CLEMENT empowered to take to a police station in these circumstances?

A Both drivers may be taken to the police station to conduct the test as they have been involved in a road traffic accident.

B MARINER as he is suspected to have alcohol in his breath or body.

C Neither person as this power is only available in respect of a person who is suspected to be unfit to drive through drugs.

D Both drivers may be taken to a police station as this power is available in respect of any person who is required to cooperate with one of the preliminary tests.

Question 22.12

Constable PENG is trained to conduct preliminary impairment tests. He was called to assist another officer who had stopped a motor vehicle which was being driven erratically by WENGER. The officer had administered a breath test which was negative; however, WENGER's behaviour led the officer to believe that he was under the influence of either drink or drugs. On his arrival, Constable PENG gave instructions to WENGER as part of the test but WENGER was not able to complete the test because of his condition.

Would Constable PENG be able to arrest WENGER now (using his powers under s. 6D of the Road Traffic Act 1988) for failure to complete the impairment test?

A Yes, provided the officer suspects the presence of alcohol or drugs.

B No, as he has not refused to take the impairment test.

C Yes, regardless of whether the officer suspects the presence of alcohol or drugs.

D No, the officer would have to arrest him under s. 4 of the Act.

Question 22.13

Constable TAYLOR was called to an accident in a shopping centre car park which was open to the public. SINGH had reversed his car into the path of a dumper truck being driven by WALSH. WALSH was working on an adjacent building site and the dumper truck he was driving was not manufactured for use on roads.

From whom, if anyone, may Constable TAYLOR require a breath test (under s. 6 of the Road Traffic Act 1988) in these circumstances?

A SINGH only, provided she suspects he has alcohol in his body.

B Neither driver as the accident did not occur on a road.

C Both drivers as they have been involved in an accident.

D SINGH only, whether or not she suspects he has alcohol in his body.

Question 22.14

GRANT was arrested and taken to a police station after failing to provide a specimen of breath at the roadside. At the station, it was decided that for medical reasons GRANT should provide a urine sample.

Which of the following statements is correct in relation to the provision of the urine sample under s. 7(5) of the Road Traffic Act 1988?

A GRANT must provide two separate samples within an hour of being requested to do so.

B GRANT must provide two samples from the same act of urinating within an hour of being requested to do so.

C GRANT must provide two separate samples within an hour of providing the second breath sample.

D GRANT must provide two samples, which may or may not be from the same act of urinating, within an hour of providing the second breath sample.

Question 22.15

RADCLIFFE was taken to hospital from a custody block, having been in police detention following a positive breath test. RADCLIFFE had suffered a suspected heart attack while about to provide samples for the station breath test procedure. Following tests, it was decided that RADCLIFFE had most likely suffered an anxiety attack and would need to remain on a ward in hospital for observation. The arresting officer, Constable SAMPSON, spoke to the medical practitioner in charge of the ward about the breath test procedure. Constable SAMPSON was told that obtaining a sample of blood could be detrimental to RADCLIFFE's medical health. The officer decided to contact the custody officer for advice about how to proceed.

Considering s. 7 of the Road Traffic Act 1988, which of the following statements is correct in respect of the options open to Constable SAMPSON?

A A police medical practitioner should be called to the hospital to take a sample of urine from RADCLIFFE.

B A police medical practitioner should take the urine sample, but if one is not available, a medical practitioner at the hospital who is not in immediate charge of RADCLIFFE's case should take it.

C A sample of urine may not be requested in these circumstances; such a sample may only be requested at a police station.

D A sample of urine may be requested in these circumstances and it may be taken by a police officer.

Question 22.16

Constable COLE attended a road traffic accident involving a car which had struck a wall. There were two occupants in the vehicle: PEARSON, the owner of the car, and his friend, STUART. Constable COLE could smell intoxicants on both persons but neither admitted being the driver of the vehicle at the time of the accident. PEARSON and STUART provided screening samples of breath which were both positive. They were arrested and taken to the police station.

From whom, if either, could a specimen of breath for analysis be requested under s. 7 of the Road Traffic Act 1988 (provision of specimens for analysis)?

A Both, provided it is believed that one of them was driving.
B PEARSON only, as the owner of the vehicle.
C Both, regardless of who was suspected to be the driver.
D Neither, Constable COLE should not have breathalysed both persons.

Question 22.17

FOSTER was arrested under s. 4 of the Road Traffic Act 1988 and was taken to the police station. FOSTER provided one specimen of breath but then the machine malfunctioned. The custody officer, Sergeant CANNON, considered transferring FOSTER to another police station to complete the station procedure.

Would Sergeant CANNON be able to transfer FOSTER to another station in these circumstances?

A Yes, FOSTER may be transferred and may be required to supply two further specimens of breath.
B No, FOSTER must now be asked to provide a sample of blood or urine at the current station to replace the specimen of breath.
C Yes, FOSTER may be transferred and may only be required to supply one specimen of breath.
D No, a person may only be transferred to another station if there is no one available to conduct the station procedure.

Question 22.18

RAY pleaded not guilty in court to an offence of failing to provide a urine sample, citing that the police had failed to properly issue a warning under s. 7(7) of the Road Traffic Act 1988 (failure to provide the specimen may render a person liable to prosecution). Whilst in custody, it had been decided that, for medical reasons,

RAY should provide a specimen of urine. Sergeant HAYES commenced the procedure and issued a warning under s. 7(7); however, the sergeant was called away to other duties before the specimen was taken and the procedure was passed over to Constable PIERCE who did not issue a further warning before requesting the sample. RAY failed to provide a specimen and was charged with the offence.

Which of the following statements is correct in relation to the fact that Constable PIERCE did not issue a warning?

A A warning by Constable PIERCE was not required in these circumstances.

B The person conducting the procedure (Constable PIERCE) should have given a warning.

C The warning under s. 7(7) is irrelevant as it only relates to the provision of samples of breath.

D The warning under s. 7(7) is irrelevant as it only relates to the provision of specimens of breath or blood.

Question 22.19

Sergeant DONELLY was conducting the station breath test procedure for BEECH, who had provided one sample of breath. However, BEECH stated that he was tired and fell asleep before providing a second sample. Sergeant DONELLY tried to wake BEECH, without success, and in the end placed him in a cell. BEECH was later charged with driving with excess alcohol, based on the reading provided which was 150 microgrammes of alcohol in 100 millilitres of breath.

Which of the following comments is correct in relation to the offence BEECH has been charged with?

A Charging BEECH with the offence of driving with excess alcohol was the correct decision by Sergeant DONELLY.

B BEECH should have been charged with failing to provide a sample but his drunken condition may provide a defence.

C BEECH should have been given the opportunity to provide a sample of blood or urine when he was sober enough.

D BEECH should have been charged with failing to provide a sample and would have no defence arising from his drunken condition.

Question 22.20

WEBBER was at a hospital having been involved in a road traffic accident. Having consulted with the medical practitioner in immediate charge of WEBBER's case,

Constable O'SHEA required WEBBER to provide a specimen of breath but she refused. Constable O'SHEA arrested WEBBER for failing to provide a specimen. After further consultation with the medical practitioner, Constable O'SHEA asked WEBBER to supply a specimen of blood.

Has Constable O'SHEA complied with the requirements of s. 9 of the Road Traffic Act 1988?

A No, because WEBBER was under arrest, the request for blood should have been made at a police station.

B No, Constable O'SHEA should not have arrested WEBBER while she was still a patient at the hospital.

C Yes, as the medical practitioner has agreed to both specimens being requested, Constable O'SHEA has complied with the Act.

D Yes, but there was no need to ask permission on the second occasion as permission had already been granted.

Question 22.21

PEARCE has been charged with an offence of driving with excess alcohol (under s. 5 of the Road Traffic Act 1988) and is still in custody. Sergeant REVERS is considering whether or not to detain PEARCE at the custody office because the lowest reading of the sample provided by PEARCE was 130 microgrammes of alcohol in 100 millilitres of breath.

What matters should Sergeant REVERS take into consideration before detaining PEARCE under s. 10(1) of the Road Traffic Act 1988?

A Sergeant REVERS has a statutory power to confiscate PEARCE's car keys under this subsection, to prevent her from committing an offence under s. 5 or s. 4 of the Act.

B Sergeant REVERS has a statutory power to detain PEARCE until she has provided a negative screening test, to prevent her from committing an offence under s. 5 or s. 4 of the Act.

C PEARCE may be detained provided Sergeant REVERS has reasonable grounds to believe she will commit an offence under s. 5 or s. 4 if she were to drive a motor vehicle on a road.

D PEARCE may be detained provided Sergeant REVERS has reasonable grounds to believe she will commit an offence under s. 5 or s. 4 if she were to drive a mechanically propelled vehicle on a road.

Question 22.22

NEWMAN is in custody and is suspected of being unfit to drive through taking drugs (under s. 4 of the Road Traffic Act 1988). NEWMAN has provided a specimen of blood which the custody officer, Sergeant BURKE, intends to submit for analysis. NEWMAN will not be charged until the results of the analysis are known and, therefore, Sergeant BURKE intends to release him on bail for the period. However, NEWMAN has stated his intention to drive when released. Sergeant BURKE suspects that NEWMAN would still be unfit if he were to drive a motor vehicle on a road.

What does s. 10 of the Road Traffic Act 1988 say in relation to the advice Sergeant BURKE should seek before detaining NEWMAN further until he is fit to drive a motor vehicle on a road?

A Sergeant BURKE may make this decision herself; she does not need to seek advice from anyone.

B Sergeant BURKE may seek advice from a police medical practitioner and must act on any advice given.

C Sergeant BURKE may not detain NEWMAN under this section as he has not been charged or reported for an offence.

D Sergeant BURKE must seek advice from a police medical practitioner and must act on any advice given.

Question 22.23

LLOYD and TINNION are drinking in TINNION's house. TINNION has passed out but LLOYD is still awake even though he has drunk the entire contents of a large bottle of vodka. LLOYD decides to get some food from a nearby chip shop and picks up the keys to TINNION's Nissan Micra motor vehicle which is parked directly outside TINNION's house on a road. LLOYD leaves the house and staggers towards TINNION's car. He opens the driver's door, sits in the driver's seat and puts the keys into the ignition and turns the key. There is a mechanical fault with the ignition meaning that the Micra will not start. At that moment, PC GRAY (on uniform foot patrol) passes the vehicle and sees LLOYD trying to start it and notices the drunken condition LLOYD is in. LLOYD gets out of the vehicle, pushes past PC GRAY and runs into TINNION's house.

Has LLOYD committed an offence under s. 4 of the Road Traffic Act 1988?

A No, the offence under s. 4 can only be committed by a person who drives a mechanically propelled vehicle whilst unfit through drink or drugs.

B Yes, although expert medical evidence must be provided as to LLOYD's degree of impairment or the case will not be proved.

C No, as there is no likelihood of LLOYD being able to drive the vehicle due to the fault with the ignition.

D Yes, and PC GRAY may force entry into TINNION's house to arrest LLOYD as long as he believes LLOYD is on the premises.

Question 22.24

DC NEVIN (who is dressed in plain clothes) is part of a murder investigation and is driving along a road on her way to speak to a witness. The officer is waiting at a set of traffic lights (showing red against her) when a Ford Focus motor vehicle (driven by MARLOW) bumps into the back of the officer's police vehicle causing minor damage to MARLOW's vehicle, but no damage to the police vehicle DC NEVIN is driving.

Could DC NEVIN require MARLOW to cooperate with a preliminary test (under s. 6 of the Road Traffic Act 1988)?

A Yes, DC NEVIN may require MARLOW to cooperate with any preliminary test, but as the officer is in plain clothes she could not administer it.

B No, unless DC NEVIN suspects that MARLOW has alcohol or a drug in his body or is under the influence of a drug.

C Yes, DC NEVIN may require MARLOW to cooperate with any preliminary test and, in the circumstances, the officer can also administer such a test.

D No, as the accident did not involve injury to any person.

Question 22.25

PC BATTY is on uniform mobile patrol and is driving his marked police vehicle on a road travelling behind a Toyota Hilux motor vehicle. PC BATTY observes the Toyota Hilux being driven through a red traffic light (a moving traffic offence) and stops the vehicle a short distance from the scene of the offence. PC BATTY speaks to FRAYLING (who is the driver of the Toyota Hilux) and makes a requirement for FRAYLING to cooperate with a preliminary drug test. FRAYLING refuses to take the test.

Could PC BATTY arrest FRAYLING (under s. 6D of the Road Traffic Act 1988) for this failure to cooperate with the preliminary drug test?

A No, the power of arrest under s. 6D only applies where a person takes a preliminary breath or drug test and fails that test.

B Yes, as refusing to take any preliminary test following the commission of a moving traffic offence generates a power of arrest under s. 6D.

C No, not unless the officer reasonably suspects FRAYLING has alcohol or a drug in his body or is under the influence of a drug.

D Yes, but in order to do so PC BATTY must reasonably believe that FRAYLING is under the influence of a drug.

Question 22.26

DC EBDALE (who is dressed in plain clothes) parked her unmarked police vehicle on a road and was sitting in the driver's seat when a Volkswagen Golf motor vehicle, driven by TAYLOR, struck the rear of the officer's vehicle causing slight damage to both vehicles in the process. DC EBDALE then saw TAYLOR get out of his vehicle and run into a nearby house. DC EBDALE contacted her control room and PS HARMON (on uniform mobile patrol) attended the scene of the accident. DC EBDALE informs PS HARMON of the circumstances of the accident.

Does s. 6E of the Road Traffic Act 1988 provide a power of entry into the house that TAYLOR ran into in order to impose a requirement for TAYLOR to take a preliminary test under s. 6(5) of the Act?

A Yes, and that power of entry could be exercised by DC EBDALE or PS HARMON.

B No, the power is not available in these circumstances unless there is a suspicion that the accident involved an injury to any person.

C Yes, PS HARMON (as an officer in uniform) could exercise the power; DC EBDALE (who is in plain clothes) could not.

D No, as s. 6E only provides a power of entry to arrest a person who has taken and failed a preliminary test after being involved in an accident in which a person was injured.

Question 22.27

PINK is arrested for an offence of attempting to drive his motor vehicle (a Toyota RAV4) on a road whilst over the prescribed limit (contrary to s. 5(1)(a) of the Road Traffic Act 1988). Throughout his time in custody, PINK states that the police are 'out of order' for arresting him and he maintains that there was no likelihood of him driving the vehicle at the time the offence is alleged to have been committed because he had broken his left arm and it was in plaster and, in addition, the front offside wheel of the vehicle was so badly damaged that it was impossible for the vehicle to be driven on a road. PINK is charged with the offence.

In relation to the statutory defence under s. 5 of the Road Traffic Act 1988, which of the comments below is correct?

A The fact that PINK was injured and that his vehicle was damaged will not afford him a statutory defence to a charge under s. 5(1)(a) of the Act.

B The court may, in determining whether there was any likelihood of PINK driving whilst over the prescribed limit, disregard any injury to PINK and any damage to his vehicle.

C The court may, in determining whether there was any likelihood of PINK driving whilst over the prescribed limit, disregard any injury to PINK.

D The court may, in determining whether there was any likelihood of PINK driving whilst over the prescribed limit, disregard any damage to his vehicle.

Question 22.28

PC EVERTON is on uniform patrol when she stops KOBEL, who is driving a BMW Z4 motor vehicle on a road. KOBEL gets out of the vehicle and speaks to the officer. KOBEL is somewhat unsteady on his feet and seems to be very animated in his actions. PC EVERTON forms the opinion that KOBEL has taken some kind of drug and is about to arrest KOBEL for an offence under s. 4(1) of the Road Traffic Act 1988 (driving or attempting to drive a mechanically propelled vehicle when unfit through drink or drugs) when KOBEL runs away from her and into a nearby house.

Can PC EVERTON enter the house to arrest KOBEL for an offence under s. 4 of the Road Traffic Act 1988?

A No, PC EVERTON cannot enter the house unless KOBEL has been involved in a road accident.

B Yes, PC EVERTON may enter and search the premises for the purpose of arresting KOBEL but only because she is in uniform.

C No, there is no power of entry to arrest an individual for an offence under this section of the Act.

D Yes, PC EVERTON may force entry to the house for the purpose of arresting KOBEL for an offence under s. 4 of the Road Traffic Act 1988.

Question 22.29

PC STEWART (who is appropriately trained and authorised to deliver a preliminary impairment test) is on uniform mobile patrol when he sees INNES driving his Land Rover Discovery motor vehicle in an erratic fashion. This causes PC STEWART to reasonably suspect that INNES has alcohol in his body or is under the influence of a drug and consequently the officer stops the vehicle. PC STEWART decides that he will test INNES (as per s. 6 of the Road Traffic Act 1988).

In respect of the tests that can be administered to INNES, which of the following statements is correct?

A PC STEWART could administer a preliminary impairment test to INNES at a police station specified by PC STEWART if he thinks it expedient.

B PC STEWART could administer a preliminary breath test to INNES at a police station specified by PC STEWART if he thinks it expedient.

C PC STEWART could administer a preliminary impairment test to INNES but this must be carried out at or near the place where the requirement to cooperate with the test is imposed.

D PC STEWART could administer a preliminary impairment test to INNES regardless of whether he is in uniform or not.

ANSWERS

Answer 22.1

Answer **A** — Under s. 5(1)(a) of the Road Traffic Act 1988, a person who drives or attempts to drive a motor vehicle on a road or other public place after consuming so much alcohol that the proportion of it in his breath, blood or urine exceeds the prescribed limit is guilty of an offence. There can be no offence, therefore, under s. 5, and answer B is incorrect.

However, under s. 4(1) of the Act, a person who, when driving or attempting to drive a *mechanically propelled vehicle* on a road or *other public place*, is unfit to drive through drink or drugs is guilty of an offence. There *can* be an offence, therefore, under s. 4, and answers C and D are incorrect.

General Police Duties, paras 3.22.2, 3.22.3

Answer 22.2

Answer **D** — The power of entry in connection with an offence under s. 4 is found in s. 17(1)(c)(iiia) of the Police and Criminal Evidence Act 1984, which states:

> Subject to the following provisions of this section, and without prejudice to any other enactment, a constable may enter and search any premises for the purpose of
> ...
> (iiia) section 4 (driving etc. when under influence of drink or drugs) or section 163 (failure to stop when required to do so by constable in uniform) of the Road Traffic Act 1988.

This means answers A and B are therefore both incorrect.

'Premises' would include a vehicle; answer C is therefore incorrect.

Note that the power of entry under this section is only exercisable if the constable has reasonable grounds for believing that the person whom he/she is seeking is on the premises (s. 17(2)(a)).

General Police Duties, para. 3.22.2

Answer 22.3

Answer **B** — This question deals with whether a 'reasonable suspicion' would provide sufficient evidence to arrest a person and prove an offence under s. 4 of the

Road Traffic Act 1988, when that evidence is provided by a 'lay' witness. In *R v Lanfear* [1968] 2 QB 77, it was held that while evidence of impairment must be produced by the prosecution, that evidence *may* be provided by a 'lay' witness, who would not need to be an expert on such matters (also *R v Davies* [1962] 3 All ER 97). Answers C and D are therefore incorrect.

However, that witness *may* not be required to give expert testimony or to *comment on the defendant's ability to drive*. Answer A is therefore incorrect.

General Police Duties, paras 3.22.2, 3.22.2.2

Answer 22.4

Answer **A** — The circumstances in this question are similar to those in *DPP v Robertson* [2002] EWHC 542 (Admin). In that case, the officers had breathalysed the defendant who produced a negative result. However, on talking to the officers further, the defendant slurred his speech when giving the name of his solicitor. The officers then arrested the defendant under s. 4 and took him to a police station where he provided an evidential sample of breath which was over the prescribed limit.

The magistrates held that the defendant had been unlawfully arrested and the prosecutor appealed on a number of grounds. However, the Administrative Court held that it was quite conceivable to have a case where, notwithstanding that a driver had given a negative screening breath test, he/she was seen moments later staggering in a way that gave rise to a suspicion of unfitness. In such a case, the law (s. 4) clearly gave a constable a power to arrest if what he/she had witnessed amounted to reasonable cause to suspect that the person was impaired, regardless of whether the impairment was due to drink or drugs. Answers C and D are therefore incorrect.

There would be no requirement for the police to require a further breath sample from the driver in these circumstances; therefore, answer B is incorrect.

General Police Duties, para. 3.22.2.2

Answer 22.5

Answer **A** — The Divisional Court has held that there is some positive duty on a person to inquire whether a drink contains alcohol before drinking it if that person intends to drive afterwards (*Robinson v DPP* [2003] EWHC 2718 (Admin)).

Answers B, C and D are therefore incorrect.

General Police Duties, para. 3.22.3

Answer 22.6

Answer **C** — Section 5A(3) of the Road Traffic Act 1988 states that it is a defence for a person ('D') charged with an offence under this section to show that:

(a) the specified controlled drug had been prescribed or supplied to D for medical or dental purposes,
(b) D took the drug in accordance with any directions given by the person by whom the drug was prescribed or supplied, and with any accompanying instructions (so far as consistent with any such directions) given by the manufacturer or distributor of the drug ...

As part of the defence, the defendant would also have to show that he/she was not in unlawful possession of the controlled drug (according to s. 5(1) of the Misuse of Drugs Act 1971), a condition a defendant should be able to satisfy if the drug was prescribed.

Therefore, provided the defendant is able to demonstrate that he/she followed any directions given when the drug was prescribed and followed any manufacturer's instructions accompanying the drug, the defence may be available even if the drug is listed in the 1971 Act as a controlled drug. Answer A is therefore incorrect.

This is a slightly more testing defence than simply being able to prove that the drug was lawfully prescribed; therefore, answer B is incorrect.

These are the only two requirements for this statutory defence so answer D is therefore incorrect.

Note that the court must assume that the defence is satisfied unless the prosecution proves beyond reasonable doubt that it is not (s. 5A(5)).

General Police Duties, paras 3.22.3, 3.22.3.1

Answer 22.7

Answer **B** — Section 5A of the Road Traffic Act 1988 deals with driving or being in charge of a motor vehicle with a concentration of a specified controlled drug above the specified limit. Where a person drives, attempts to drive or is in charge of a *motor vehicle* on a road or other public place and there is in that person's body a specified controlled drug (which includes cocaine), he/she is guilty of an offence if the proportion of the drug in his/her blood or urine exceeds the specified limit for that drug (s. 5A(1) and (2)).

Under s. 6(2), a constable may require a person to cooperate with any one or more preliminary tests (including the test to detect drugs) if he/she reasonably suspects that the person has been driving, attempting to drive or in charge of a *motor vehicle* on a road or other public place while having alcohol or a drug in his/her body or while unfit to drive because of a drug, and still has alcohol or a drug in his/her body or is still under the influence of a drug.

However, as with the power to require a preliminary breath test, a request for a preliminary drugs test will only be lawful if the person is or has been driving etc. a *motor vehicle* on a road or other public place (that would apply to the requirement if made under s. 6(5)—relating to an accident on a road or public place). Of course, the officer could still arrest the person for an offence under s. 4 of the Act in these circumstances since that section *does* apply to mechanically propelled vehicles.

Answers A, C and D are incorrect for this reason.

General Police Duties, paras 3.22.4, 3.22.4.2

Answer 22.8

Answer **A** — This is a bit of a trick question—no apologies for that! Section 6 of the Road Traffic Act 1988 outlines the circumstances in which a person may be required to cooperate with any one of the preliminary tests, e.g. where the person is reasonably suspected:

- to be driving, attempting to drive or in charge of a motor vehicle on a road or other public place and has alcohol or a drug in his/her body, or is under the influence of a drug (s. 6(2)); or
- *has been* driving etc. in these circumstances and *still* has alcohol or a drug in his/her body or is still under the influence of a drug (s. 6(3)); or
- *is* or *has been* driving etc. in these circumstances and has committed a traffic offence while the vehicle was in motion (s. 6(4)).

In each of these circumstances, the officer *making the requirement* does not have to be in uniform; however, the officer *administering the test* must be in uniform (s. 6(7)). Under s. 6(5), where an accident occurs owing to the presence of a motor vehicle on a road or other public place, and it is reasonably believed that the person was driving, attempting to drive or in charge of the vehicle at the time of the accident, the officer making the requirement *and* administering the test does not have to be in uniform.

Therefore, the *earliest point* at which DC PARR would have been entitled to require BAKER to cooperate with one of the preliminary tests was when the person sat in the car, and was in charge of a motor vehicle on a road and had alcohol or a drug in his/her body.

Answers B, C and D are therefore incorrect.

General Police Duties, paras 3.22.4, 3.22.4.3

Answer 22.9

Answer **B** — The facts in the question are similar to the case of *Ridehalgh* v *DPP* [2005] RTR 26. In this case, the defendant (a police officer) argued that the questions asked prior to the breath test procedure constituted an interview and, as he had not been cautioned, Code C, paras 10.1 and 11.1(A) of the Codes of Practice had been breached. It was held that no interview had taken place and that there had been no breach of Code C. It was held that the questions regarding driving and whether he had been drinking first were merely preliminary and had been made with the intention of finding out the possibility of whether an offence had been committed. On appeal, the Divisional Court held that a necessary precondition of the giving of a caution was that there had to be grounds for the suspicion of a criminal offence and that the magistrates were correct. The police officers merely suspected that the defendant had been drinking alcohol; they had no indication as to how much alcohol had been consumed, or whether he had actually driven. The ruling followed an earlier, similar decision in the case of *Whelehan* v *DPP* [1995] RTR 177. Answers A, C and D are therefore incorrect.

General Police Duties, para. 3.22.4.1

Answer 22.10

Answer **A** — It has been held that where a constable innocently fails to follow the manufacturer's instructions, it will not render the test or any subsequent arrest unlawful (*DPP* v *Kay* [1999] RTR 109). Answer B is therefore incorrect. Answer C is also incorrect as the arrest was not unlawful.

In addition to the case of *Kay*, it was decided in *DPP* v *Carey* [1970] AC 1072 that failing to comply with the manufacturer's instructions on the use of an approved device will mean that the person *has not provided* a preliminary breath test and *may* be asked to provide another; refusing to do so will be an offence. Answer D is incorrect as the case is not authority for the view that a person *must* be made to take another test. Since the purpose of the test is to indicate whether there is a *likelihood* of an offence being committed, an arrest in these circumstances is appropriate as the test did show a positive result.

General Police Duties, para. 3.22.4.2

Answer 22.11

Answer **A** — The three tests that the driver may be required to cooperate with under s. 6 of the Road Traffic Act 1988 are:

- preliminary breath test (s. 6A);
- preliminary impairment test (s. 6B); and
- preliminary drug test (s. 6C).

A preliminary breath test under s. 6A may only be administered at or near the place where the requirement to cooperate with the test is imposed. The other two tests, under ss. 6B and 6C, may be administered at or near the place where the requirement to cooperate is imposed *or*, if the constable imposing it thinks it expedient, at a police station specified by the constable. Answers C and D are therefore incorrect.

There are separate provisions under s. 6(5) relating to drivers where an accident occurs owing to the presence of a motor vehicle on a road or other public place and a constable reasonably believes that the person was driving, attempting to drive or in charge of the vehicle at the time of the accident. In such cases, a preliminary *breath* test (under s. 6A) may be administered:

(a) at or near the place where the requirement to cooperate with the test is imposed; or
(b) if the constable who imposes the requirement thinks it expedient, at a police station specified by the constable (see s. 6A(3)).

This provision applies to *any* driver who has been involved in such an accident, regardless of whether or not that person is suspected of having alcohol in his/her breath or body, and answer B is therefore incorrect.

General Police Duties, paras 3.22.4.2, 3.22.4.3

Answer 22.12

Answer **A** — Under s. 6B of the Road Traffic Act 1988, an appropriately trained officer has the power to require the driver of a motor vehicle on a road or public place to submit to a preliminary impairment test in order to observe the driver's behaviour. Such observations may be used as evidence in any subsequent court cases—but will not provide absolute proof of a person's guilt.

A person who fails to cooperate with a preliminary impairment test commits an offence under s. 6(6) of the Act. A person does not cooperate unless his/her cooperation is sufficient to allow the test to be carried out (s. 11(3)). In the question, the driver's behaviour meant that the test could not be carried out even though he did not refuse to take it. Answer B is therefore incorrect.

A constable may arrest a person who has failed to cooperate with a test under this section, *provided* the constable reasonably suspects that the person has alcohol or drugs in his/her body or is under the influence of drugs (s. 6D(2)). Answers C and D are therefore incorrect.

General Police Duties, paras 3.22.4.2, 3.22.4.4, 3.22.4.5

Answer 22.13

Answer **D** — The power to conduct a breath test under s. 6(5) of the Road Traffic Act 1988 applies where an accident has occurred owing to the presence of a motor vehicle on a road or public place. Since WALSH was driving a mechanically propelled vehicle and not a motor vehicle, there is no power to request a breath test from him. Answer C is therefore incorrect. As s. 6 applies to accidents that occur in a public place as well as on a road, answer B is also incorrect.

There is no need for the officer making the inquiry to suspect or believe that the driver has been drinking, or that he has committed an offence, in order to require a breath test following an accident. Answer A is therefore incorrect.

General Police Duties, para. 3.22.4.3

Answer 22.14

Answer **A** — Urine samples must be provided within an hour *from the time the request is made* (s. 7(5)). Answers C and D are therefore incorrect.

The defendant must provide two distinct samples (as opposed to two samples taken during the same act of urinating) (*Prosser* v *Dickeson* [1982] RTR 96). Answers B and D are incorrect for this reason also.

Note that the defendant must be given the opportunity to provide the urine within the one-hour period (*Robertson* v *DPP* [2004] EWHC 517 (Admin)).

General Police Duties, para. 3.22.5.1

Answer 22.15

Answer **D** — Under s. 7(3) of the Road Traffic Act 1988, a requirement to provide a specimen of blood or urine can only be made at a police station or at a hospital. Answer C is therefore incorrect.

Urine samples do not need to be taken by a medical practitioner. The samples will be admissible as long as they are provided within the time set out under s. 7(5) and may be taken by a police officer. Answers A and B are therefore incorrect.

General Police Duties, para. 3.22.5.1

Answer 22.16

Answer **A** — It was held in the case of *Pearson* v *Metropolitan Police Commissioner* [1988] RTR 276 that the requirement under s. 7 may be made of more than one person (in this instance three people were involved) in respect of the same vehicle. Answers B and D are therefore incorrect. However, it must be believed that one of them was driving the vehicle, and for that reason answer C is incorrect.

General Police Duties, para. 3.22.5.2

Answer 22.17

Answer **A** — If the machine being used at one station is unreliable by virtue of the fact that it will not calibrate the reading correctly, it will be 'unavailable'. In this case, the driver may be taken to another station, where another machine is available, even if the driver has already provided two specimens on the inaccurate machine (*Denny* v *DPP* [1990] RTR 417). Answer B is incorrect for this reason.

When a person is transferred in such a way, the procedure will start again and the defendant may be required to provide two further specimens (logically, the sample from the first station could not be used as the machine has malfunctioned). Answer C is therefore incorrect.

A person *may* be transferred to another station if there is no trained officer to operate the machine (*Chief Constable of Avon and Somerset* v *Kelliher* [1986] Crim LR 635). However, this is not the only circumstance in which a person can be transferred and answer D is therefore incorrect.

General Police Duties, para. 3.22.5.4

Answer 22.18

Answer **A** — Under s. 7(7) of the Road Traffic Act 1988, when a constable is requesting the provision of a specimen under s. 7(3), a warning must be given that a failure to provide the specimen may render a person liable to prosecution. This warning is generally critical to a successful prosecution for failing to provide a specimen.

Answers C and D are incorrect because the warning relates to *any* specimen requested under s. 7 (breath, blood or urine).

In *Bobin* v *DPP* [1999] RTR 375, it was held that as long as the information is provided by a police officer, it does not matter which police officer. Therefore, the warning under s. 7(7) might be given by, for instance, the arresting officer or by the custody officer who makes the requirement for the relevant specimen. There was no requirement in these circumstances to provide a further warning and answer B is incorrect.

General Police Duties, paras 3.22.5.5, 3.22.5.6

Answer 22.19

Answer **D** — Sergeant DONELLY has not acted correctly in these circumstances. Where a driver provides one specimen only and fails without a reasonable excuse to provide the second sample, he/she has committed the offence of 'failing to provide' a sample (*Cracknell* v *Willis* [1988] AC 450). Answers A and C are incorrect for this reason.

'Mental impairment' may provide a reasonable excuse for failing to provide a sample. However, being drunk or under stress is not in itself enough to provide a 'reasonable excuse' for failing to provide a specimen (*DPP* v *Falzarano* [2001] RTR 14). This is confirmed by the case of *DPP* v *Beech* [1992] Crim LR 64, where it was decided that where the defendant's mental capacity to understand the warning was impaired by his/her drunkenness, this was not a 'reasonable' excuse. Answer B is therefore incorrect.

General Police Duties, para. 3.22.5.11

Answer 22.20

Answer **B** — While a person is at a hospital as a patient, he/she shall not be required to cooperate with a preliminary test or to provide a specimen under s. 7 of the Road Traffic Act 1988, unless the medical practitioner in immediate charge of his/her case agrees. Section 7 applies to both breath samples and samples of blood/urine.

However, if a patient provides a positive reading or fails to provide a sample at a hospital, he/she cannot be arrested while still a 'patient' (s. 6(5)). Answer B is therefore correct and answer C is incorrect as, even though the officer sought permission to take the second sample, the arrest that preceded it was unlawful.

Since the arrest was unlawful, answer A is incorrect as the patient should not have been taken to a police station in these circumstances. However, if the person had been arrested after ceasing to be a patient, she could have been taken to the station to provide a sample (*Webber* v *DPP* [1998] RTR 111).

Answer D is incorrect as permission must be sought from a medical practitioner for each sample that is required under s. 9(1).

General Police Duties, para. 3.22.6

Answer 22.21

Answer **D** — Section 10(1) of the Road Traffic Act 1988 states that a person required to provide a specimen of breath, blood or urine may afterwards be detained at a police station (or if the specimen was provided otherwise than at a police station, arrested and taken to and detained at a police station) if the constable has reasonable grounds for believing that, were the person to drive or attempt to drive a *mechanically propelled* vehicle on a road, he/she would commit an offence under s. 4, 5 or 5A of the Act. Answer C is therefore incorrect.

Although the provision of a negative screening test would be a good indication that the person would not commit an offence under s. 4, 5 or 5A, there is no specific power to demand such a sample. Answer B is therefore incorrect. Similarly, there is no statutory power to retain a person's car keys to prevent them from driving (although this is common practice) and therefore answer A is incorrect.

General Police Duties, para. 3.22.7

Answer 22.22

Answer **D** — Section 10 of the Road Traffic Act 1988 allows for the detention of a person who has provided a specimen of breath, blood or urine, until it appears to a constable that were the person to drive a mechanically propelled vehicle on a road, he/she would not be committing an offence. The power does not apply if it appears to a constable that there is no likelihood of the person driving such a vehicle on a road. There is no mention of a person having been charged or reported for an offence, merely that they have been required to provide the relevant sample. Answer C is therefore incorrect.

Under s. 10(3), a constable *must* consult a medical practitioner on any question arising under this section concerning whether a person's ability to drive properly is or might be impaired through drugs. The constable must act on such advice. This is mandatory; therefore, both answers A and B are incorrect.

General Police Duties, para. 3.22.7

Answer 22.23

Answer **D** — The Criminal Attempts Act 1981 (s. 1) states that if a person does an act which is *more than merely preparatory* to the commission of an offence, then he/she is guilty of attempting to commit the offence. This approach is taken when deciding if someone is attempting to drive, i.e. is what this person is doing *more than merely preparatory to the act of driving*? The general approach to attempts under s. 1 of the Criminal Attempts Act 1981 is that one can attempt the impossible. This is also the case when considering whether someone is attempting to drive, so when an unfit driver, who had no ignition key, sat in the driver's seat and attempted to insert other keys into the ignition, he was held to be properly convicted of attempting to drive (*Kelly* v *Hogan* [1982] RTR 352). There can be little argument that in this case LLOYD is attempting to drive.

The offence under s. 4(1) and (2) of the Road Traffic Act 1988 is committed by a person who, when driving, attempting to drive or being in charge of a mechanically propelled vehicle on a road or public place, is unfit to drive through drink or drugs—this makes answer A incorrect.

There is a defence available in relation to being in charge of a mechanically propelled vehicle under s. 4(3) if the defendant proves that at the material time, the circumstances were such that there was no likelihood of his/her driving so long as he/she remained unfit to drive through drink or drugs. But as this is only available to 'being in charge', it would not apply to this offence. Further, the likelihood of driving is not an element of the offence itself; the intention of the defendant is only material to the statutory defence, meaning that answer C is incorrect.

It is not an evidential requirement that expert medical evidence be provided as to LLOYD's degree of impairment—evidence of impairment can be given by expert or lay witnesses, making answer B incorrect.

Answer D is correct as s. 17(1)(c)(iiia) of PACE provides a power to enter and arrest a person for an offence under s. 4 of the Road Traffic Act 1988 but it is only exercisable if the constable has reasonable grounds for believing that the person sought is on the premises (s. 17(2)(a)).

General Police Duties, paras 3.22.2 to 3.22.2.2

Answer 22.24

Answer **C** — Section 6(5) of the Road Traffic Act 1988 states that a constable may require a person to cooperate with any one or more of the preliminary tests if an accident occurs owing to the presence of a motor vehicle on a road or other public place and a constable reasonably believes that the person was driving, attempting to drive or in charge of the vehicle at the time of the accident; this makes answer B incorrect. The meaning of an 'accident' is not restricted to that given to a 'reportable' accident, meaning that literally any occurrence that could be described as an 'accident' will be viewed as such—here an 'accident' has occurred even though the only vehicle damaged was the one driven by MARLOW and this makes answer D incorrect. When a preliminary test is administered under s. 6(2) to (4) of the Act, the officer administering the test must be in uniform—this test is being administered under s. 6(5) and there is no requirement for the administering officer to be in uniform, making answer A incorrect. In these circumstances, DC NEVIN can require and administer any of the preliminary tests (correct answer C).

General Police Duties, paras 3.22.4, 3.22.4.3

Answer 22.25

Answer **C** — Under s. 6(4) of the Road Traffic Act 1988, a constable may require a person to cooperate with any one or more preliminary tests administered to the person by that constable or another constable if the constable reasonably suspects that the person is or has been driving, attempting to drive or in charge of a motor vehicle on a road or other public place and has committed a traffic offence while the vehicle was in motion. So in the circumstances, PC BATTY is entitled to require FRAYLING to take a drug test.

Section 6D(2) of the Road Traffic Act 1988 states that a constable may arrest a person without warrant if the person fails to cooperate with a preliminary test in pursuance of a requirement imposed under s. 6 (as FRAYLING has) and the constable reasonably suspects that the person has alcohol or a drug in his/her body or is under the influence of a drug. This makes answer A incorrect.

Refusing to take a preliminary test after committing a moving traffic offence would mean that the person concerned has committed an offence under s. 6(6) of the Act (failing to cooperate with a preliminary test) but the fact that the failure comes after committing a moving traffic offence does not, in itself, create a power of arrest under s. 6D, making answer B incorrect.

The power of arrest under s. 6D(2) allows any officer to arrest a person who fails to cooperate with any preliminary test imposed under s. 6 provided the officer *reasonably suspects* that the person has alcohol or a drug in his/her body or is under the influence of a drug. Without this reasonable suspicion, s. 6D(2) provides no power of arrest for failing to cooperate with a preliminary test (correct answer C). Answer D is incorrect as it is the suspicion of the officer rather than a belief which generates the power of arrest.

General Police Duties, paras 3.22.4, 3.22.4.4, 3.22.4.5

Answer 22.26

Answer **B** — The power of entry under s. 6E of the Road Traffic Act 1988 states:

(1) A constable may enter any place (using reasonable force if necessary) for the purpose of—
  (a) imposing a requirement by virtue of section 6(5) following an accident in a case where the constable reasonably suspects that the accident involved injury of any person, or
  (b) arresting a person under section 6D following an accident in a case where the constable reasonably suspects that the accident involved injury of any person.

This means that answer D is incorrect as there are several circumstances that would enable entry to be made to premises, amongst which is to impose a requirement by virtue of s. 6(5) of the Act (procedure following an accident). The power of entry under s. 6E(1)(a) could be exercised by an officer in or out of uniform (taking option C out of the equation) but options C and D are incorrect as the power could not be used in these circumstances alone. If there was a suspicion that the accident involved injury to any person, then it would be available (making answer A incorrect).

General Police Duties, paras 3.22.4.3, 3.22.4.6

Answer 22.27

Answer **A** — The statutory defences available under s. 5 of the Road Traffic Act 1988 are available in answer to a charge under s. 5(1)(b) of the Act—that is, *being in charge* of a motor vehicle whilst over the prescribed limit. There is no statutory defence to a charge under s. 5(1)(a) (driving or attempting to drive a motor vehicle whilst over the prescribed limit) so answers B, C and D are incorrect.

General Police Duties, para. 3.22.3.1

Answer 22.28

Answer **D** — Whether there has been a road accident or not does not affect the fact that there is a power of entry to arrest for this offence (under s. 17(1)(c)(iiia) of the Police and Criminal Evidence Act 1984), making answer A incorrect. As there is a power of entry, answer C is incorrect. An officer does not have to be in uniform to arrest a person for an offence under s. 4(1) of the Road Traffic Act 1988, neither do they have to be in uniform to exercise the power of entry, making answer B incorrect.

General Police Duties, para. 3.22.2

Answer 22.29

Answer **A** — A preliminary breath test can only be administered at or near the place where the requirement to cooperate with the test is imposed, making answer B incorrect. Answer C is incorrect as a preliminary impairment test can be carried out at a police station if the constable making the requirement thinks it expedient (as per answer A). Answer D is incorrect as the constable administering the test under s. 6 of the Road Traffic Act 1988 must be in uniform (unless the test is administered after an accident (s. 6(5) of the Act)).

General Police Duties, para. 3.22.4.2

Question Checklist

The following checklist is designed to help you keep track of your progress when answering the multiple-choice questions. If you fill this in after one attempt at each question, you will be able to check how many you have got right and which questions you need to revisit a second time. Also available online; to download visit www.blackstonespoliceservice.com.

	First attempt Correct (✔)	Second attempt Correct (✔)
1 Stop and Search		
1.1		
1.2		
1.3		
1.4		
1.5		
1.6		
1.7		
1.8		
1.9		
1.10		
1.11		
1.12		
1.13		

	First attempt Correct (✔)	Second attempt Correct (✔)
1.14		
1.15		
1.16		
1.17		
2 Entry, Search and Seizure		
2.1		
2.2		
2.3		
2.4		
2.5		
2.6		
2.7		
2.8		
2.9		

Question Checklist

	First attempt Correct (✔)	Second attempt Correct (✔)
2.10		
2.11		
3 Powers of Arrest		
3.1		
3.2		
3.3		
3.4		
3.5		
3.6		
3.7		
3.8		
3.9		
3.10		
3.11		
3.12		
3.13		
4 Protection of People Suffering from Mental Disorders		
4.1		
4.2		
4.3		
5 Offences Relating to Land and Premises		
5.1		
5.2		
5.3		
5.4		
5.5		
5.6		

	First attempt Correct (✔)	Second attempt Correct (✔)
5.7		
5.8		
5.9		
5.10		
6 Licensing and Offences Relating to Alcohol		
6.1		
6.2		
6.3		
6.4		
6.5		
6.6		
6.7		
6.8		
6.9		
6.10		
6.11		
6.12		
6.13		
7 Protecting Citizens and the Community; Injunctions, Orders and Police Powers		
7.1		
7.2		
7.3		
7.4		
7.5		
7.6		
7.7		

	First attempt Correct (✔)	Second attempt Correct (✔)
7.8		
7.9		
7.10		
7.11		
7.12		
7.13		
7.14		
7.15		
7.16		
7.17		
7.18		
7.19		
7.20		
8 Processions and Assemblies		
8.1		
8.2		
8.3		
8.4		
8.5		
8.6		
8.7		
9 Public Order Offences		
9.1		
9.2		
9.3		
9.4		
9.5		
9.6		

	First attempt Correct (✔)	Second attempt Correct (✔)
9.7		
9.8		
9.9		
9.10		
9.11		
10 Sporting Events		
10.1		
10.2		
10.3		
10.4		
10.5		
11 Domestic Abuse		
11.1		
11.2		
11.3		
11.4		
11.5		
11.6		
11.7		
11.8		
11.9		
11.10		
12 Hatred and Harassment Offences		
12.1		
12.2		
12.3		
12.4		
12.5		

	First attempt Correct (✔)	Second attempt Correct (✔)
12.6		
12.7		
12.8		
12.9		
12.10		
12.11		
12.12		
13 Offences and Powers Relating to Information and Communications		
13.1		
13.2		
13.3		
13.4		
13.5		
13.6		
13.7		
13.8		
13.9		
13.10		
13.11		
13.12		
13.13		
13.14		
13.15		
13.16		
13.17		
13.18		
13.19		

	First attempt Correct (✔)	Second attempt Correct (✔)
14 Offences Against the Administration of Justice and Public Interest		
14.1		
14.2		
14.3		
14.4		
14.5		
14.6		
14.7		
14.8		
14.9		
14.10		
14.11		
15 Terrorism and Associated Offences		
15.1		
15.2		
15.3		
15.4		
15.5		
15.6		
16 Diversity, Equality and Inclusion		
16.1		
16.2		
16.3		
16.4		
16.5		
16.6		
16.7		

	First attempt Correct (✔)	Second attempt Correct (✔)
16.8		
16.9		
17 Complaints and Misconduct		
17.1		
17.2		
17.3		
17.4		
17.5		
17.6		
17.7		
17.8		
17.9		
17.10		
17.11		
17.12		
17.13		
17.14		
18 Unsatisfactory Performance and Attendance		
18.1		
18.2		
18.3		
18.4		
18.5		
18.6		
18.7		
18.8		

	First attempt Correct (✔)	Second attempt Correct (✔)
18.9		
18.10		
19 Road Policing Definitions and Principles		
19.1		
19.2		
19.3		
19.4		
19.5		
19.6		
19.7		
19.8		
19.9		
19.10		
19.11		
19.12		
19.13		
19.14		
19.15		
19.16		
19.17		
20 Key Police Powers Relating to Road Policing		
20.1		
20.2		
20.3		
20.4		
20.5		

	First attempt Correct (✔)	Second attempt Correct (✔)
20.6		
20.7		
20.8		
20.9		
20.10		
20.11		
20.12		
20.13		
21 Offences Involving Standards of Driving		
21.1		
21.2		
21.3		
21.4		
21.5		
21.6		
21.7		
21.8		
21.9		
21.10		
21.11		
21.12		
21.13		
22 Drink, Drugs and Driving		
22.1		
22.2		
22.3		

	First attempt Correct (✔)	Second attempt Correct (✔)
22.4		
22.5		
22.6		
22.7		
22.8		
22.9		
22.10		
22.11		
22.12		
22.13		
22.14		
22.15		
22.16		
22.17		
22.18		
22.19		
22.20		
22.21		
22.22		
22.23		
22.24		
22.25		
22.26		
22.27		
22.28		
22.29		